SUCCESSFUL GARDENING WITH PERENNIALS

BOOKS BY HELEN VAN PELT WILSON

A GARDEN IN THE HOUSE

HOUSE PLANTS FOR EVERY WINDOW (with Dorothy H. Jenkins)

THE JOY OF FLOWER ARRANGING

CLIMBING ROSES

ROSES FOR PLEASURE (with Richard Thomson)

THE NEW PERENNIALS PREFERRED

FLOWER ARRANGEMENT DESIGNS FOR TODAY (editor)

THE JOY OF GERANIUMS

THE FRAGRANT YEAR (with Léonie Bell)

AFRICAN-VIOLET AND GESNERIAD QUESTIONS
   ANSWERED BY TWENTY EXPERTS (editor)

1001 AFRICAN-VIOLET QUESTIONS
   ANSWERED BY TWELVE EXPERTS (editor)

HELEN VAN PELT WILSON'S AFRICAN-VIOLET BOOK

FLOWERS, SPACE, AND MOTION

JOYFUL THOUGHTS FOR FIVE SEASONS (anthology)

HELEN VAN PELT WILSON'S OWN GARDEN AND LANDSCAPE BOOK

HOUSE PLANTS ARE FOR PLEASURE

SUCCESSFUL GARDENING IN THE SHADE

SUCCESSFUL GARDENING WITH PERENNIALS

DOUBLEDAY & COMPANY, INC.
GARDEN CITY, NEW YORK
1976

HELEN VAN PELT WILSON

SUCCESSFUL GARDENING WITH PERENNIALS

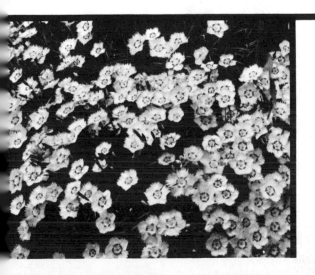

**HOW TO SELECT AND GROW
MORE THAN 500 KINDS
FOR TODAY'S YARD & GARDEN**

ISBN 0-385-06358-X
Library of Congress Catalog Card Number 76–2831
Copyright © 1975, 1976 by HELEN VAN PELT WILSON
All Rights Reserved
Printed in the United States of America
BOOK DESIGN BY BENTE HAMANN
First Edition

FRONTIS FLOWERS

ABOVE LEFT: Oriental Poppies.
ABOVE RIGHT: Christmas-roses.
CENTER: Hosta 'Royal Standard'.
BELOW LEFT: Shasta Daisies.
BELOW RIGHT: Dianthus Hybrids.

THIS ONE IS FOR SUSAN

WITH GRATITUDE

To Daniel T. Walden, first and foremost, for helping me in every possible way to make this study of perennials as accurate, inspiring, and attractive as I wanted it to be. He has not only meticulously edited my text, but also counseled me on the selection and placement of the illustrations. I complete this book with my warmest thanks to him, and also

To Helen B. Krieg, my secretary and friend for some fifteen years, who has lifted my flagging and exhausted spirits as needed, while she flawlessly typed copy.

Others have generously shared their expert knowledge with me, giving critical reading to certain chapters. For this I am grateful to:

Joseph J. Maisano, Jr., extension agent for Fairfield County Extension Service in Connecticut, who patiently led me through the chemical maze of pest and disease controls.

Toms Home & Garden Center in New Canaan, for recommendations of trade products containing chemicals for pest and disease controls.

Phyllis Walsh of Lapolla Greenhouses in New Canaan, for her enthusiastic interest and help in the planting of my new garden.

Louis Smirnow, for sharing his extensive knowledge of peonies, both herbaceous and tree types.

Grace Mack, a hybridizer of chrysanthemums for Yoder Brothers, Inc., for opening her extensive trial gardens to me, and to

Bill Aulenbach of that company, who sent me trial plants and made a number of useful suggestions.

To Robert Schreiner of Schreiner Gardens for helpful guidance on iris culture, and

To Bea Warburton, of The Median Iris Society, who increased my knowledge of the many fine smaller irises.

As always, my friends and their gardens have taught me much, so again my thanks to Edna J. Payne, whose extensive plantings of day-lilies, irises, and lilies offered me a wealth of practical information as well as inspiration, and

To Helen Muller, who is one of the wisest gardeners I know—and in many areas. In every season, her interesting borders, designed by her husband, Theodor Muller, F.A.S.I.D., A.I.A., have been a joy to visit, and I am grateful to him too for the sketch he prepared of their borders.

To Kathleen Bourke, both gardener and artist, I give special thanks for her careful drawings that give guidance for ways to use perennials, and to

Eloise A. Ray, L.A., who designed the new small garden that now provides me with a different kind of perennial pleasure.

Contents

Lists and Charts

Drawings

The true gardener is never overmuch disquieted by bad seasons, whether they are seasons of drought or of frost. The half-hearted gardener thinks that all is lost when he has lost one season; but the wise man's caution has a very wide meaning: *He that observeth the wind shall not sow, and he that regardeth the clouds shall not reap.* The fair-weather gardener, who will do nothing except when wind and weather and everything else are favourable, is never a master of his craft. Gardening, above all crafts, is a matter of faith, grounded, however, (if on nothing better), on his experience that somehow or other seasons go on in their right course, and bring their right results.

CANON ELLACOMBE

Helen Van Pelt Wilson's garden on a sunny, summer day. BUKOVCIK PHOTO

THE SOLACE OF A GARDEN

Life being what it is, full of stress as well as distress, I sometimes wonder how people get on without a garden to comfort them in the worst times. I'm sure I couldn't manage. Now my new small garden makes constant, though hardly inordinate, demands upon me, and I welcome them to relieve me of the sorrow and anxiety in a time of personal problems.

Making notes of the color schemes as they change, the possibilities of better ones, setting out new but familiar plants and others I've never grown before, is so engrossing that I am removed from reality to the imaginative world of the perfect garden that always exists in the gardener's vision. So I consider if apricot pansies should be introduced in the right-hand garden as an edging for a bed of blue hyacinths and whether in the left-hand garden more pink flowers aren't needed, tulips perhaps to set off the bleedinghearts and forget-me-nots.

Then I keep making discoveries. When I moved a few ferns and some feverfew plants from Stony Brook Cottage, my former home, I also brought along, unknowingly, two plants of Jack-in-the-pulpit, a few cherished erythroniums, not in evidence in late June when I dug the others, and tiny clumps of wild geranium. Yesterday I spied a single bleedingheart and, having disciplined myself to but one plant of this big grower, I happily indulged myself for this extra, especially as it was then so small.

Today I am lucky to have a couple of hours of outside "digging help" once a month, plus the occasional assistance of my plant-loving granddaughter, Susan. Even so, pleasing effects have been possible, and I know if I plan wisely, I can find emotional satisfaction in *limited* hours of work in a *limited* garden. What is vitally important for us all is to be realistic. I emphasize perennials; they are indeed for pleasure, whether used simply as landscape plants in the yard or, well chosen for their health and duration of bloom, in narrowed borders or a more formally planned small garden. Unlike my frantic earlier years of strenuous gardening hours when I rarely gazed but always worked, now I often view my perennial efforts from a rocking chair, with our kitten, Snug, sleeping on my lap, and *facing* my garden instead of with my back turned as I used to so as to avoid seeing things that still had to be done.

Of course, I am not alone in finding a garden vastly comforting. My friend Ruth Spears says, "I weeded my way through many of life's problems," and Adelaide Baker, a former neighbor of mine in Westport and a great gardener, just before her death wrote: "If you have an outlet in a love of nature that can blunt the edge of the hard things in life, then you can't go under. I can always walk out into my garden and get restored."

In this trying world, I take no newspaper to my terrace. In the early dawn-sweet hours (I am a 5:30 A.M. riser) I could draw no solace from my garden if I attempted to alternate a dire front page with the fragrance and beauty of the flowers, the music of the birds. Rather I confess I bring along a volume of poetry, not contemporary verse, but sometimes Shakespeare's *Sonnets,* "Shall I compare thee to a summer's day?," sometimes Wordsworth's, "The world is too much with us." With such companions, how agreeable are the first private hours in my garden, what detachment, what solace can be found there.

1975   H.V.P.W.

SUCCESSFUL GARDENING WITH PERENNIALS

Dianthus allwoodii hybrids, variously marked and colored in pink, rose, red, and white, fragrant and floriferous all summer long, happily set off against the cool green foliage of tall bearded iris. GENEREUX PHOTO

1

PERENNIALS FOR TODAY'S
YARD AND GARDEN

Probably no aspect of gardening has changed more in the past thirty years or so than the way we use perennials. When I wrote my first book about them in 1945, I gave eight rules for the development of perennial borders with plans for 8-foot-wide sections, like mine at that time, with a five-deep lineup of plants, and I stated, "That is little enough planting depth when the aim is continuous color. A 10-foot bed would simplify the task." In England I admired 20 feet, and there great gardeners like Gertrude Jekyll could expand to their heart's content. Rereading one of her books, I was amused to come on this account of her method with a favorite perennial:

"Every year, before replanting, the Primrose ground is dug over and well manured. All day for two days I sit on a low stool dividing the plants; a certain degree of facility and expertness has come of long practice. A boy feeds me with armfuls of newly-dug-up plants, two men are digging in the cooling cow-dung at the farther end, and another carries away the divided plants tray by tray, and carefully replants them." Four helpers!!!!

The way I garden today is vastly different from the way I gardened in the 1940s, when help was not only plentiful but even experienced. Then many of us had a worker at least several days a week. At that time wide perennial borders for continuous colorful bloom could be carefully plotted through winter evenings, and then gradually brought into being from April on with the help of a local gardener. In the years when I went to England every September, I made it a practice to study from both the far and near view the magnificent herbaceous borders in the Savill Gardens at Windsor. I recall how impressed I was by the then new-to-me *Achillea* 'Coronation Gold' and the way the fresh colors of the borders lasted well into October.

Christopher Lloyd's handsome gardens at Great Dixter in Surrey provided one of my recent lessons. From Mr. Lloyd I learned about the useful perennials he called the Weavers. He wrote they "flower continuously for three, four, or even five months without exhausting themselves, but do so from ever-lengthening stems. These filter through their neighbours, whether at the same level or higher. If the latter, a plant that you may normally think of as ground-hugging sometimes peers out from among the stems of its supporter at a height of 3 or 4 foot. The long-flowering qualities of these plants are obvious but they are also invaluable for knitting the units in your border together. No one wants to see gaps between groups of plants, at the height of the growing season. Naked earth is almost an indecency. The plant weavers do a splendid integrating act. They appear to enjoy themselves and make your border look fun to be in. Sometimes they have to be controlled; their enjoyment goes too far." His favorite weaver is the *Viola cornuta alba* that blooms "in moist shade from May til November," a greater wanderer than the violet-colored *V. cornuta*. My sprawling apricot pansy has proved to be a good weaver for me.

More important and really invaluable for continuing color are the perennials I call my Big Four. Peonies, Iris, Daylilies, and Chrysanthemums alone can make a place colorful from mid-May into November, and these four are always featured in my own planting plans. If the picture can be strengthened with some other perennials, perhaps Christmas-roses for winter, poppies, columbines, and candytuft for spring, the riotous daisies and the less-demanding kinds of delphiniums and phlox for summer, and dependable hardy asters for fall, a brilliant and continuous panorama can be developed. With these favorites, I grow colonies of hardy spring bulbs —crocus, hyacinths, narcissus, and scillas—that once planted produce for years, and also several annuals as they appeal to me. I usually buy flats of in-bud pansies, petunias, and impatiens.

Plans for Perennials

Today in this country the herbaceous border has shrunk considerably.

In front of shrubbery planting along the boundary of a property a perennial border 3 to 5 feet wide can be effective. Of course, the wider it is the more work it will require.

Now 2-foot strip gardens are more popular. They can be laid out on each side of a path that moves through sun and shade with appropriate, fairly low plants for each location.

Island beds of irregular form and without backgrounds are popular in England today and are becoming so here. These are colorful, forthright collections of plants growing right in the middle or the side or the end of a lawn or garden area, the same way beds of cannas were used in Queen Victoria's time.

Less ambitious—and less work—but so satisfactory are tuck-in groups of perennials in "coves" along the edge of shrub boundaries or set between big growers, or used as accent clumps like small shrubs beside steps or in otherwise bare corners.

To grow and display her two specialties, my friend Edna Payne has developed a 3-foot-wide iris-and-daylily border to run along the length of her driveway. A foot-wide grass strip behind it makes cultivating easy for the back of the bed. Beyond the grass strip is a shrub-and-evergreen boundary planting, 5 feet wide, with spaces between for tall perennials. In Chapters 5 and 6 on iris and daylilies, Mrs. Payne's handsome plantings are discussed in detail.

Another friend, Helen Muller, benefiting from the design advice of her architect husband, has developed a fascinating uphill path garden with sinuous beds like arabesques. These take the place of the uncompromising 6-foot-wide block plantings that she inherited from an earlier day. They were lovely in her mother's time, but how much more interesting is this new free-form design filled with suitably lower-growing perennials.

We all know that perennial means "through the years," that the word refers to these wonderful plants that mostly die down in winter but grow again from hardy roots when the soil warms up in spring. Perennials are essential to the permanent garden, most of them requiring division and replanting only every third year or so, and some, peonies, for example, almost never. The majority do not have the long blooming period of annuals, rarely more than six weeks, but perennials are much less trouble and much more interesting, I think.

A Five-foot Perennial Border in Front of Shrubbery

Astilbe hybrid
Peach Blossom
(light pink)

Tall
Bearded Iris
Celestial Glory
(gold-to-orange)

Peony
Gold Standard
(white-to-yellow)

Creeping Phlox
subulata
(rose)

Hybrid Delphinium
Cliveden Beauty
(light blue)

Achillea
Coronation Gold
(yellow-gold)

Columbine
Spring Song hybrids

Hemerocallis
Little Cherub
(yellow)

Hardy Aster
Julia
(lilac pink)

Peony
Bowl of Cream
(white)

Hemerocallis
Clarence Simon
(pink-melon)

Flax
Heavenly Blue

Cushion Mums
Jackpot (yellow)

Monarda
Snow Queen
(white)

Papaver Orientale
Helen Elizabeth
(rose)

Petunias
(pink and lavender)

Dwarf Iris mixed

Baptisia
australis
(blue)

Tall
Bearded Iris
Primrose Drift
(yellow)

Columbine
Spring Song
hybrids

Phlox
paniculata
Starfire
(red)

Chrysanthemum Maximum
Alaska
(white)

Chrysanthemum
Starlet
(orange-buff)

Dwarf Iris (mixed)

Cushion Mums
Jackpot (yellow)

Hardy Aster
Harrington's Pink
(pink)

Daylily
Chetco
(creamy yellow)

Bearded Iris
Eleanor's Pride
(powder blue)

Creeping Phlox subulata
(rose)

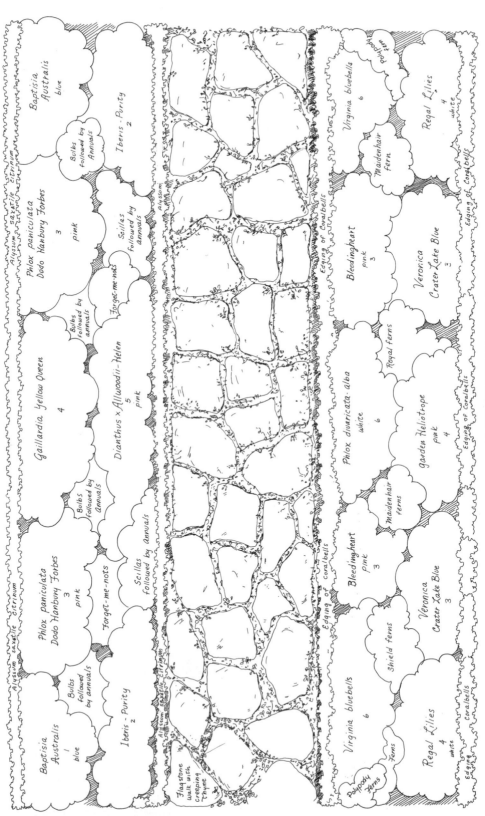

3-foot x 15-foot SUN STRIP TO BORDER A WALK

Baptisia Australis blue

Bulbs followed by Annuals

Iberis - Purity 2

Phlox paniculata Dodo Hanbury Forbes 3 pink

Scillas followed by annuals

Forget-me-nots

Bulbs followed by annuals

Gaillardia Yellow Queen 4

Alyssum saxatile Citrinum

Dianthus x Allwoodii-Helen 5 pink

Scillas followed by Annuals

Forget-me-nots

Bulbs followed by annuals

Phlox paniculata Dodo Hanbury Forbes 3 pink

Iberis - Purity 2

Baptisia Australis 1 blue

Alyssum saxatile Citrinum

Alyssum saxatile Citrinum

Flagstone walk with creeping Thyme

Edging of Coralbells

3-foot x 15-foot SHADE STRIP TO BORDER A WALK

Virginia bluebells 6

Polypody fern

Maidenhair fern

Regal Lilies 4 white

Bleedingheart pink 3

Royal ferns

Veronica Crater Lake Blue 3

Phlox divaricata-alba white 6

Maidenhair ferns

Garden Heliotrope pink 4

Edging of Coralbells

Bleedingheart pink 3

Shield ferns

Veronica Crater Lake Blue 3

Virginia bluebells 6

Ferns

Polypody Ferns

Regal Lilies 4 white

Edging Coralbells

Edging of Coralbells

Island Bed for Peonies
10 feet wide x 16 feet deep

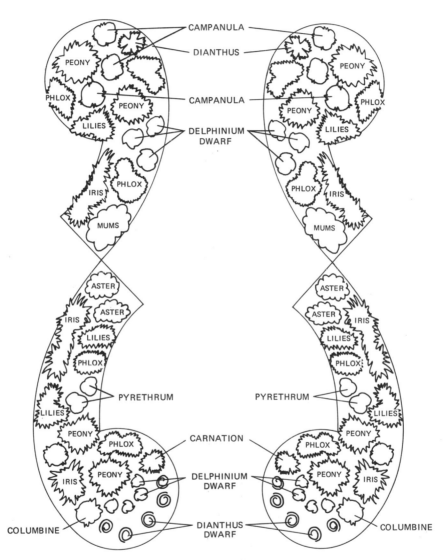

Plan for The Muller Garden by Theodor Muller, A.I.A.

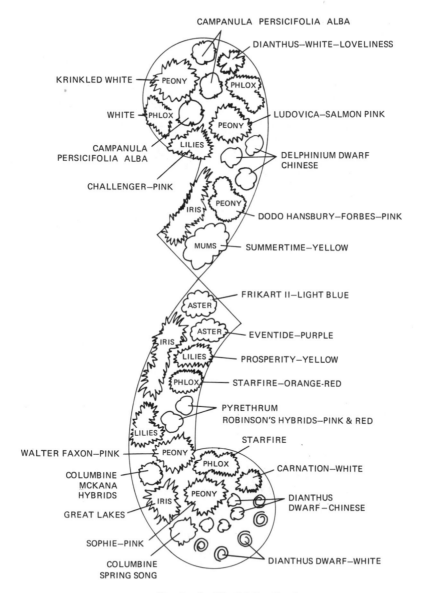

CAMPANULA PERSICIFOLIA ALBA

DIANTHUS—WHITE—LOVELINESS

KRINKLED WHITE — PEONY

PHLOX

WHITE — PHLOX

LUDOVICA—SALMON PINK

PEONY

CAMPANULA
PERSICIFOLIA ALBA

LILIES

DELPHINIUM DWARF
CHINESE

CHALLENGER—PINK

IRIS

PEONY

DODO HANSBURY—FORBES—PINK

MUMS — SUMMERTIME—YELLOW

FRIKART II—LIGHT BLUE

ASTER

ASTER — EVENTIDE—PURPLE

IRIS

LILIES — PROSPERITY—YELLOW

PHLOX — STARFIRE—ORANGE-RED

PYRETHRUM
ROBINSON'S HYBRIDS—PINK & RED

LILIES

STARFIRE

WALTER FAXON—PINK — PEONY

PHLOX

COLUMBINE
MCKANA
HYBRIDS

CARNATION—WHITE

IRIS

PEONY

DIANTHUS
DWARF—CHINESE

GREAT LAKES

SOPHIE—PINK

DIANTHUS DWARF—WHITE

COLUMBINE
SPRING SONG

Planting for The Muller Garden

How you will enjoy perennials today depends, of course, on your own preferences, and the possibilities of your site. In any case you won't get bogged down with the hard-to-cope-with, old-fashioned wide herbaceous border. The new ways are delightful ways, stimulating and full of promise whether we are designing narrow borders, strip plantings, or bold islands that we can enjoy from every angle. And the newer, smaller perennials suit the new ways, low single peonies, English delphiniums half as tall as the early Blackmore and Langdon hybrids, cushion chrysanthemums under a foot, and at least one phlox that measures but 8 inches. Since it is good design to have plants only half as high as the width of the beds, the lower perennials are perfectly suited to the contemporary picture.

Christmas-roses beside the terrace step in early February. TALOUMIS PHOTO

CHRISTMAS-ROSES
FOR THE WINTER GARDEN

In January I keep peering out of my breakfast-table window to see what is going on with the Christmas-roses just below. Early in the month firm white unfolded blooms can *sometimes* be detected nestling low among the evergreen leaves. Then—and usually on a Sunday, for this plant has the religious tradition of having bloomed the first Christmas Eve—in the second or third week of January the utterly lovely, pink-tinged white blossoms *may* open in a great bouquet above the 12-inch, deep green palm-like leaves. In some years this budding may not occur until February. No summer garden plant is more effective. Like the old-time postman "neither snow, nor rain, nor heat, nor gloom of night" delays its swift accomplishment. In a snowstorm the Christmas-rose may draw back a little, but then it will arise again and again and again, quite perfect, and go on being so well into spring, having gradually turned a deep rose-pink. Usually I don't cut off the faded flowers until early May. In propitious years, I have counted as many as forty-one flowers on a well-established, older plant. In other areas bloom may commence in December.

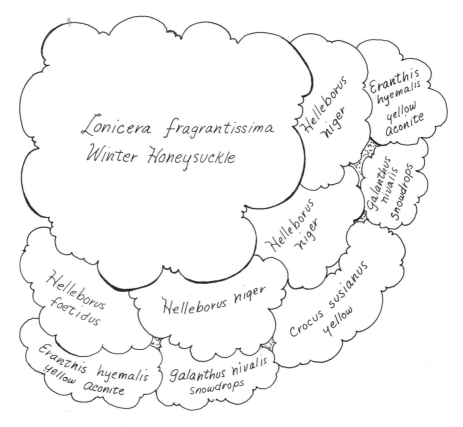

Christmas-roses for the Winter Garden

I suppose if I dared say I had a favorite perennial it would be the intrepid *Helleborus niger,* and I wish I could convince you that it would also give you tremendous pleasure. I don't think it belongs in a border, rather planted as you would a small evergreen shrub, at a doorstep perhaps but close to a south- or east-facing wall for warmth and association with other very early bloomers. You can enjoy something quite special if you plant a corner with the winter honeysuckle shrub (*Lonicera fragrantissima*), which opens piercingly sweet flowers from late February to April for background, and yellow aconite (*Eranthis*) tubers, also cold-defying in February, as underplanting. There are other pleasing companions, such as yellow crocus 'Cloth of Gold' and the lavender *Crocus tomasinianus,* snowdrop *Galanthus nivalis,* and where it prospers, the little fragrant *Iris unguicularis* (*stylosa*).

Helleborus lividus (corsicus) produces bright green flowers that last well when cut and are fine for a St. Patrick's Day arrangement.

Hellebores to Collect

Some years ago before growers' listings were necessarily reduced, you could locate a number of hellebores. Today in local nurseries and by mail order (see Where to Buy), you can locate at least three others besides the nigers. All are interesting and, if you have the space, well worth planting, although they are not so handsome as the nigers. The species, *Helleborus niger*, and the big white form of it I now have, variety *altifolius*, are still the most beautiful. Others that I have grown include *H. lividus* (*corsicus*).

Helleborus foetidus, a 12-inch mound-shaped plant, lifts purple-edged, nodding green flowers above the snow.

The Lenten-rose *Helleborus orientalis,* opens pale green to rose to dark purple
flowers on 18-inch stems about Easter time. Drawings by Kathleen Bourke

This produces bright, truly green blooms on 24-inch stems above hollylike leaves; it is fine and lasting for a St. Patrick's Day arrangement. Nodding green flowers edged with purple appear on thick 2-foot stems above the fernlike evergreen foliage of *H. foetidus.* This plant makes a pretty 12-inch mound above the snow. Several stems spring from each crown in four- or five-year-old plants, thus producing the effect of a small shrub, which is reminiscent somehow of leucothoe and just as attractive for the foreground of a rhododendron planting.

The Lenten-rose, *H. orientalis,* opens later, around Easter. Blooms are pale green to rose to dark purple, with several on each 18-inch stalk unlike other hellebores that produce flowers singly. *H. o. atrorubens* is a purple Lenten-rose. The Millet Hybrids include a mixture of colors with some blooms speckled and striped. The 12-inch palmate foliage of orientalis inclines to die down once very cold weather sets in in January.

All these hellebores produce cut flowers that last for ten days to two weeks at least, and it is certainly a delightful experience to gather garden flowers in winter. I avoid taking much foliage then; instead I use sprays of yew or English ivy or pachysandra. Because winter flowers are so valued, it's worth trying to revive a wilted spray. I have managed an extra ten days by steeping freshly cut stems for five minutes in a cup of boiling water and then plunging them into a tall vase filled with ice water.

In the beginning it takes patience with these hellebores. If specimens are quite small, they may not bloom either the first or even the second year after planting. Therefore, try to get hold of "big clumps" or "extra large" plants. The point is that before setting buds, hellebores must not only attain a fair degree of maturity but must also make themselves completely at home. It is therefore important at the outset to select permanent quarters for them. Elegant and unusual as they are, there is no great skill required in raising hellebores. In average garden soil they will do well enough, but because of the permanency of their residence, it seems worthwhile to prepare an ideal plot of loam mixed with plenty of leaf-mold and sand until it feels coarse and light but is reliably moisture-retentive; then mulch with compost.

Most important is location, some sun in winter and a cool, moist, light shaded spot in summer. Hot, dry soils are fatal to Christmas-roses, and in Zone 7 they will grow only at higher altitudes. Protection from north and west winds, which tend to burn foliage, is important. The closer plants are to a protecting wall, the earlier they will bloom. Most of my hellebores, now eight years old or so, flourish in an angle of kitchen and terrace wall.

Set plants out in spring or late August or September but with time to develop roots before frost. Let the roots stretch down, not out, in each

16-inch hole (depth *is* important), with the crown of the plant just under the surface of the soil. Good drainage is the great essential; standing water will not be tolerated by the fleshy roots.

When a plant has reached the ten-to-twelve-leaf stage, it may be ready to be divided. Sometimes the buds on niger come up so thickly they can hardly find space in which to open. Even in the first year of flowering after division, there may be six or seven blooms to a good-sized plant. In the course of a decade one *H. niger* specimen will be capable of sufficient division to provide a great many plants. However, hellebores are generally slow-growing perennials and are better if separated only for good reason.

Perhaps you will want to try to grow some from seed. This is, indeed, a tedious business and not recommended to the impatient or to the easily discouraged. Even experienced gardeners have a hard time with commercial seeds, for germination may take two years. But when you own mature plants set seed for you, results are likely to be very good.

In spring cut back the "evergreen" foliage of winter as it disintegrates while fine, new, light-green leaf clusters thrust up through the center of the plants. The faded flowers now bend low to perfect and drop their seeds. For the sake of looks in my small garden, I cut off most of the blooms at the ground line, letting only a few remain. The soil below these is then not disturbed. Early the next spring, after the necessary freezing period of winter, germination will have occurred, and tiny plants showing seed leaves will appear. By summer true leaves will have developed, and the new small hellebores can then be safely transplanted. However, they are far from flowering size; in fact, bloom should not be expected for two years or more. Even so, your expensive original plants will now have earned their keep. (At most nurseries these plants are at least half again as expensive as average perennials.)

Through summer your hellebores will change little. They seem simply to wait for autumn. In times of prolonged drought, soak them deeply to avoid wilting of foliage. In my experience hellebores are easy to grow, and they never get anything, either pest or disease. I keep plants mulched with compost or small wood chips, and I fertilize with an all-purpose mixture in spring, as I do all my perennials.

Hellebores, too rarely seen in gardens, are grand plants, capable of late January to early May bloom. When my neighbors have winter parties, they bring their guests over to see my "summer" garden of Christmas-roses. You too are bound to enjoy this great favorite of mine, so do plant hellebores at your earliest convenience.

The true perennial forget-me-not, *Myosotis scorpioides*. FITCH PHOTO

3

APRIL EMPHASIS,
MAY TRANSITION

Although technically spring begins with the vernal equinox on March 21 and ends with the summer solstice on June 21, for us who garden in the Northeast, March is usually too chilly for much activity among our perennials. Our spring doesn't usually begin until early or mid-April when, comforted by a sweater, we poke around to see what's what and at that time find a good many plants up and budding, some even blooming in a tentative way.

In our perennial borders the wave of color moves from the edge in April toward the center of the beds through May and June, and becomes a crescendo along the back in September and October. The edging plants, except for the Cushion chrysanthemums and dwarf asters, are plants of spring. But there are many other edging plants we will want for later bloom, and some space must be reserved for them. Usually we tend to plant excessively while garden fever runs high.

Blue phlox with lily-of-the-
valley in early May.
TALOUMIS PHOTO

White *Iberis* and *Viola
cornuta* 'Apricot' in late
April. GENEREUX PHOTO

Spring Color

Right on the heels of the fading Christmas-roses come the lovely, low-growing, late April-blooming perennials. Besides the alyssum, candytuft, and rockcress for the outer rim of our plantings, and entrancing blue forget-me-nots for bedding, there are other small treasures to tuck in as we can for early-spring enjoyment—the pasque-flower and creeping phlox, sweet violets, and perennial pansies.

The pasque-flower, the small *Anemone pulsatilla,* opens purple cups with fuzzy golden centers on plants 9 to 12 inches high. April is its month, and it will show early if the location is warm, as in a sheltered rock garden. Do plant where you can glimpse it from a window. Then there are two small relatives of the familiar tall garden phlox—the mat-forming ground-pink, *Phlox subulata,* pink, rose-purple, or white, a spreader in the sun and sometimes blooming late in March, and the wild blue Canadian phlox, *P. divaricata,* really lavender or white. Twelve inches high, this phlox with its excellent foliage makes a lovely April to May carpet, a fine foil for the early carmine-tinted, ivory waterlily tulip, *T. kaufmanniana,* and the white and cherry-red lady tulip, *T. clusiana.* I have also appreciated clusters of early yellow narcissus in the midst of the big stretch of blue phlox that grew beside my brook. Here, in my new garden, the yellow narcissus is in bloom when the Norway maple is shedding its golden pollen, and Snug's gray coat, as well as the brick walks, is covered with it.

Where your beds are partly shaded or you want something to finish off a shrub border, an area where the sunlight hardly reaches, do try some of the cultivated violets that will also prosper in the sun. Varieties of *Viola odorata,* the sweet violet, are unlikely to survive where temperatures occasionally drop to zero but anyway are worth a trial. The dark purple variety *semperflorens* lives up to its name all summer long. 'Royal Robe' produces long-stemmed, fragrant flowers even before winter ends; 'White Czar' and the pink 'Rosina', said to bloom again in autumn, are charming companions. The hardy perennial pansies, *V. cornuta,* carry on where they are content, from April to October. I plant mine in the sun, trim back the leggy, early-summer growth, and take care to dose plants regularly with a soluble fertilizer, but not during extremely hot weather, which they don't care for. The lavender 'Floraire' is likely to bloom right after the snow melts, also the indefatigable apricot 'Chantreyland', my favorite, not only for good looks but also for good behavior. You will find plants of this one at roadside stands, not to date in catalogues, but you can buy seed for it or for 'Apricot', which both Park and Burpee offer. All the violas want soil rich in compost or leafmold and plenty of water if the season is dry.

Virginia bluebells in May.
GOTTSCHO-SCHLEISNER
PHOTO

For me an indispensable picture for late April into May is composed of tall bleedinghearts and Virginia bluebells, planted side by side, with the yellow doronicum (or leopardsbane) in front to enliven the scene, maidenhair ferns to conceal the departure of these early actors, blue forget-me-nots for carpeting, and the flushed rose tulip for accent. (In Chapter 14 on shade plants, I have more to say of these favorites.)

Peonies, irises, and the earliest daylilies come into their own late in May, and the yellow-to-orange, 24-inch globeflower, *Trollius europaeus,* a handsome buttercup cousin, can now add interest to a garden of these more

Earliest of the daisy
flowers, the soft-yellow
Doronicum caucasicum.
TALOUMIS PHOTO

familiar subjects. The globeflower is also just the plant to lighten a shaded,
somewhat damp area, and I enjoyed it along the brook. I hope you will
make the acquaintance of this delightful perennial as well as the spiderwort, *Tradescantia virginiana*. They are about the same height, but the
spiderwort is not for season-long placement because it must be cut back
after bloom. However, it makes a fine showing when fall comes, and is up
by March in spring. The improved varieties are lovely in mixture or
separately, as the mauve 'Pauline', white and lavender-flushed 'Iris Pritch-
ard', or the newer 'Red Cloud'. I do enjoy tradescantias.

May into June

Late in May, as color moves toward the center of the border, columbines provide an airy contrast to the stalwart forms of peonies. Yet who would seek a reason beyond their own attractiveness to plant columbines? Captivating in their own right, these spurred and birdlike blossoms pendant on airy stems are charming for garden or vase. In May and June they bloom just after the tulips and, since their heights—according to the species or variety—vary from low to medium, their place is in the foreground of the border just behind the edging plants.

There are three species you will enjoy if you have room for them: the 30-inch yellow *Aquilegia chrysantha,* which is likely to go on blooming to July; the 20-inch Rocky Mountain, lavender *A. caerulea,* a lovely thing; and the 6- to 8-inch white fan columbine, *A. flabellata nana alba.* Where only one kind is possible, you will probably want an improved strain like the 18-inch Dwarf Dragonfly, the McKana Giants to 3 feet, or the 30-inch Spring Song Hybrids that usually have more than a single row of petals. These delight me in my present garden with wild blue phlox in front of them and yellow azaleas in back.

Columbines thrive in full sun or light shade but are not drought resistant and so need summer watering even after the flowering sprays have been cut down. Plants are not long-lived, hardly beyond two years, but they come easily from seed, so it's a good plan to keep a crop coming with sowings every other June.

I hope your plants will be spared leafminer attack. Mine recovered from the labyrinthine tunnelings of these pests when I was constant about cutting off attacked foliage and sprayed plants several times with Malathion. If you are using a contact spray elsewhere for aphids, this should destroy the leafminer too. I am now trying Isotox, systemic insecticide granules sprinkled around my plants and watered in well. I work the systemic lightly into the soil because our kitten, Snug, is so terribly inquisitive that I have to be constantly careful. But systemics are far less trouble than sprays, they can't wash off, and they last about six weeks, which is long enough for columbine protection. However, if you wish to spray, Malathion or Sevin does a good job.

True Blues

Along with the columbines, a stretch of forget-me-nots or of *Brunnera macrophylla* (formerly *Anchusa myosotidiflora*) in front of the feathery flax or linum beside them will be lovely, for these three offer true-blue, not

Long-spurred columbine 'Rose Queen' in late May. ROCHE PHOTO

lavender, spring flowers, and this rare blue is enchanting with every other color in the garden. From early spring to early summer, the 12- to 18-inch brunnera with its forget-me-not flowers, is a charming sight in light shade. Plants need space, for they develop tremendous foliage after the flowers fade. From the living room windows I enjoyed a big blue spread of this under a white birch tree; it was a lovely sight.

The 18-inch feathery *Linum perenne*, blooming from May into August, is charming, with white or yellow tulips and with white phlox 'Miss Lingard' in a foreground planting. Its azure shower of fine petals is as pretty on the plant as on the ground, which it literally "blues" around it every morning. By removing almost at the earth line the shoots that have bloomed, you can induce thicker growth and longer flowering. I couldn't say of this blue flax that it is as indispensable as is peony or iris, only that you'll love it and treasure it for color and pleasant individuality.

June into Summer with Poppies

If you have space for plants of three weeks' bloom and six weeks' disappearance, plant the oriental poppies. As spring slips into summer, from late May through June, these poppies make a garden sing with color. But a well-grown, 30-inch or taller specimen needs almost as much space as a peony, and furthermore requires later-blooming plants such as phlox, hardy asters, or babysbreath to cover up its long rest period. In its favor, I must add that the flowers are stunning and the plants are winter hardy, thrifty, and undemanding. In fact, if your garden were all poppies, you wouldn't need spray or dust gun, hose, or even fertilizers, which only induce rank growth. Planted 2 to 3 inches deep in a sunny or lightly shaded garden bed, in well-drained soil, originally well prepared with leafmold and bonemeal, poppies can be trusted to carry on beautifully by themselves for many years. Mid-July to late September is the best planting time, and do keep locations marked so that you won't forget and let other plants crowd them out during July and early August.

Three of the older varieties go well together—'Barr's White', pink 'Helen Elizabeth', and cerise 'Watermelon', or you might prefer the new deeper pink 'Salome' to 'Helen Elizabeth'. If you have a separate spot for a red and white planting of the vermilion 'Surprise' or orange-red 'Bonfire' with 'Barr's White', you will have something spectacular. But I would never advise buying these poppies in mixtures, and I don't care for the doubles.

As cut flowers the single, crinkled, satiny blooms are excellent if properly

Carefree but spectacular oriental poppies for May–June transition. GENEREUX PHOTO

treated. Gather them just as the buds show color and before the bees get to them, either in the evening or early morning. Sear the cut ends of stems as promptly as possible over a gas flame until the lower inch or so is charred. Or follow my plan of taking a lighted candle and a pail of water to the garden for poppy cutting at dusk. I sear each stem as I cut and immediately plunge it up to the neck of the flower in warm water. The pail is then placed on the porch next to the house wall where no early eastern sun will touch the buds. Indoors then in the morning the bouquet is made. The buds open their glowing chalices quickly and the flowers stay fresh four days or more.

Six- to 12-inch blossoms, 2- to 4-foot plants, colors that make the rainbow a pallid arc, and a month's succession of cut flowers—all this, with less than usual routine care, makes the oriental poppy a perennial prized by every knowing gardener whose space permits its brilliant presence.

A handsome pure-white semidouble Japanese tree peony. GENEREUX PHOTO

4

THE EVER-BEAUTIFUL PEONIES

If any herbaceous plant can be considered indestructible, surely it is the peony. Of ancient lineage—*Paeonia lactiflora* was grown in China at least 2,500 years ago and *P. officinalis* for centuries in southern Europe and western Asia—hybrids of these two species later were known popularly as "Chinese" peonies in gardens of northern Europe and England. They became a cherished subject in American colonial gardens. Thomas Jefferson records them in his *Garden Book, 1771*. One form created in France in 1851, the rose-flecked, fragrant double white 'Festiva Maxima', is still a jewel of a plant and a resident of every garden I have ever planted.

I like to think of this variety enduring through decades in the peony hedge that bordered my garden in Philadelphia long before I came there. And who has not been amazed to find blooming plants beside the foundations of houses long given over to decay, or in overgrown, deserted gardens. Today the windows of my study look out on such a garden. The dwelling, in a protected historic area, and the two thriving boxwoods, sentinels of a once-important garden path, indicate a planting at least half a century old; yet there in June in a heavily weed-infested area the peony plants produce flowers lovely enough for the neighbors' bouquets.

Indestructible is indeed the word for the modern descendants of this Chinese plant, *P. lactiflora.*

John C. Wister remarks in his Introduction to *The Peonies:* "Herbaceous peonies are among the few really dependable and truly long-lived hardy perennials. They do not maintain themselves by spreading out into new areas, but instead exist decade after decade in the same spot, yielding divisions which their owners can pass on to children and friends. It is not unusual to see one of these long-lived and sturdy plants which has expanded to four or five feet across. Such a large specimen has obviously been flourishing undisturbed in the same position for many years. Under most circumstances it is good garden practice to divide and reset the plants after ten or twelve years."

Modern hybrid peonies accommodate themselves to a wide climatic range, flourishing through our north temperate areas, especially in the cold Dakotas and Minnesota, as well as in western Canada. However, they are not successful in the sub-tropical areas of Florida and southern California, where no cold winters occur to satisfy their need for a dormant rest period.

Botanists classify peonies as Double, Semidouble, Single, Japanese, and Anemone-flowered, but most of us simply select our garden peonies as Doubles or Singles. We are not too concerned as to whether those great golden cushions in the centers of the usually five-petaled semidoubles and singles are composed of pollen-bearing stamens, stamenodes, or carpels. We just like the contrasting effects of white, pink, or red petals and prominent yellow centers.

Familiar to all of us are the so-called Chinese doubles: their great massive blooms, globular or bomb-shaped, are spectacular wherever they are planted. And certainly the double varieties have tremendous vitality. Catalogues offer today the same ones I enjoyed more than thirty years ago, such as the white 'Festiva Maxima' "largest and gayest," and the pink 'Mons. Jules Elie', whereas among chrysanthemums, for instance, I find today not one familiar face of those that pleased me in earlier gardens.

The semidoubles and the various singles, usually listed together in catalogues, are more suited to today's smaller gardens and strip plantings than the great handsome doubles, which are great for the "new" island beds. I have enjoyed the singles for years but see them too seldom in other gardens. I value them for their simple elegance and their often lower stature. They do not overwhelm limited spaces, and all make excellent cut flowers.

In addition to these herbaceous peonies, there are the tree peonies, which are really shrubs, with similar flowers produced on a woody framework that does not die down in winter—but more presently on these.

HANDSOME CHINESE DOUBLE PEONIES

Selecting a few double peonies is a mind-boggling business in view of the many gorgeous and *dependable* varieties available today. It is estimated that more than a thousand named horticultural varieties of *P. lactiflora* have been produced (some of them probably duplicates) in the past 150 years. Furthermore, the old varieties—1851 for 'Festiva Maxima', 1881 for 'Felix Crousse'—are still listed because they are still worthwhile. Anyway, after prayer and fasting, I suggest the following ten for long-season fragrant bloom in a wide color range. Perhaps I should delete 'Therese', which is on few commercial lists, but I can't. This one is indispensable to me. It was introduced in France in 1904, and fifty years later was still the highest rated of all pink peonies. Because peonies last well indoors and are strongly fragrant there, they are excellent bouquet flowers. I wish you could have all ten—and one other of your own discovery!

TEN FINE DOUBLE PEONIES

E—Early; M—Midseason; L—Late; F—Fragrant;
VF—Very Fragrant

Name	Color	Season	Fragrance
Bowl of Cream	Glistening cream-white, rose type	M	VF
Felix Crousse	Red bomb type, brilliant	L	F
Festiva Maxima	Crimson-flecked white	E	F
Moonstone	Large, white outside, delicate pink inside, among best	M	F
Mons. Jules Elie	Large deep pink, bomb type	E	VF
Mrs. Franklin D. Roosevelt	Rose form, deep pink, fringed petals	E	VF
Philippe Rivoire	Small, deep red, rose form	M	F
Sarah Bernhardt	Dark pink, very fine	M	VF
Therese	Light pink to lilac white, large and lovely	E	VF
Walter Faxon	Pure bright rose, medium height	M	F

Since season of bloom is important to all of us who pursue the impossible dream of continuous color, here is an approximate sequence of peonies that you may find helpful as you make your selection for May to June peony color. And with your peonies, you will probably want plants of the tall bearded irises.

Sequence of Double Herbaceous and Tree Peonies

May 10–30	Japanese Tree Peonies, *Paeonia suffruticosa* (Moutan) and Herbaceous Hybrids
May 20–30	Lutea Tree Peonies, *P. suffruticosa x P. lutea,* especially var. *ludlowii*
May 25 on	Early Chinese Double Peonies, *P. lactiflora* (*albiflora*) Hybrids
May 30 on	Midseason Double Chinese Peonies
June 5	Late Chinese Double Peonies

Sequence of Tall Bearded Irises

Early Peonies bloom with midseason Irises, beginning about May 23
Early-midseason Peonies bloom with medium-late Irises, beginning about
  May 27
Midseason Peonies bloom with late Irises, beginning about May 31
Late Peonies bloom with those very long-season Irises still in flower in
  June

SINGLE PEONIES FOR SMALLER PLACES

The singles are, indeed, favorites of mine, and have been for years. I wish they could find their way into your yard or garden, too. The singles —including the Japanese, Anemone-flowered, and some like 'Silvia Saunders', often listed as semidouble—have a delicate air compared to the massive doubles, and the golden-centered flowers are light enough to hold their heads up unassisted after a driving spring rain.

In a 2- or 3-foot strip border these singles are both suitable and attractive. I like to plant the pink 'Silvia Saunders' with an edging of deeper pink coralbells, the white Isani-Gidui with yellow epimedium, and the brilliant red 'Sword Dance' with white candytuft. The lower border irises are also good associates for these single peonies, as the pink 'Lace Valentine' and lavender 'Moonshade'. The miniature daylilies like the yellow 'Bitsy' or pink 'Curls' provide a two-season effect.

Here then are singles that are bound to please you. If you are only familiar with the big doubles, do plant a few.

SOME FINE SINGLE PEONIES

Ama-No-Sode, very large, pink, yellow-touched petals
Gay Paree, pink and white bicolor
Gold Standard, tall, white, tinted yellow, handsome (expensive)
Isani-Gidui, "like a large white poppy," perhaps the best
Le Jour, large loose crinkled white
President Lincoln, heavy-textured dark red, rounded petals
Primavere, enormous white, full golden center
Seashell, tall, light satiny-pink, a favorite
Silvia Saunders, "semisingle," pink petals, white at base
Sword Dance, brilliant, late-flowering red

THE HERBACEOUS HYBRIDS

Here I must say a word about what used to be known as the new herbaceous hybrids. Actually they are no longer new, some of my favorites going back to 1939. The species—*P. albiflora, officinalis, tenuifolia, macrophylla,* and others—have been used to create these fine double, triple, and quadruple hybrids. I prefer the varieties with single flowers, although some doubles like 'Auten's Red' and the semidouble rose-pink 'Ludovica' are also to be considered. These hybrids are not so commonly available today as other peonies, but I find them well represented in Louis Smirnow's catalogue. (See address under Where to Buy.) Here is a list of lovely singles, particularly useful for your strip or other narrow plantings when 2-foot-high rather than 3-foot-high plants are desirable.

LOW-GROWING SINGLE HERBACEOUS HYBRIDS

Avant Garde, salmon-pink, to 18 inches
Campagna, white goblet, green tones, fringed petals, to 25 inches
Cardinal's Robe, shining scarlet, to 26 inches
Coralie, coral-pink, crinkled, to 21 inches
Good Cheer, pink to orange, to 21 inches
Green Ivory, unusual, two-tone, to 26 inches
Laddie, scarlet, early, ferny foliage, to 22 inches
Lavender Strain, with pink tones, to 22 inches
Le Printemps, yellow to pink, to 18 inches

Some Charming Associations

Peonies need space, up to 4 feet for each tall grower and hardly less then 30 inches for the smaller kinds. If you have a fence or wall, a planting of peonies alone running the full length will delight your heart all through June, the foliage thereafter until frost, a fine, enduring green. Or you may plant peonies in front of your shrubbery border of lilacs, mock oranges, deutzias, and rugosa roses, with annuals in front of the peonies, to give you flowers from July on. In August, peony foliage can be a perfect setting for *Lilium henryi* and *L. tigrinum* interplanted and rising above them. Peonies are also attractive in the fore of foundation plantings or along a not-low-enough terrace where the supporting wall would other-wise be unpleasantly bare or around a "ground floor" terrace. They have particularly pleased me edging a long driveway with a line of dianthus in front that offered color well into fall after the peonies were only a respectable green.

In the yard or garden, peonies have many values. If their primary use is for bouquets, one plant each of an early, midseason, and late variety in favorite colors, plus one or two of the early fernleaf species, *P. tenuifolia,* may be set out in a cutting row. These will bloom from early May through June. For boundaries or low hedges one variety looks best, unless the line is long. Then it may be composed of groups of different colors but all blooming at the same season. For example, an early-flowering boundary

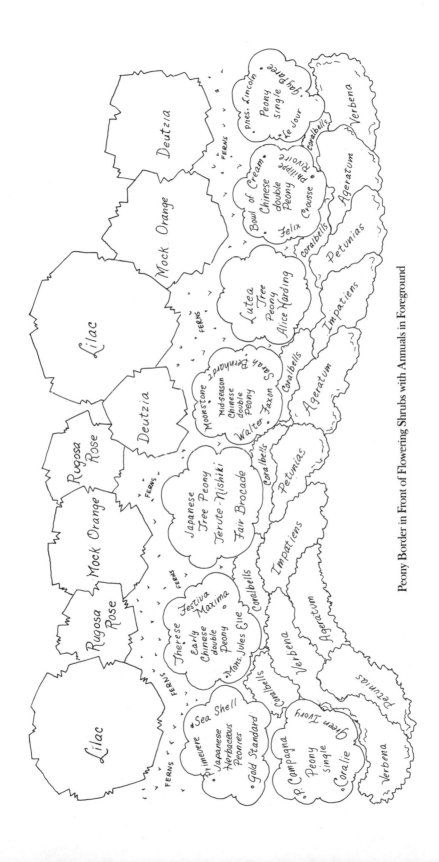

Peony Border in Front of Flowering Shrubs with Annuals in Foreground

could be made of white, blush, and rose peonies with groups of 'Festiva
Maxima', 'Therese', and 'Mons. Jules Elie', or a one-color effect for
midseason obtained from the very handsome red 'Philippe Rivoire'.

Where there is room for these big doubles, the glistening white 'Bowl
of Cream' is stunning with a tall, yellow iris (like 'Brightside') and clusters
of forget-me-not brunnera for foreground.

The pink 'Sarah Bernhardt' is well accompanied by a tall *Iris sibirica,*
such as the bright blue 'Gatineau', with low *Nepeta mussinii* before it. Or
if the pink 'New Dawn' climbing rose grows in your garden, try this group
in front of it for June beauty. Broad masses of blue baptisia, yellow
thermopsis, and the white and fragrant garden heliotrope, *Valeriana
officinalis,* also form pleasing backgrounds for peonies.

Peonies look well in beds by themselves, since their foliage from April
reddish tint to final September green never falters. Perhaps you will
want the new look of an island bed on your lawn. For this the double
stalwart peony bushes would be ideal, with the lowest-growing Cushion
chrysanthemums for the edge, and, if there is room, an intermediate
planting of *Aster frikartii.* Your island would then be colorful from late
May far into September. If you plant peonies near a porch or open
windows or for cutting, by all means select very fragrant varieties.

Planting and Care

Today, ease of culture is nearly always our first requisite in selecting
plants; in this regard the peony is pre-eminent. It is also adaptable to
various situations. Important for the taller kinds is protection from wind
and a fair amount of sunlight. Full sun is usually recommended, but I
have had fine bloom from plants receiving only a few hours of early
sunshine and then light but no direct sun through the afternoon.

Well-rooted two-year-old plants with three to five eyes are the only
reliable kind to buy, and mid-September to early October is considered
the best time to plant, although I have successfully moved them at my
convenience in spring, even in early summer. Good drainage is essential.
Dig the beds deep, at least 1 foot, deeper if you can manage it for this
quite permanent planting. Mix in compost liberally.

When you set out peonies, place the growing points—pink buds called
"eyes" protruding from the roots—just below the soil surface so that the
buds will be about 2 inches deep in firm clay loam and certainly no more
than 3 inches down in very light soil. As I have said, allow 3 to 4 feet
for the full development of each plant. (You can use the space between

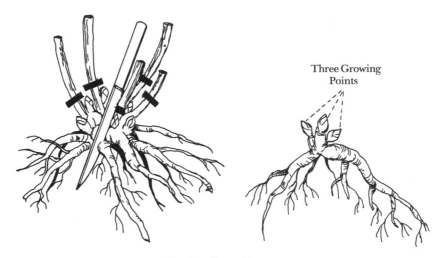

Three Growing
Points

Dividing Peony Roots
Three Eyes for Each Division

for groups of early narcissus.) Allow two weeks between soil preparation and planting; if little or no rain, soak the new bed thoroughly to hasten settling. Sinking is dangerous afterward, since it results in the burial of crowns that should remain near the surface.

Take all possible care with this planting operation. Hollow out sufficiently large holes for each clump and work the soil firmly around the roots with your fingers so as to leave no air pockets. Finally, *tramp* the soil down well and water deeply. Remember, you are not planting a perennial that is to be reset in a year or so but one that is to dwell in the same place for ten years or more.

When in the course of years it may be necessary to divide clumps, choose a new location or else remove the exhausted soil in the present one and replace it with fresh before resetting the stock. Separate the clumps with a sharp knife into strong natural divisions containing at least three growing points. Don't hesitate to discard very old material, since this seldom yields worthwhile stock.

In October, as a sanitary measure, cut off all peony foliage and stems and *burn* them to destroy any possibly lingering fungus spores. Then work a trowelful of bonemeal into the soil around each crown. Except for the first year, provide no winter covering. When the ground freezes hard that first year, mound soil several inches over the plants after tops have been cut down. Or spread evergreen boughs, not leaves, over the plants.

A trowelful of wood ashes, saved from your fireplace, and half a handful per plant of a commercial plant food—4-8-8 or 4-8-10 or 20 per cent superphosphate—in spring supplements the autumn feeding of bonemeal and, in all, affords for an average-size plant a very square meal indeed. Peonies of great size or peonies that are being reconditioned can do with three times as much food. Or if a complete fertilizer is being used in the garden, the peonies can be given this in spring.

Disbudding may be another spring chore. If you want large-sized flowers for cutting, remove the two side buds as each group of three forms. If the flowers are to stay on your plants, as mine are, don't disbud at all and the blooming period will be longer and more effective, quantity-wise.

By all means put supports in place early for the doubles. I always thrust double-ring tripods (see page 188) around the big peonies when growth first appears. Otherwise I may find myself so busy in spring that suddenly the peonies are in full and heavy bud and handling them then is a terrific chore involving not me alone but two of us. Incidentally, don't worry about ants on the buds. They are after the honey exuding there and do no harm at all.

Be sure plants are kept well watered. Sometimes a drought occurs in spring as well as in summer. I get busy then with a slow-running hose moved on the half hour from plant to plant.

Why They Don't Bloom

Perhaps you are not nearly so keen as I am about peonies because for you they have been plants that simply will not bloom. Don't give them up on this account. There is probably a definite reason for their failure, which you may well be able to discover.

If plants are in deep shade or growing where they must compete for food and moisture with tree and shrub roots, by all means transplant them to an open, sunny location where very likely they will start to bloom after a year's stay. If you suspect that they have been planted deeper than the allowed 2 or 3 inches, reset them. If they are very old plants in a starved condition, you might try to revive them with generous spring and autumn doses of plant food, but replacing them with a few stalwart new plants will probably give you a lot more satisfaction.

If buds drop prematurely and stems discolor or rot off at the base, or if buds turn brown while small, suspect botrytis blight and spray every ten days with Benlate from the time shoots are a few inches high until buds appear. Then, in fall, cut stalks at ground level and destroy them. A further precaution would be to remove carefully the soil from around the crowns to a depth of 2 to 3 inches and to replace it with new. And to prevent the spread of trouble in the spring, cut off and drop in to a paper bag all imperfect buds as well as any open flowers just before they shatter. Then *burn* everything.

Sometimes failing plants reveal, on examination of roots, galls or knots that pathologists say are caused by nematodes. If such roots are dug up and immersed for thirty minutes in water heated to 120 degrees Fahrenheit, they may be saved. Crown and root rot can be similarly checked; sterilized plants are reset in fresh soil and preferably in a new location. Only I confess if I had to do all this I'd just throw the plants out and either get a few new ones or conclude there were other perennials for me.

Finally, your peonies may not bloom because they are too small and young. The first year after they have been planted, there may be no flowering or only a meager showing and the blooms not typical of the variety. If the divisions you set out included less than three eyes, there may be no bloom for a year or two. Quite obviously then, your only remedy is an attitude of patient anticipation. But when they are in full swing and healthy, you will find they have been well worth the waiting, for they are handsome plants, indeed, in or out of bloom, and there is never a shabby spring-to-autumn moment on the peony calendar.

TREE PEONIES

These aren't herbaceous perennials, the main concern of this book, but they are certainly peonies, producing on their enduring woody frames, flowers similar to those of the familiar garden peonies that die down in winter. The tree peonies, *Paeonia suffruticosa* (Moutan), have given me so much pleasure that I cannot disregard them here while freely admitting they are indeed deciduous shrubs. Plants of great distinction, and much too rarely included in gardens, the tree peonies in my experience are as easy to grow as their herbaceous cousins, and they have the advantage of advancing the peony season by ten days or so, usually opening their elegant buds before mid-May.

Tree peonies, from 3 to 4 feet high and about as broad in maturity, are garden aristocrats, expensive and worth their cost. They (or it) are to be chosen with considerable care for you want to be sure you have flowers you like to dwell upon. Try to select plants in bloom; they will be with you for years; indeed, I always marvel at their longevity. In some Philadelphia gardens that date back to the Revolution are tree peonies known to be 150 years old. Others are upstarts, tracing their origins only to the Centennial Exposition of 1876. All, like true philosophers, have gained in beauty with age and have refused to succumb to the rigors of time.

The species is of Chinese and Japanese origin and was first introduced into England, via the East India Company at Canton, in 1789. Today, somewhat artificially, tree peonies are considered of three types: Chinese, Japanese, and Yellow Hybrids (from *P. lutea,* discovered much later in western China). From these types many cultivars have been derived. The Chinese are large, opulent, shaggy, and heavy flowers; the Japanese flowers are not so huge, single, semidouble, or double, but held on strong, erect stems. The Yellow Hybrids, now including other colors and some very dark ones, are the last to bloom.

Plants are characterized by fine narrow leaves and large, broad-petaled, crinkle-tipped, single, semidouble, or "double" flowers displaying a prominent cushion of golden anthers in the less heavy varieties. Actually there are few true doubles in this group, but the semidoubles have a double look with their full set of pistils and stamens in the center surrounded by rows of ruffled petals, usually ten or more in two or three rows; and most catalogues describe these as doubles.

Single Japanese tree peonies have up to eight or nine petals but look five-petaled. The finest, most luminous whites are in this Japanese class, and here you will do well to make your first selection. The tall, double, pure white 'Renkaku' (Flight of Cranes) has been a long delight for me. Also a little later the glistening white 'Gessekai' (Kingdom of the Moon). When you are selecting, do have a look also at the white, rose-stained, fragrant 'Shuchiuka' (Flower in Wine), the pure pink 'Terute Nishiki' (Fair Brocade), the glistening scarlet 'Nisshow' (Sunshine), the clear violet 'Kamada Fuji' (Wisteria of Kamada), and the famous, brilliant, royal purple 'Rimpo' (Sacred Bird).

The Lutea hybrids are the result of crosses of *P. suffruticosa* varieties with the species *P. lutea.* Here are the gorgeous yellows that have given me so much pleasure beside the terrace where they are protected from the wind. You will be charmed by such singles as the fragrant 'Argosy', 'Canary', and 'L'Esperance'; semidouble 'Mme. Louis Henry', and "doubles" like 'Souvenir de Maxime Cornu' and 'Alice Harding', perhaps the most popular of all.

Selecting your investment will, indeed, be difficult, so take your time.

How to Plant

Take pains when you set out these treasures, preferably in mid-September or seven to ten days earlier in those regions where first frosts are likely to occur before mid-October. It is worthwhile to prepare a good-sized hole 18 inches deep and 30 inches across if possible with a filling of rich topsoil mixed with plenty of bonemeal. Since the tree-peony root is grafted on a thick herbaceous peony root, you want to set the knobby graft, where the two roots are joined, 6 to 7 inches down. Let the soil line of the plant guide you. Planted deep, the stringy, brittle, tree-peony roots will take over. Spread them out when you plant, water liberally, and keep the soil damp, not wet, until there is a heavy frost. In the interim the tree-peony roots will have time to grow and become established. Be careful not to harm the woody top; on the development of a tall, free-branching frame depends the abundance of the flowers.

Full sun is not essential to free flowering. As Gertrude Jekyll wrote: "The Moutans do best with even a little passing shade at some time of the day." An evergreen planting or similar shield behind them protects plants from the full sweep of the wind and forms a barrier to a late touch of frost. Louis Smirnow recommends for "half shade to almost full shade" the pink 'Gosho Zakur' (Cherries of the Imperial Palace), red 'Ruby Delight', and purple 'Rimpo' (Sacred Bird). He thinks 'Stolen Heaven' the best white for shade, but I found my 'Renkaku' (Flight of Cranes) a glistening marvel. If the names affright you, don't be afraid to buy by color alone, and notice that the Japanese tree peonies may also be listed as Chinese.

Peonies, herbaceous or woody, can be the colorful mainstay of your May to June yard or garden. Properly planted at the start, they are almost never disappointing as to flowers for cutting or outdoor display, and their undemanding nature and enduring foliage make them indubitably one of the best of our chosen Big Four.

Iris germanica in a dooryard garden with a picket fence. ROCHE PHOTO

5

THE STATELY IRIS

On a cool morning in late May or early June, a tall bearded iris sparkling in the sunlight is one of the most beautiful flowers in the garden, for the blossoms, especially the paler ones, have a glistening quality that adds to their brilliance. The first of the important Big Four perennials to bloom, today's tall bearded irises are of easy culture and most rewarding, since they can be effective in many ways, in gardens large or small. To the collector, they offer an astonishing variety of color patterns and combinations.

Bearded Irises in Use

Perhaps you have a little plot enclosed by a picket fence. Iris and a picket fence are natural companions. Or you may want a fairly narrow but colorful border to enjoy as you walk along the path to your house. Perhaps your backyard has a big center grass plot that you'd like to surround with a colorful shrub and perennial border. There big accenting clumps of several kinds of bearded iris in your favorite colors—I am always selecting the paler ones in melting shades of cream, yellow, pink, and lavender, but you may like the deeper shades—will give you pleasure through weeks of May to June bloom. Later the fine upright lance foliage will be a good foil for masses of phlox and asters. If you have a narrow but sunny strip between your house and a walk, bed it with bearded irises or set good-sized clumps of some favorite kind to accent a flight of steps or the corners of your terrace.

A garden planted mainly to irises with all else secondary in spring is quite intoxicating. Such are the great· borders of my friend Edna Payne, where late May to mid-June (her diary records May 20 to June 17) is brilliant with tall bearded irises, and July and August glorious with daylilies. These two plants are more than a hobby for Mrs. Payne; they are almost her way of life. In winter she studies the catalogues—and what handsome color these present—to make her selections among ·the newer kinds of irises and daylilies; in spring she plants; in summer she tends, working hard over plantings beside the driveway that are 3 feet wide and 50 feet long. At the back of the border is a convenient foot-wide path that separates it from a wider planting of evergreens and azaleas. These are ·interplanted with tall white foxgloves, lofty blue Pacific Hybrid delphinium, a medley of chrysanthemums, and apricot Connecticut Yankee lilies that offer fine background color to the green summer foliage of the irises.

For her newer trials, Mrs. Payne has planted another bed, some 4 by 20 feet, with the great 'Pink Pearl' lilac beside it. I sat beside this harmony one day in early June making notes of new favorites and entranced by the colors and the scents of irises, particularly of the blues, and of the tall pink shrub. The fragrances seemed similar to me, both pleasantly musky. The day before, Mrs. Payne and I had traveled together some two hundred miles to visit the Martin Viette Nurseries in East Norwich, Long Island. The same gorgeous irises kept appealing to me in both places. On pages 50–51 is a selective list of early, midseason, and late varieties. These can extend the season of iris pleasure for you who may want to make the tall bearded the emphatic plant in your garden.

For best effect, you have to be controlled in your choices, repeating groups of a few varieties, perhaps the white 'Christmas Time,' the pale-yellow 'Brightside', the powder-blue 'Eleanor's Pride', and that old favorite, the pink 'Esther Fay'. Of course, there's nothing wrong with a medley if irises are your hobby and you like studying many kinds or if you are growing for exhibition rather than garden splendor.

In a border planting, where the picture is the thing, you can get a handsome—and enduring—effect with colonies of irises interrupted with specimen plants of fountainous daylilies or the broader and deeper green

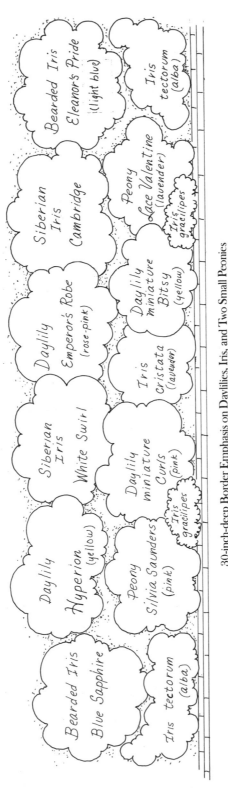

30-inch-deep Border Emphasis on Daylilies, Iris, and Two Small Peonies

foliage of peonies. Or you can emphasize the spring to summer iris picture with the lesser perennials. Tall airy columbines—McKana or other fine hybrids—pink pyrethrum, pink or white gasplant, *Dictamnus,* and rosy coralbells are lovely with a pink iris. I like the apricot-toned pansies or perennial violas with the lavender varieties. With an iris like 'Royal Gold' you may like the strong contrast of light-blue flax and dark-blue anchusa. With a dark, almost-red iris, tradescantias, both purple and white, are good companions, although with them you must allow for their weeks of August disappearance. The rich "crimson lake" hues of 'Frontier Marshal' are set off by blue lupines and white meadowrue. Of course, tulips are natural iris companions, especially for the early intermediate irises, the 15-to-18-inch kinds, and for narrow or wide beds, I do like an edging of white hardy candytuft, the ranging *Iberis semper-virens* where there is space, a small cultivar like 'Purity' for a quite narrow stretch.

The Categories

The tall beared irises are not all of a kind; particularly if you are exhibiting you need to distinguish the show categories as set up by the American Iris Society. If you are selecting for your garden, the categories won't matter to you, and you will probably emphasize the selfs, bitones, and blends.

Self is a flower of uniform color like 'Blue Sapphire', pink 'Esther Fay', and yellow 'Primrose Drift'. In the average garden planting the selfs seem to me to give the best effect.

Bicolor has upright petals, called standards, of a light or medium color, and drooping or flaring petals, called falls, of a deeper, contrasting hue; 'Touché' is a pink-and-blue example.

Bitone has two tones of the same color as the lavender and violet 'Came-lot'.

Blend is a *subtle* combination of two or more colors, one always being yellow, as in 'Commentary'.

Plicata has a stitched or stippled margin color on a white or yellow background. 'Stepping Out', white with purple margins, is a great favorite.

Among these types are varieties that are handsomely *ruffled*. In fact, most of the newer bearded irises are not only huge but also ruffled or fluted or crinkled, for hybridizers are striving to produce larger, more elaborate, and spectacular blooms.

Texture refers to the sheen or glisten of the petals, **substance** to their thickness. The **beard** is a small tuft of hair on the midribs at the point where these converge. Sometimes the beard is in decorative contrast, as the vermilion area on 'Christmas Time'; sometimes the beard is a self color, as in 'Blue Baron' or 'Royal Gold'.

Culture of the Tall Beardeds

Good drainage and plenty of sunshine spell success with tall bearded irises. If drainage is questionable, raise beds 3 to 4 inches. The beardeds are not overly particular about soil. Providing it is in good "tilth," it may be alkaline, neutral, or mildly acid. Prepare new beds 10 to 12 inches deep, preferably with plenty of well-rotted compost. Lacking compost, incorporate commercial cow manure in the soil, but this should go where feeding roots will reach it but well below the rhizomes. Touching them, manure may cause rot. For extra food, I always sprinkle bonemeal around the plants in fall and superphosphate or a balanced fertilizer in spring when this is applied to the other perennials. A 5–10–5 or 5–10–10 is good; a high-nitrogen fertilizer is not advisable, for it promotes lush growth that inclines to rot.

To insure good early root development for these big plants, set them out in July and August, except in hot sections of the South, when September may be a preferable time for garden work. Space plants about 2 feet apart. What is absolutely essential is shallow planting. "As a duck swims" was the old advice. Set the rhizomes almost on top of the soil or with no more than an inch of soil over them. The rhizome likes to bake in the sun; the feeding roots want the cool, damp earth below. Planted too deep, irises will not bloom well, and, of course, not much can be expected the first year after planting.

Face rhizomes (those fat underground stems enlarged by food storage and with roots attached) all the same way, preferably south so leaves won't shade flowers. In any case, avoid planting in a circle around an open area, for the center never fills in. Spread the fine feeding roots out circularly; don't pull them straight down. Don't cultivate but weed by hand and do keep the plantings "clean"; otherwise iris rot may occur or borers be attracted to a too-shaded rhizome. After plants bloom, you can remove a few of the now-drooping side leaves, and you can shorten the remaining leaves when transplanting or dividing in August, but don't cut down the fans until late fall, for leaves are the constant source of nourishment for the plants.

Borer Controls

Except for their attraction to borers, the tall bearded irises are perfect plants for ease of culture. Borers can be, but need not be, the flies in the ointment. On borer control, there are several points of view, but all are emphatic on keeping plantings cleaned up, and by hand. It is particularly important to get rid of every speck of debris in the fall when you cut down the fans. Now this is the borer story. The borer is one phase in the life cycle of a night-flying moth that lays eggs that overwinter at the base of the iris stalks. Remove the nesting sites in fall and you will go far toward avoiding trouble. Eggs that remain hatch early in spring. Then the larvae crawl up the outside of the iris leaves and puncture them. It is those pinholes that are certain evidence of borer trouble. As the borer devours the soft tissues of foliage, it looks like a thin white worm. Gradually it works its way down toward the rhizome, growing fat as it feeds. Unchecked, it will enter the rhizome, feed voraciously, swell to a 2-inch grub, and turn a pinkish tan. Inevitably rot develops in the damaged rhizome, which must now be lifted, the soft parts removed, and the cuts covered with a fungicide like Captan.

How to avoid borer trouble? Mrs. Payne depends on no chemicals, and there are few borers in her *very clean* plantings. If a puncture in a leaf and a watery appearance of the main fan indicate borer presence, she gives her plantings a meticulous examination, removing flowering stalks all the way down. Then she cuts off any leaves showing borer trouble, strips them open, and dispatches the culprit borer by hand. I've seen her do it. (Ugh!)

You may prefer the method advised by many iris specialists. Spray or dust with an insecticide like Malathion or Sevin, when new spring growth is about 3 inches high and you have cleaned up your planting. Then spray or dust twice more at weekly intervals until buds form. Of the soil systemics, at this time, none is definitely available that is strong enough to cope with the iris borer in the soil, although I have heard that Di-Syston granules have been successful in some instances. The Connecticut Extension Service advises me that "there are no systemics cleared for use for iris borer control. The best control for this insect is to keep the top of the tuber open [to the air], which will also help in control of rot diseases."

Rhizome rot may also develop from poor drainage in the beds or in a weed-ridden situation. The tall bearded iris needs sun on stems and leaves, and moisture but not wetness in the soil. A muggy season may also cause brown spotting of leaves and withered tips. This condition is unsightly but usually harmless, a response to humid weather.

When to Divide

Healthy plantings hardly need division before the third or fourth year, when deteriorating bloom indicates the need for more space. Any time from July to September is suitable. Trim fans back to about 5 inches, and with a sharp knife cut away the hard old sections of rhizome. This will leave you with L-shaped sections, the new growth starting from the angle of the L, and bloom stalks growing from this "heel." As you plant, face the sections in the same direction. As I have said, avoid open-center plantings.

The first winter after planting, mulch lightly, but afterward omit this protection unless you live in a subzero area. In spring, however, go over the beds early to press back into the soil any frost-heaved plants. Although established irises are quite drought tolerant, newly set plantings will need watering during dry spells until the roots take hold. Sometimes, too, brown leaf tips on older plants in times of drought indicate the need for a thorough soaking. Finally, make it a routine matter to relieve plants promptly of the stems of faded flowers at the ground line. This helps to let into each clump more health-giving sun and air.

To Help You Choose

The selective list in this chapter is by color and reflects my own preference. For the most part, I prefer the paler hues, maybe a few browns to go with the yellows, mostly the selfs and the bitones; no magentas, no shocking bicolor combinations, no dotted varieties. You may want the darker beardeds for contrast in your plantings, and certainly I have seen collectors sigh with pleasure over a dark brown like 'Dutch Chocolate', a magenta like 'Mulberry Wine', the so-called-red 'War Lord', even the "black" 'Patent Leather' and 'Licorice Stick'. Most plicatas strike me with horror, but the violet and white 'Stepping Out' was first on the American Iris Society's popularity poll in 1973 and continues to be favored there. It has won several awards, including the Dykes Medal (England) in 1968. What it seems to come to is that many gardeners prefer drifts of soft colors. We select irises differently from the collector who is thrilled by each triumph of the hybridizers' art and delights in stunning plant-by-plant variance. So, to each his own. Among bearded irises are kinds to please us both.

Some of my favorites, such as the powder-blue 'Eleanor's Pride', awarded the Dykes Medal (English) in 1961, have been around for some years. It is still one of the best but costs comparatively little. Newest beardeds may be introduced at twenty-five dollars. If these attract you, be patient. As the supply increases, especially if awards are given, the price will go down. In this list are irises that have received many awards, but I have indicated only those honored by the Dykes Medal (DM).

If possible, try to select your irises from fields of them in bloom as in the large Martin Viette Nursery in East Norwich, Long Island, or White Flower Farm in Litchfield, Connecticut; at Schreiner's in Salem, Oregon; at Wild's in Sarcoxie, Missouri. The full-color catalogues of iris specialists are also helpful guides. (Addresses are given in Where to Buy at the end of this book.)

A SELECTION OF HANDSOME TALL BEARDED IRISES

E—Early; M—Midseason; ML—Midseason to Late; L—Late

Blooming times vary somewhat with region and weather but this sequence will pretty much remain. DM indicates a Dykes Medal award.

Variety	Season	Height in Inches	Remarks
WHITE TO CREAM			
Christmas Time	M	40	Choice, frosty white corsage iris.
Cup Race	ML	38	Strong, superb white, pale lemon beard.
Winter Olympics	EM	38	Sparkling ruffled self, DM '67.
PALE YELLOW TO GOLD			
Brightside	EM	37	Pale, shimmering lemon yellow, lacy edge.
Celestial Glory	M	36	Gold to orange, orange-red beard, ruffled standards, handsome.
Fluted Lime	M	33	Flaring "green cast" yellow.
Green Quest	ML	36	Handsome chartreuse, clear yellow beard.

Variety	Season	Height in Inches	Remarks
(PALE YELLOW TO GOLD cont.)			
New Moon	M	36	Lemon yellow, heavily ruffled, expensive, DM '72.
Primrose Drift	ML	42	Fine light-yellow self, even the beard, DM '64.
Rainbow Gold	ML	36	Sunny yellow, crinkled, tangerine beard.
LAVENDER TO DEEP "BLUE"			
Babbling Brook	M	38	Fine light blue, lemon yellow beard, DM '72.
Blue Baron	M	40	Outstanding dark marine blue, self beard.
Blue Sapphire	E	40	Silvery, ruffled, has stood test of time, DM '58.
Eleanor's Pride	M	38	Glistening powder blue, graceful, majestic, DM '61.
Sky Watch	ML	38	Exquisite lavender-blue self, expensive, DM '70.
LIGHT TO DARK PINK			
Cashmere	ML	37	Lovely, deep rose, beard deeper color.
Esther Fay	M	35	Pink self, ruffled, reddish-pink beard.
Fashion Fling	L	36	Deep pink, tangerine beard.
Heartbreaker	ML	36	Flamingo, creamy cerise blend.
Pink Taffeta	EM	32	Light rose pink, heavily ruffled, expensive.

Smaller Beardeds in Five Figures

Be sure to consider the fine lower-growing beardeds, now featured in some catalogues. These don't produce as large rhizomes or increase as rapidly in the East as do the taller irises. They are therefore not such good commercials but are still excellent for gardens, especially if one's space is limited. These miniature dwarf beardeds, sometimes called wee ones, are

Miniature dwarf bearded
iris in a pavement planting.
GENEREUX PHOTO

under 10-inch cushion plants; they bloom a full month before the tall May beardeds, bringing bright April color to the edges of the garden or a rock slope or as a ruffle around an evergreen. The flowers on most of them are quite large in proportion to the dwarf plants. The yellow 'Bee Wings', 'Blue Frost', white 'Crispy', yellow 'Fashion Lady', and lilac and purple bicolor 'Grandma's Hat'—such an amusing name—would make a pretty grouping. With these miniature dwarfs pink ground phlox, *P. subulata,* is an excellent groundcover.

The standard dwarf beardeds or Lilliputs grow taller, 10 to 15 inches, and bloom early in May soon after the smallest beardeds. They are of mixed derivation, vigorous and colorful, again for front-of-the-border or rock garden. They are likely to bloom for some three weeks along with the latest daffodils and the very earliest tulips. You might select from among these: the pansy-purple 'Cherry Garden', white 'Cotton Blossom', 'Gingerbread Man' (if you like a brown iris), 'Greenspot', a white with a green spot as named, pink 'Lenna M' (still expensive), the bitone yellow 'Pamela Ann', light blue 'Sky Baby', yellow 'Stockholm', and red 'Wee Lad'.

The intermediate beardeds are taller with larger flowers. Their great advantage is their time of bloom, which precedes that of the tall beardeds and coincides with the early tulips. You can plan very pretty garden pictures with these. The lavender *Phlox divaricata* is excellent with them, also various violas. Flower size is in fairer proportion to plant height than with the lower-growing beardeds. Here you find varieties of clear and sparkling color. A nice start would be the purple 'Annikins', which branches right from the ground up, the light blue self 'Dilly Dilly', the red 'Indian Fire', and apricot 'Lilliput'. The 24-inch 'Arctic Ruffles' is a charming white, the 19-inch 'Toy Money' a fine gold.

Any of these, also the tall beardeds, may rebloom in August and September, but this is a maybe-yes, maybe-no situation in cold regions. Certainly there are good records for some of the Lilliputs. Apparently rebloom depends first on climate. In California a second showing is easily accomplished. Here with a cultural program that emphasizes water and feeding it is sometimes successful, but the second bloomings I have seen here were hardly good enough.

Border and table irises are also appealing, both 15 to 28 inches tall and blooming at the same time as the tall beardeds. The blue-on-white 'Embroidery', a plicata, pink 'Lace Valentine', and lavender 'Moonshade' are pretty border types with flowers in proportion to the plants. 'Dainty Bluebells', the white 'Dainty Dora', and the rosy 'New Idea' are attractive table varieties, their 2½-inch flowers on wiry stems. But do study the catalogues that feature these interesting smaller irises; the detailed descriptions are fascinating. Both border and table irises are particularly useful for narrow beds and strip plantings where the tall beardeds are likely to be out of scale. The lower-growing peonies, especially the single hybrids and the miniature daylilies, are fine companions for these too-little-planted smaller irises.

Other Smaller Delights

Two early-flowering bulbous irises have pleased me through the years. In protected places, touched by the late winter sun, both bloom in March, sometimes in late February, and how much appreciated are these first flowers! The 24-inch fragrant *Iris reticulata,* the netted iris, is purple with gold markings and four-angled stems. It may even appear while there is snow. Set it close to a house wall for protection and warmth. 'Joyce' and 'Violet Beauty' provide light and dark purple flowers. Also in March the rather tricky *I. danfordiae* may open bright yellow flowers

Iris cristata, low and appealing, for a dense groundcover even after the flowers have gone.

about the size of a species crocus, its 12-inch leaves appearing afterward. It needs a slightly acid soil. The reticulatas prefer an alkaline condition, so I dust the soil around these plants with lime every year after flowering. Where acid soil is called for, I don't bother, as I always seem to be dealing with soil of that condition.

Following these two bulbous irises is the 3- to 4-inch *I. cristata* that I plant now as a groundcover in partial shade under a little rose tree. It is such a charmer, lavender or the white *alba;* it thrives in moist soil, rich in humus. You will enjoy it, as I have, along with an early narcissus.

Two other crested irises add to the May picture. The 10-inch *I. gracilipes* is a tiny gem of a plant, lavender on white, and pretty for a rock garden or an informal border edging with its excellent foliage. Alas, it is rare today, and as far as I know, not available from catalogues. You may find it, as I have at a local nursery or in the older garden of a friend who will share it with you. *I. tectorum,* which in China and Japan covers thatched roofs, grows a little taller, mine to 12 inches, with frilled lavender-blue or white flowers in late May or early June. I like it as a specimen border plant, the foliage a little too lusty for a rock garden. Alternately grouped with lavender *Phlox divaricata,* it has been a pretty sight in a lightly shaded place and in soil from the compost pile. A clump of it is in exactly right scale for a small garden and it is easily grown from seed. The pure white form is considered by some iris enthusiasts as unsurpassed in balance and perfect symmetry.

'Snowcrest', a yellow Siberian iris with gleaming white standards. FITCH PHOTO

Siberian Iris

If you and your garden require some absolutely carefree plants of unfailing good looks and excellent bloom, do consider the beardless Siberian iris. I have treasured it for years, but I rarely see it in other people's gardens. Flowering in June for two weeks at least, the majority develop strong clumps to 3 feet with slender, grassy foliage and a quantity of individual stems carrying delicate white, lavender, or deep violet blooms.

Opening just before the later tall bearded varieties, the Siberians have real garden value. I have grown the older varieties like 'Perry's Blue', 'Snow Queen', and 'Caesar's Brother' for years and years in a richly prepared bed as well as in less mellow shrubbery borders; in both places they have provided quantities of bouquets. Although there was, of course, a difference in flower quality, both plantings required little beyond a few deep soakings prior to blooming if the season was dry, the clipping off of faded flower stems, and an application of a low-nitrogen fertilizer in spring. Rarely do these thick-rooted perennials require division, perhaps once in ten years, and for the most part they are disease-free and pest-free (certainly the older varieties have been so for me, but I am told that borers do sometimes get into the Siberians). After the first winter, you do not even have to bother with a cold-weather covering.

Their garden uses are, indeed, multiple. When you plant Siberians, space several single divisions 3 to 4 inches apart to form a clump. Even one clump of each color will afford quantities of cut flowers. Bea Warburton, an authority on irises and a world traveler viewing them in foreign lands, writes, "We who breed Siberians try to increase the bud count; the best new ones have probably four buds." Newer varieties have longer periods of bloom, up to five weeks. Useful dwarfs to 12 inches, and semidwarfs to 20 inches are becoming available, mainly from England and the West Coast, where they are far more satisfactory than in the East. The Siberians are well worth the hybridizer's attention. You can naturalize the 26-inch 'Blue Brilliant' delightfully or fit the deep blue 20-inch 'Perry's Pygmy' or the 2-foot 'Snow Queen' into the landscape design as a facing-down for shrubs or along a low porch to conceal foundations.

Siberians can also be used in separate beds where after flowering their foliage continues excellently green. Or they may be combined with other perennials. The clear blue 'Cambridge' and 'White Swirl' with its touch of yellow are handsome with such early daylilies as the dwarf yellow 'Little Cherub'; the shaded blue 'Sea Shadows' is a lovely companion for the crimson-flecked, fragrant, white 'Festiva Maxima' peony. 'Snow Queen' sets off red or deep pink oriental poppies, which are not always easy to place in a border. If you want to cut down on upkeep, select a favorite Siberian variety and have perhaps just one big clump to enjoy from a window, as I used to. It will give you great pleasure.

Japanese Iris

Really exquisite are the hybrids of the beardless Japanese Iris, *I. kaempferi,* also called oriental. I have loved them for years. From late June through July, after the pageantry of the tall bearded irises has subsided, this completely different type comes into beauty. Blooming for the most part after the first delphiniums and before summer phlox, the large, flat flowers—6 to 10 inches across—bring strong color to the border, and they

Japanese iris in the early July garden. GENEREUX PHOTO

are unbelievably beautiful as cut flowers. Especially to those who are adept at arrangements in the oriental manner is the kaempferi iris challenging material.

Plants vary in height from 3 to 5 feet. I favor the singles that have three large and three small petals, like 'Great White Heron' and the doubles like 'Gold Bound', which has long been a pleasure in my garden. The orchid 'Queen of Blues' and light 'Pink Frost' make a charming picture. In general, colors run from luscious deep, deep blue-purple through burgundy and pink shades to soft blues and whites with striking yellow markings. Indeed, I cannot recall seeing any variety I could dislike, and even mixtures are pleasing. In *The Iris Book,* Molly Price notes that the Marhigo and Payne strains have superior qualities; the stiffer flower stems better branched, resulting in more flowers per stalk and longer bloom. The flowers themselves, though no larger than the old favorites, have improved substance, are rain-resistant, and last much longer in the garden.

Success with this *I. kaempferi* is dependent on three factors: a well-drained site, an *acid* soil rich in organic matter and spread 2 inches over the crowns, and above all—and this is the real key to success—abundant moisture during the period of bud and bloom. But make certain the situation is not wet in winter; here in the North plants sometimes suffer injury under such conditions. The Japanese iris seems to require more food than other types. When I feed the azaleas in spring with an acid-type fertilizer, I apply this also to the Japanese iris.

If you include this iris in occasional sentinel clumps through the border, you will find the yellow lupinelike *Thermopsis caroliniana* a pleasing companion. I have also liked white oriental iris varieties and the blues with yellow meadowrue, *Thalictrum glaucum,* 'Bristol Fairy' babysbreath, regal lilies, and dark purple petunias. And many daylilies bloom handsomely with the Japanese iris, as 'Little Cherub' and 'Placer'. To make certain of fine flowering in the border all through the spring and up to blooming time, let the slow-running hose rest for several hours weekly among the plants. If you have a pool or stream, as I have had, by all means plant oriental irises beside it, not only because reflection doubles the beauty of the iris but also because plenty of water keeps it culturally content. In such a situation, ferns and astilbes are good associates.

Each year notice the quality of the blossoms. If with good culture they tend to get smaller and stems shorter, you had better decide upon division. This is usually advisable every three to four years, preferably just after flowering in July, although any time before October is safe, if a later date is more convenient for you. Separate each large clump into two or three sections, not into single pieces, or you will lack flowers completely for the next year or so. Water well, following division, to stimulate strong rooting before frost.

Spurias and Two Flags

Recently I have been planting the long-neglected but very hardy group of beardless spuria irises that bloom after the last tall beardeds. Reaching some 36 to 50 inches, they also require good drainage, rich compost, moisture in spring and summer, and deeper planting than the beardeds require. I cover mine with 2 inches of soil and give them a location in full sun. Sun is essential for good bloom, and August or early September planting for proper root development, not spring. The flowers are handsome for arrangements and also for corsages. Cut in bud, blooms open beautifully indoors in water and last a long while.

For me it is the garden beauty of the spurias that counts most. The tall white-and-yellow *Iris ochroleuca gigantea* plant just inside my picket fence is an old favorite, but there are many other beautiful varieties like the pure gold 'Sunny Days', copper-on-gold 'Indian Pueblo', ruffled white-and-gold 'Lydia Jane', and the pale blue 'Morning Tide'. If any plant can be said to be permanent, it is this spuria iris, which spreads and spreads without requiring your attention to thinning out.

Finally, I must say an appreciative word for the wild blue flag, *I. versicolor,* which naturalized in light shade along the wet brookbank and bloomed charmingly there late in June. The yellow flag, *I. pseudacorus,* also grew on the bank. This one and its white and lavender varieties will also thrive standing in water, which makes them useful plants for relieving the harsh outline of a pool.

From winter reticulata to midsummer flags and spurias is a long and entrancing iris season; not too long, however, for us who have enjoyed irises in the garden over many years. Omit the odd little species if you will, but consider almost indispensable the tall beardeds, the Siberian, Japanese, and spuria types, which bloom in about that order. Irises not only afford the border weeks of rich, pure color but their foliage also gives strength to the garden composition throughout the entire growing season.

For July, an effective mass planting of cool yellow 'Hyperion' daylilies.

THE INDISPENSABLE DAYLILY

One of the pleasant experiences of July is a mile drive along a narrow, winding country road with Susan to exercise her horse, Amber, and our kitten, Snug, asleep on my lap. On each side of the way the tawny daylily, *Hemerocallis fulva,* is a brilliant sight among the green woods ferns, and this display lasts for weeks. Daylilies are indeed *the* midsummer flower, but much earlier, in May, another species, the old-fashioned, very fragrant lemon-lily, *H. flava,* has opened in my garden, and these are only two of the more than one dozen species that hybridizers have employed to produce the thousands of cultivars available today. Now they come in rainbow colors from near whites, green-tinted whites, through yellows, pinks, melons, lavenders, and reds to almost blacks. Heights vary from the early 15-inch 'Little Cherub' to the very late 45-inch 'Fidelity', the majority in the 30-inch range, and there are night bloomers for your evening pleasure, and dormant, semidormant, and evergreen kinds, these last and those that repeat mainly for Southern gardens. I have never seen a satisfactory second blooming here in the North, although 'Becky Sharp', 'Mystic Mood', and 'Heirloom Lace' make an effort. If early fall flowers are wanted, it is better to select varieties that bloom in September. Among these are 'Changing Tide', 'Fidelity', and 'Postlude'.

The great value of daylilies lies in the glorious summer display they so easily afford. From late June well into September, they offer a wealth of color, a time when other perennials perform less freely. Iris and peonies are past and most chrysanthemums are not yet in color. For one thing, not many plants can so beautifully endure the vagaries of heat, drought, and also flooding rains that too often characterize summers here. But the daylilies, needing no staking, immune to insects, and in my long experience immune to disease as well, perform well year after year with a modicum of our attention. Those enduring green fountains of foliage, so important to the good looks of any flower bed, are another asset. Indeed, the perennial that offers fine foliage as well as fine flowers is twice blessed—and so is the gardener who grows it.

Where to Plant

Now, where can you plant daylilies to best advantage? Not in a cutting garden, I think, unless you want the flowers, as I do, for bouquets, not arrangements where linear proportions and centers of interest are bound to be disturbed as the faded daily blooms are removed. Massed with ferns in my old brown country pitcher, they please me enormously and decorate the hall for a week, new flowers opening each day.

Since daylilies bloom well in full sun or light open shade, many locations are agreeable to them. I admire them as important spaced accents in borders or associated with peonies as a follow-up in beds where these two perennials are dominant. They make excellent facing-down subjects for shrub borders or placed to fill odd corners where weeds might otherwise take over. As specimens beside steps or at corners of the terrace, I have enjoyed them, and in beds featuring spring bulbs that would otherwise be flowerless later without them. Used alone along the top of a retaining wall, daylilies are effective or in front of a New England stone "fence," as I saw them in glorious profusion at White Flower Farm in Litchfield, Connecticut. They are also appropriately lovely associated with water. I planted them along the brook, and I have seen them beside pools, large and small, where the recurved foliage crowned with colorful lily-form flowers looked charming. Such varieties as 'Hortensia', 'Luminaire', and 'Moon Dancers' that remain open in the evenings ("o.e." in the catalogues indicates "open evenings") are particularly desirable in plantings around the home swimming pool and terrace, where their faces gleam and glow under outdoor lighting.

The miniatures, which usually start to bloom before the standard varieties, are a good choice for small gardens because the plants, though 20 to 30 inches high, have an airy effect due to their thin stems and 2-inch flowers, and these can be grown to the fore of perennials with heavier foliage. Some miniatures like the yellow 'Bitsy', orange-yellow 'Daily Bread', and dark red 'Little Wine Cup' bloom the summer through; some others give a good spring and fall performance but rest in summer.

Perhaps my favorite layout is the 50-foot driveway planting designed by my friend Edna Payne. She is a collector, and every clump is carefully labeled. Studying the plants there is an education in daylilies, especially of recent kinds, for she frequently discards the old in favor of the new. In fact, my beloved and fragrant 'Hyperion' is no longer included.

Daylily sizes and shapes are varied. 'Winning Ways' has overlapping petals and sepals; 'Melon Balls' and 'Renee' are rounded; 'Treasured Lace' is triangular. 'Frances Fay' has smooth, recurving petals; 'Cartwheels' is huge and flat, 'Lilly Daché' is recurved with pointed petals. 'Lady Inara' and 'Chitco' bear small flowers rather like those of the gladiolus. 'Hortensia' is richly ruffled and crimped. Oddly enough, with these lilylike forms, true lilies can be used for contrast, provided they are tall, with *rounded,* not pointed blooms. In back of Mrs. Payne's 3-foot-wide daylily (and iris) expanse rise at long intervals great clumps of the 4-foot, early July-blooming apricot 'Connecticut Yankee' lily. This is followed by the 5-foot yellow-green 'Nutmegger', which carries into August. Tall evergreens and deciduous azaleas, blooming before the midseason daylilies, provide an effective green backdrop.

Which Daylilies for You

Height and season of bloom affect your selection and then, of course, color. If you can see the plants in bloom in a garden, that will be fine, but daylily catalogues are also wonderfully informing and almost too tempting with their handsome illustrations in color. If you are a novice gardener, you will probably be wise to select the older varieties that are still excellent but offered at low cost; if you have grown daylilies for a long time and are perhaps a collector, newer varieties like 'Master Touch' with a high price tag may deplete your budget but add to your fun. Of course, the high prices go down as supplies go up, and also as awards are won.

As for colors, my leaning is to the yellows, pale and golden, the melon pinks, pastels like 'Satin Glass' and 'Nob Hill', the green-tinted creams (no pure whites yet), and the delicate lavenders, like 'Lavender Flight' and

'Little Wart', but you may prefer stronger hues like the red 'Bess Ross', 'Chipper Cherry', 'Royal Game', or that enormous orange-brushed cinnamon, 'Invictus'. Dark purples like 'Derby Bound' and the "mahogany" varieties all appear more attractive in the garden if they are interspersed with pale yellow or cream daylilies that set them off. There are also certain odd variegations, "wine red with a chartreuse throat," "peach-buff pastel with a maroon eye zone above a green throat." These are not for me, for collectors perhaps; in any case, as with iris, to each his own.

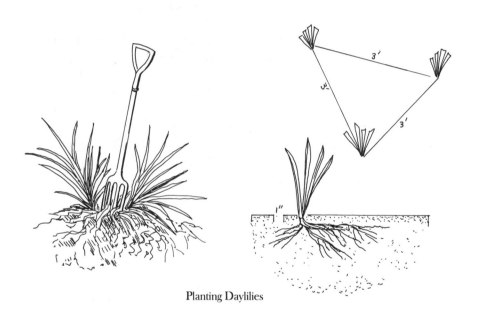

Planting Daylilies

Separate the clump of roots with a fork, using two forks if the clump is large. Divide the loosened roots by hand into pieces having only one fan of leaves.

Easy Culture

Success with daylilies does not depend on an arduous routine. Under the most average conditions they are bound to thrive. They are not particular about a sweet or acid soil, provided it is well drained. Loosen it about 10 inches deep, work in some commercial humus or garden compost and a little bonemeal or commercial cow manure. Set the big growers 2 feet or more apart so you won't have to divide and transplant for four or five years. To get splendid bloom, you might sprinkle superphosphate or an all-purpose fertilizer high in phosphorus around the plants in spring as new shoots appear. A mulch is desirable. In autumn, let the tops remain (if they don't look too untidy), as a protective mantle along with the collecting leaves till spring cleanup time.

You can plant or transplant at your convenience, spring, summer, or early fall, just so long as there is time for good root development before frost. Divide in August and early September or after bloom if the weather is not too hot and dry. Set the plants shallowly. Spread the roots out in a wide hole so that the point where roots join foliage, the so-called crown, is not covered more than an inch when the soil is filled in and firmed. Roots are spread wide and downward. Never plant daylily roots straight down, or bloom will be inhibited.

Ongoing care consists of slow, deep watering in times of summer drought, particularly if plants are forming buds, for you want to assure a full three to four or more weeks of bloom. Staking is not necessary even for the tall growers. For looks, it's a good idea to pinch off each day's faded crop of flowers and, when the whole stem or scape has bloomed, to cut it off at ground level.

Propagation

Division of a big plant is the easiest way to increase your supply, and inevitably you will have plenty to share with friends. Some of my old favorites greet me throughout the neighborhood. However, if you have acquired some fairly expensive varieties, you may wish you could increase them before they are of a size for sensible division. In that case, you might try the proliferation method. If you let flower stalks remain on some varieties, you may see little rootless plants developing along the stems in the axils between the rudimental stem leaves and the drying stalks. Cut off these plantlets with about 2 inches of stem. Pot each one separately in a good growing mix, barely covering the base of the proliferation. Set the pots in a sheltered place, and water as you do other potted plants outdoors, taking care not to let the soil dry out. Transplant to a garden bed as soon as you see that roots have developed adequately for survival. The new plants will probably bloom next year; it rather depends on how much of a start they have this year.

Such a do is for the most part quite unnecessary. Division is the easy-easy way, but if you have indulged yourself in, say, the seven-fifty 'Winning Ways', the twenty-five-dollar 'Viola Parker', or just possibly a fifty-dollar gem, like 'Warner House', the proliferation method will appeal as a way of increasing your supply of these expensive beauties.

One of my great favorites is still the lovely, fragrant, yellow 'Hyperion'. Mrs. Payne accuses me of a nostalgic affection, but it *is* beautiful and will always be, I suppose, on any recommended list of mine. When I was inspecting a glorious border of daylilies at White Flower Farm, one tall handsome yellow particularly appealed to me. Thinking it was something new, I sought the label, and there it was—'Hyperion'.

All very busy people loving gardens turn naturally to daylilies for summer color. I sympathize with Millicent Taylor's account in the *Christian Science Monitor:* "In my former New England garden I had a 50-foot border in part shade in front of an evergreen hedge. After a few seasons of raising in it various demanding perennials and annuals, and having to make more time for vegetables and plants elsewhere on the place, I planted the entire border to daylilies, with groundcover and a few low things in front. It was grand to enjoy their beauty as they kept performing with nothing but watering and appreciation! . . . Here in my smaller Ohio garden I have room for only about half a dozen, but I put them in promptly on moving here and they remain a joy and still my favorites, as they are with many other homeowners."

Daylily Companions

An invaluable combination for the spring garden is a planting of early daylilies in front of spring bulbs. As the bulbs' foliage matures and becomes unsightly, the unfolding daylily foliage beautifully conceals the retreat.

Many attractive color combinations can be planned with daylilies. In June, tall white foxgloves are attractive with yellows and pinks. In July the

Platycodon, the long-
blooming purple bellflower
(also its white variety), is
an excellent foil for most
daylilies. GENEREUX PHOTO

pink 'Winsome Lady' is set off by the purple bellflower, platycodon, or 'Blue Star' stokesia. A lavender shrub-althea, 'Heavenly Blue', makes a beautiful background plant for yellow, salmon, and near-white varieties, these again in contrast to the spires of white foxgloves or blue delphiniums. Various daisy plants are attractive with daylilies because they offer good form contrast, and even if the area is somewhat shaded, most daisies, like the daylilies, will bloom well. And I like big clumps of phlox, especially the whites, with any color of daylilies, this combination of course, for a sunny site. With bicolor daylilies, like the notable yellow-throated, rich pink 'Emperor's Robe', you can get a pleasing effect if you plant a mass of it with some yellow perennials to emphasize the yellow in the throat, as 'Yellow Queen' gaillardia, 'Moonshine' achillea, or 'Sunburst' coreopsis.

DAYLILIES TO DELIGHT YOU

Here are highly recommended beautiful daylilies in a variety of colors, heights, and blooming times. A specialist's catalogue will show you most of these in color. (See Where to Buy for names and addresses.)

E—Early; M—Midseason; ML—Midseason Late; L—Late;
VL—Very Late; EV—Evergreen; OE—Open Evenings

Name	Color	Height in Inches	Season
Annie Welch	Blush pink to flesh	24	E M
Amazing Grace	Cream, green throat	26	E
Bambi Doll	Pale pink, green heart	28	E M
Cartwheels	Huge, flat, gold	24	M
Changing Tide	Apricot	26	VL
Clarence Simon	Melon pink	28	M, EV
Emperor's Robe	Rose pink, yellow throat	25	E M
Exalted Ruler	Deep rich coral pink, rose throat	32	E M– ML
Green Glitter	Greenish-yellow, apple-green throat	24	M
Heirloom Lace	Deep gold, green throat	30–34	M, OE
Hope Diamond	Near white	14	E M
Hortensia	Medium yellow, crimped	34	M, OE
Hyperion	Lemon-yellow, fragrant	48	M
Ice Carnival	Near white, green heart	28	M, OE
Lavender Flight	Deep lavender, greenish-yellow throat	34	E M, Semi– EV
Little Cherub	Ruffled light yellow, fragrant	15	E
Little Wart	Deep lavender, green heart	20	E
Love That Pink	Light pink	26–28	E M
Winning Ways	Greenish yellow, green heart	32–34	E M, OE
Winsome Lady	Bluish pink, green heart	24	E

Phlox 'Iceberg', white with a rosy center, for weeks of bright July bloom.
TALOUMIS PHOTO

7

PHLOX

FOR SUMMER SCENT AND COLOR

"Summer is a seemly time," a Scottish poet wrote, and so it is in gardens where billows of phlox and verticals of delphinium proclaim the season's height of fragrance and color. Flowering perennials, even carelessly set about, can be pleasing, but when plantings are organized with attention to the different growth forms and to attractive color associations, our pleasure is greatly increased. So it is that we alternate the masses and the verticals for subtle effect and set the misting babysbreath, feverfew, and sea-lavender between them.

Let us think first of the wonderful possibilities of phlox, later of the glorious delphinium. The flowering of phlox is a symbol of high summer, and sunny borders cannot have too much of this undemanding perennial, so easy to grow, so brilliant to bloom. Phlox is no modest, shrinking subject, to be appreciated in a shady nook. Flamboyant, friendly, and sunloving, it brings a wealth of brilliant midseason color to our gardens. Even in deserted country dooryards it may be seen reverted to magenta or shades of rose, purple, and white, neglected yet beautiful, with gray, weatherbeaten walls of some forsaken homestead for background. Obviously self-reliant and persistent, such descendants of hardy phlox planted years before do not readily succumb to the quirks of fate.

Do reserve space for lavish dealings with phlox. Especially if your summers are spent at home, you will enjoy this sturdy perennial either in a mixed border or in an area of its own. The early *Phlox carolina* (*suffruticosa*) 'Miss Lingard', with shining leaf and fine white flower, gives a June effect ahead of the more diversified *P. paniculata,* and goes on blooming well into July. It is particularly effective with delphinium blues and salmon-pink sweet William, also with the brilliant red 'Starfire', another early phlox, but a paniculata variety.

Varieties and Harmonies

Following 'Miss Lingard', various other low-growing paniculatas bring long summer color to foreground plantings. Hybridizers have now provided us with a fine array of these 2-foot or lower plants that are better suited to our smaller places and narrower borders than such 4-foot varieties as 'Dresden China' and 'Lilac Time'. These have their place in front of shrubs, high walls, or fences. Among shorter phloxes are the crimson-eyed pale pink 'Bright Eyes', lavender-pink 'Juliet', 'Orange Perfection', 'Snowball', deep purple 'Amethyst', 'Pinafore Pink', 'Starfire', and 'White Admiral', though this one may reach 30 inches.

The paniculata season extends from late June through September, sometimes into October; it depends on the advent of frost. Many colors are so brilliant and clashing in this group that varieties must be selected with caution and grouped with care. There can be no artless beauty achieved by the careless flinging about of phlox or the planting of "mixtures." But if color harmonies are thoughtfully considered and perhaps some misting perennials placed to harmonize the strongest hues, delightful pictures will result either with various phlox or associations of phlox with other perennials.

In selecting the handsome "reds," note whether they are vermilion—that is, with a yellowish cast, as 'Orange Perfection' or 'Starfire'—or crimson—that is, with a bluish tone, as 'Prince Charming' or 'Windsor'. For harmony's sake, don't combine these two kinds of reds, and with either, plant some placating whites, as 'White Admiral' or 'Mary Louise'. Along the same line, consider the difference between rose pinks like 'Dodo Hanbury Forbes' and the salmon-pink 'Sir John Falstaff'. You can set off the brilliant dark violet shades of 'Amethyst' and 'Royalty' with whites, or light blends like 'Starry Skies' and the paler lavenders like 'Lilac Time' with the shell-pink 'Dresden-China' or, more interesting perhaps, one of the gray-leaved perennials like the misty *Artemisia* 'Silver King.'

Lilium centifolium associates beautifully with summer phlox. GENEREUX
PHOTO

Keeping in mind the supplementary shadings, select other perennials to subtly emphasize these. Yellow daylilies or the golden meadowrue *Thalictrum glaucum* will bring out the yellow tones of the salmon-pink 'Sir John Falstaff' and harmonize with 'Orange Perfection'. 'Sun Gold' gaillardias and 'Yellow Supreme' marigolds will be pleasing companions for the salmon-orange 'Cecil Hanbury'. The clear pink 'Dodo Hanbury Forbes' will be right with hardy aster 'Eventide' or with lavender hostas. With 'Starfire', one of the most brilliant of all phlox varieties, plant white regal lilies and clouds of babysbreath. Emphasize the lavender-pink 'Juliet' with purple platycodon and single lavender petunias. The imperial purple 'Royalty' is handsome with a white variety like 'Mary Louise' and the pale pink crimson-eyed 'Bright Eyes'. A charming low-growing group might include 'Snowball', 'Pinafore Pink', and 'Juliet'. And for peacemaking amid the rival brilliance of purple, rose, or red phlox, you might select 'Mt. Everest', white with a faint rose eye that gives a pale, blending effect.

In my gardens three white varieties—'Miss Lingard', 'White Admiral', and 'Mary Louise'—have given me particular pleasure. On moonlit evenings, these shine out luminous and lovely, together dispensing a sweet fragrance. The scent has an indefinable reaching quality, a light, musty sweetness that belongs to phlox alone. Coolly beautiful, white phlox is a refreshing sight on the most humid night. In fact, among white flowers, white phlox is pre-eminent, a beautiful summer emphasis.

In the Landscape

I also find phlox a charming landscape plant. One memorable colony was effectively set in a small green-and-white plot that was primarily a bird sanctuary. For background, there was a graceful hemlock tree and a clump of hybrid rhododendrons. To the fore stood strong clumps of 'Miss Lingard', with an underplanting of lily-of-the-valley. In the midst stood a birdbath. From June on, it was the white phlox that made intermittently lovely this quiet spot at the end of the vista from a study window.

To outline shrubbery or bring color along a boundary at some distance from the house, a border of phlox is excellent. Phlox has carrying power, and I am not sure that it is not really better seen in perspective. Some plants, like bleedinghearts or Christmas-roses or lilies, should be close at hand so that we can dwell on every perfect detail. Not so phlox. It serves best in a mass planting, where the individual is lost in a colorful symphony. If you plant it so, be sure the prevailing breeze will bring its sweet scent toward you.

Perennials in full-summer beauty, yellow achillea, blue delphinium, white astilbe, apricot and lavender violas, all edged by myrtle.
TALOUMIS PHOTO

For winter, spring, and early summer. TOP: Siberian iris. CENTER LEFT: Christmas-rose. CENTER RIGHT: Bleedinghearts. CHARLES MARDEN FITCH PHOTOS. BELOW: Miniature dwarf and Lilliput irises. HAMPFLER PHOTO.

LOWER LEFT: Single yellow peonies with dark red late tulips and a cluster of white gasplant. RIGHT: Tall bearded irises edged with pink coralbells. GROFFMAN PHOTOS

ABOVE: Edna Payne's handsome driveway border of the finest daylilies now available. CHARLES MARDEN FITCH PHOTO. RIGHT: Daylilies in a popular melon shade. GROFFMAN PHOTO

Phlox, the glory of the summer garden, reigns here with the contrasting form of fluffy pale yellow goldenrod for background.
GENEREUX PHOTO

Volute-shaped beds of the Muller garden are bright with campanula, phlox, Shasta

daisies, and yellow lilies.   (See design of this planting on pages 7 and 8.)   CHARLES

MARDEN FITCH PHOTOS

ABOVE: An interesting planting of yellow chrysanthemums sets off a white statue against the dark autumn foliage of oxydendrum. TALOUMIS PHOTO. RIGHT: White dwarf asters are a crisp note in the late-September garden. TALOUMIS PHOTO

About Culture

Phlox does best in full sun, and I would plant it there even though quite *open* shade is advised for the darker colors as the violet tones, which may fade a little in glaring sunshine. Plants keep both health and looks if the soil is rich, adequately prepared, and well drained. Deep watering in times of drought is essential, but overhead sprinkling is to be avoided. "Wet feet but dry clothing" is the rule.

It is also most important that each plant be allowed a full 2-foot area with a free circulation of air about it. A house wall or solid stone boundary wall that dispenses dampness is not a good location for phlox. The ills this plant is heir to are kept at a minimum under proper growing conditions. Often they do not appear at all. There are two principal ailments. Foliage sometimes appears rusty, with leaves curling under. This indicates red-spider mites. A strong hose spray directed from below the plant frequently suffices to break the tough spider webs and wash away the minute offenders. If not, a miticide (Aramite or Kelthane) should be regularly applied. Flotox or Phaltan is indicated if humid days bring the second ailment, mildew, which disfigures the plants although it does little harm. The sulphur (in these preparations) is kept as much as possible away from flower heads because it ruins color, especially reds, and it should not be applied on a very hot day.

Phlox does not, as is commonly supposed, revert in color. When lovely blues or pinks seem to change to magenta, it is because faded blooms have been permitted to go to seed and the lusty seedlings, which do not come true to the parent, have crowded out the parent. "Reversion" is prevented by prompt removal of blooms past their prime.

Phlox thrive on adequate feeding and by frequent enough division to keep the centers of the plant in a healthy growing condition. This means about every third year. September is an excellent time for separating phlox. Tough centers are then discarded and strong outside sections cut apart with a knife rather than a spade, into three to five budded divisions. These are then reset at the same height to which they grew before but in well-forked and much-enriched soil and at proper distances. If this task is completed three to four weeks before the first frost, new roots will firmly anchor the fresh divisions, and next year's display will be lavish despite the disturbance.

Since hybrid phlox does not come true from seeds, plantings are increased either by division (as above) or by cuttings. It is, indeed, a simple matter to get a fine, large crop of some favorite variety if you will take tip cuttings in July or August. I have had them form good roots in three weeks.

If size of bloom is an objective, remove at the stem line from each strong phlox clump all but four or five main shoots. These will then produce big heads of bloom, and the open plants will be healthier. Of course, phlox is not the perennial for cutting; the flowers fall too readily.

The colors and values of phlox are exciting. The culture is easy. The heat endurance is remarkable. This, I think, is the pleasant combination of attributes that makes certain summer perennials invaluable.

PHLOX FOR SUMMER COLOR

Except for the early 'Miss Lingard', these all are varieties of *P. paniculata*. S-J indicates Symons-Jeune strain from England.

Name	Height in Inches	Color	Remarks
Amethyst	24	Good, deep color	Nice with true pinks
Bright Eyes S-J	24	Pale pink, crimson eye	Good with reds
Dodo Hanbury Forbes S-J	36	Clear pink	Large pyramid, very fragrant
Dresden China S-J	48	Shell pink	Deeper pink center
Fairy's Petticoat S-J	36–42	Pale pink, darker eye	Fairly early, long flowering
Gaiety S-J	42	Bright red	Orange suffusion
Juliet S-J	24	Lavender pink	Good with purples
Lilac Time S-J	42–48	Clear lavender	With any pink
Mary Louise	30	White for Aug.–Sept.	Fragrant, excellent
Miss Lingard	30	Earliest white	For June on
Olive Symons-Jeune S-J	40	Rich rose	Orange tint, to go with yellow flowers
Orange Perfection	24	Close to pure orange	Lovely shade
Pinafore Pink	18	Bright pink	Fine for front of border with 'Snowball'
Russian Violet	24–30	Dark violet	Needs whites for contrast
Sir John Falstaff	30	Salmon pink	Brilliant effect
Snowball	20–24	White	Good with reds
Starfire	24–36	Brilliant red	Striking with whites
White Admiral	24–30	White for July–Aug.	Outstanding side branching

For the June garden, the towering white verticals of 'Sir Galahad' delphiniums (Round Table Series). ROCHE PHOTO

DELPHINIUMS
AND OTHER GARDEN VERTICALS

When a border or other perennial planting is seen from a distance, the differences in plant forms are a salient contribution to the total effect. Most important are the vertical or spire flowers that, rising above the masses of lower plants, can establish a visual rhythm. When the verticals are set as repeated accents, a pleasing continuity results, as if the same chord were struck over and over again in a musical composition.

Of course, large groups of verticals are not placed together, or the valuable pyramidal form of the individual is lost. Usually sufficient is a small clump of delphiniums or a few well-developed plants whose flowers grow in long wands or spikes. The August chimney bellflower, for instance, will send up from a single crown several purple or white rockets, while others of the steepled clan are often even more prolific.

In selecting our primary spire flowers for the various seasons we require definite qualities. Obviously the predominant characteristic must be height, not usually less than 4 feet. The blossom must be of steeple or column form, preferably with the leaves growing in a low crown so that a long line of stem is visible. Plants should be moderately sturdy, too, never even artistically loose in the manner of the carefree hardy aster or thermopsis, but some staking may be required.

For the tallest verticals for wide borders or plantings in front of shrubs or high fences there are a number of fine summer spires. Pre-eminent are the lofty delphiniums where they will grow, a few well-chosen campanulas, hollyhocks, snakeroot (which deserves a kinder name), and Spark's monkshood for fall.

Then there are the verticals I think of as secondary spires, usually not growing much above 3 feet. Blue baptisia and the pink or white gasplant for early June; lupines and foxgloves, pink, red, or white astilbes, pink loosestrife and plume poppies, pink or white false-dragonhead, violet big betony (*Stachys officinalis*), and yellow thermopsis for midsummer.

DELPHINIUMS, PRIMARY VERTICALS

Most loved, most valuable among all garden verticals is the delphinium or larkspur, its shades of ineffable blue quite indispensable. Delphiniums bring even to simple gardens a charming distinction. Whether the blue wands rise in effective isolation from a green base or present the perfect background foil to pale yellow daylilies or white masses of phlox, they are always important.

But since in our busy lives the behavior of a plant is quite as important as its beauty, we must inquire into the disposition of the delphinium. Is it exacting or is it amiable? Perhaps a charitable dictum would be: It is improving. The Pacific Hybrids, in particular, have been bred to disease resistance. However, we must realize that the delphinium is basically a native of high altitudes and cool climates, and there are limits to its powers of adjustment.

Therefore, if you live on the Pacific Coast, along the Great Lakes, or near the Atlantic Ocean in upper New England, where the humidity is high and the heat of summer days is mitigated by cool evenings, you can expect to bring to perfection the giant hybrid beauties, even grow them from seed. However, if your garden is near Philadelphia, or in some sections of the Midwest or around New York City, where the summers are sudden, droughty, and blisteringly hot, you can enjoy the handsomest hybrids only if you will be satisfied to have them behave as biennials or even annuals, as I do. There is no disgrace, indeed, in considering delphinium as a worthwhile yearly garden luxury and each spring purchasing one- or two-year-old plants from a specialist. If you are lucky, half of these plants may pull through to the second year, and usually a *few* will survive into the third. Of course, some may succumb by the fall of the first year, especially if summer heat is continuous and intense. Even so, these purchased plants will produce at least two and often three glorious periods of bloom. Then if they depart, you can still bless your delphiniums as annuals of extraordinary loveliness.

The candle or bee delphinium, *D. elatum,* with 5- to 6-foot giant hybrids, is the joy of those who live in the favored regions of cool summers, the envy of those who do not. Our own Giant Pacific Hybrids belong here, also the Round Table Series, including the white Galahad and the royal purple King Arthur; and my favorite Summer Skies Series, and the handsome English Blackmore and Langdon Hybrids. Recently this English firm has offered named varieties of dwarf hybrids. These grow to 3 or 4 feet and need staking just as the tall hybrids do. 'Blue Jade', with a brownish bee, the paler blue 'Cupid', and medium-blue 'Sabrina', these two with white bees, all growing to 4 feet, sound well worth growing where the tallest hybrids are inappropriate. However, they require the same cool climate as the other candle delphiniums.

Easier Larkspurs

The less spectacular, but still very lovely, hybrids of the garland larkspur, *D. cheilanthum formosum,* will usually prove perennial, and they too bring to the garden much-valued shades of blue, but they are not so tall as the glorious English and West Coast hybrids. The 2- to 4-foot, light blue or white Belladonna Hybrids bloom abundantly in June and again in September. 'Casa Blanca' is white, 'Cliveden Beauty' a light blue. This is enchanting in the familiar combination with white madonna or candidum lilies and with some such climbing rose as the blush-pink 'New Dawn' or the deeper 'Coral Dawn' for background, a carpeting of salmon sweet William at its feet. A more unusual picture results when, against a backdrop of evergreens, the deeper blue Belladonna strain is accompanied by white foxgloves and Shasta daisies. The garland delphiniums are better than the giant hybrids for strip borders and also for plantings close by houses of contemporary design.

For smaller gardens and for those of us who live in less acceptable climates for delphiniums, the feathery 24-inch, blue or white Chinese or Bouquet delphiniums (*D. grandiflorum*) are nice for constant summer bloom. These are extremely dependable. Easily grown from late April sowings, they blossom their first year from seed early in September when other true blues are scarce, and they require no staking. 'Cambridge Blue' and 'Blue Mirror' are light and dark varieties; *D. grandiflorum album* is white.

Then for the center of the border are the newer 'Connecticut Yankee' delphiniums. These rarely exceed 30 inches and are a bush type resembling the low-growing, branching Chinese delphiniums rather than the taller vertical hybrids. In my area, the hybrid 'Connecticut Yankee' has been marvelously successful, easy from seed and needing less staking since plants are only medium high. All through the summer they give us constant bloom—blue, lavender, purple, or white.

Location and Culture

Delphiniums, all of them, require full sun, protection from wind, and all but the bush types, secure staking, with ample spacing, say 24 to 30 inches between plants. If you grow delphiniums in a mixed border, trim back through the summer any rampant perennials or lusty annuals that crowd around them and so invite disease by preventing a free circulation of air. For cut flowers, I have always obtained the best blooms from plants grown in a garden row by themselves.

If success with delphiniums means a lot to you, you might prepare the soil an ideal 2 feet deep. But this involves a terrific amount of digging, much more than the average back can bear or the average pocketbook can afford to hire. Feel, therefore, that you have done right by your delphiniums when in a well-drained spot you improve the soil with leafmold or compost and bonemeal to a full 12-inch depth. Provide an extra 6-inch drainage area if the site requires it. Waterlogged delphiniums, of course, rarely survive. High fertility; limey, not sour, soil; perfect drainage, and plenty of moisture at flowering time are the four essentials of successful culture. Wood ashes, so rich in lime and potash, are fine for delphiniums. In early spring, feed your established delphiniums with a high-phosphorus fertilizer.

Encourage the Comeback

As the first blooms fade, cut the *flower* stalks down, but let some of the old *leaf* stalks remain to protect the upspringing new growth. When this is 12 inches high, cut back the old stalks to 6 inches.

After plants have had a fortnight's rest, sprinkle fertilizer a second time under the outer leaf spread of each one. Cultivate the soil lightly then, and water deeply. As new shoots develop, select two or three and pinch back the others. When this second flower crop fades, cut back as before, but do not attempt to force a third period of bloom with further feeding. It may appear anyway.

Meanwhile, the lofty delphiniums cannot be left unsupported. Before the fatalities of wind or rain occur, firmly insert in the soil a number of wire or bamboo stakes long enough to support the *ultimate* height of each spire. Fasten these with Twistems or raffia to the highest current point of growth.

In summer, mulch to keep the root runs cool and so reduce heat and dryness, ever the bane of delphinium. Disease and pest controls are, of course, necessary. Mites sometimes distort tip growth, particularly if the plants are not environmentally content. Mildew and blackspot often appear during humid July days. Regular dusting or spraying with one of the all-purpose mixtures concocted for roses is almost essential for the big hybrids; or Phaltan alone may suffice. In winter, *after* the first hard freeze, in very cold climates, cover plants with a sifting of coarse sand plus a little Captan or Fermate to deter fungus troubles, then spread evergreen boughs. (See Chapter 18 on controls.)

OTHER VERTICALS

The chimney bellflower, *Campanula pyramidalis,* produces porcelain blue and clear white flowers for six summer weeks, starting in August. It is biennial, and the great pyramid of bloom needs staking. It is the tallest of the bellflowers. The peach-leaved, purple or white bellflower, *C. persicifolia,* grows to 3 feet and blooms in midsummer. Unlike most campanulas, it is perennial. 'Telham Beauty' is a fine, clear purple, and 'Grandiflora' is a large-flowered white. The Canterbury bells, *C. medium,* blooming from late spring to midsummer, are also biennial and unlikely to reach more than 3 feet. They should be considered secondary spires; they can be nice blue substitutes for delphiniums.

A fourth and less familiar bellflower of great value should be noted here, *C. lactiflora.* Not a vertical spike but a long, branching panicle of light blue or white flowers on strong stems to 4 feet or more, this has been called one of the twelve best herbaceous plants.

In July "flaunts the flaring hollyhock," and to 8 feet. When the background is a white fence or brick wall, hollyhocks, *Althaea rosea,* are the inevitable choice. They are most effective, as Gertrude Jekyll has pointed

A good secondary vertical for early summer—the old-time Canterbury bells, *Campanula medium,* in blue-lavender, pink, or white. GENEREUX PHOTO

out, if the wall is not too high and the spires shoot up "telling well against the distant tree masses above the wall." Hollyhocks require a lot of room, and plants must be staked. If you have an odd sunny corner that they can fill, or if you can place them in front of evergreens or shrubs, you will enjoy their dramatic height and fine red, pink, lavender, white, and yellow flowers, but they are too tall and massive for our modern narrower borders. Short-lived perennials, they readily seed themselves. (Alas, they are

Another campanula, *C. lactiflora,* with hundreds of pale-blue or milk-white bells in branching panicles on 3- to 4-foot stems in midsummer. GENEREUX PHOTO

favorites of the Japanese beetle and hardly worth planting in beetle territory.)

The shade-loving, feathery white snakeroot, *Cimicifuga racemosa,* for July and August is a lovely but apparently unfamiliar plant. It grows to 5 feet, a tall vertical choice in rather moist soil. I like it with the old-fashioned orange daylilies in front of hemlocks and a gray stone wall.

For cool half-shady places
in August, the tall and
feathery shakeroot,
Cimicifuga racemosa. FITCH
PHOTO

Autumn Turrets

For early fall in sun or shade, I like the well-named gayfeathers. *Liatris scariosa,* 'September Glory' lifts a fine strong purple cone some 5 to 6 feet. 'White Spire' is a beauty, too. These tall ones are attractive in association with shrubs; the 3-foot spicata varieties, like 'Silver Tips', are better for narrow borders.

Finally, for later bloom, there are the shade-loving aconites, marvelous when they thrive, which could be more often. Plant them in that section of

Gayfeathers, in white or red-violet, a striking note in late summer. Sturdy stems need no staking. GENEREUX PHOTO

the border that passes under a tree; most of them fail in full sun; in the shadows, they will rise like dark blue torches. 'Sparks' Variety' is a good late-summer aconite, producing violet-blue 5-foot turrets that are usually colorful well into September. 'Barker's Variety' is an amethyst color and grows 5 to 6 feet. The tall Wilson's aconite is deep violet-blue, coming late, staying on until frost.

SECONDARY SPIRES

In addition to the tall verticals, there is a nice selection of secondary spires, most of them in the 3-foot range. These too bring distinction to perennial plantings.

For May and June

For late May and June weeks the 3- to 4-foot, sometimes a little taller, *Baptisia australis,* false indigo, is a choice plant rather like a blue lupine and reliably handsome throughout the season in full sun or light open shade. After its blue spikes fade, the feathered blue-green foliage persists. For a minimum-work garden, baptisia is indispensable, and why it is so rarely grown I do not know. It doesn't get things and almost never needs dividing, for its taproot goes deep, not wide.

The blue lupines, *Lupinus polyphyllus,* have long been June favorites of mine, but today I do not know where to find this lovely 3-foot blue perennial. The Russell lupines, which are taller, are widely obtainable as plants in mixture, or as seeds in separate colors—red, yellow, blue with white. Since the Russells do not care for my garden or thrive in any of my friends' plots, I am not well acquainted with them. Evidently even the selected American seed is still dependent on the cool humidity its English ancestors enjoyed. Of these the remark seems true, "The weather that grows corn, kills the lupine." However, where they thrive, all lupines produce fine secondary spires, so you may want to try the Russells. Lupines grow wild, acres of them, in southern Nova Scotia, a cool and foggy region.

The 30-inch gasplant is an undemanding, long-lived gem, blooming for me in late May and June. It will grow in full sun or light shade in deep, rich loam. Slow to establish, it eventually reaches 30 inches. From the midst of fine, ashlike foliage appears a rose or white turret of exquisite form and color. This is a foreground spire of undeniable worth to all who wish to garden for the future as well as the present. Here is plant quality of the finest kind. Space gasplants at 5- to 8-foot intervals just behind the edging of a border and let their companions be iris and blue flax. You will then have added a note of considerable interest to your plantings.

The foxgloves, *Digitalis,* give strength and dignity to any garden and consort well with nearly any other flower and certainly with every other color. Growing to 3 feet or a little taller, they bloom in June. The biennial

Lupine hybrids, one of the
best accent plants for the
late-spring early-June
garden. GENEREUX PHOTO

Another secondary vertical
for early summer—the
long-lived dictamnus in
white or rose.

Excelsior Hybrids and Hyacinth Hybrids are handsome choices if you don't mind mixtures of pink, rose, red, yellow, and white, some with crimson dots —which I do. If you want a crushed-strawberry shade in your border, the perennial *Digitalis mertonensis* holds its color and grows to about 3 feet. I have been searching for a dependable white. I have seen it growing handsomely in June with tall bearded irises in a friend's garden, where it was a selection from a mixed planting. It proved perennial, lasting for three years, and its seedlings stayed white. (Seeds of this spectacular white are being tested for me.) With irises white foxgloves are perfect verticals. These grew in full sun, but foxgloves also make lovely spires for moist, shaded areas and in woody settings with ferns. Recently I discovered that Thompson and Morgan, the English firm of seedsmen, offer *D. alba* as a 3-foot biennial. This too is being tested, so we shall see.

Summer Spires

Summer offers many charming verticals. The 1½- to 4-foot astilbes with their plumy spires are excellent for the center of a border in sun or in light shade, where I have enjoyed them with Japanese iris and ferns. 'Peach Blossom' is a choice pale pink, deliciously fragrant. 'Deutschland' is my favorite white; 'Fanal' is red, and 'Granat' is a salmon shade. I cannot imagine gardening without astilbes. (More about them in Chapter 14.)

The yellow thermopsis, sometimes called Carolina-lupine, blooms in June and July. It grows to about 4 feet and is lovely with all blue flowers. If you want a spire duet, plant this lower yellow thermopsis with the taller blue delphiniums. Thermopsis is not to be overlooked, but how rarely I see this fine perennial in gardens, although it is easily grown in the sun and is fine to cut.

Likewise good to cut and of long season border value are the veronicas or speedwells. These produce a fine stalwart foreground of spires of purple, rose, or white for July, August, and September. They are easily propagated by seed or division and a constant joy because of good foliage and easy culture.

It is important, however, to select veronicas with care and under no circumstances to take in gift plants whose habits are not known to you. *Veronica longifolia* is a weedy grower you will wish you had never met, but *V. longifolia subsessilis* is one of the best, 2½ feet high, with continuously good foliage and showy deep purple spikes through midsummer. 'Blue Spire' is a worthwhile improved *V. spicata* for early summer effect and

Veronica 'Blue Peter' 15 to 20 inches tall, with a profusion of purple flowers, midsummer to early fall.

In midsummer the tall spikes of yellow thermopsis on reliably strong stems.

TALOUMIS PHOTO

noteworthy for heat- and drought-resistance. The white 'Icicle' is an abundant bloomer in August and September.

These spire flowers are a fascinating group, but not all of them, of course, would be right in any one garden. Their value both outdoors and in bouquets lies essentially in the contrasts they afford. Plant them therefore near loose, massive material. Purple veronicas with white Shasta daisies, for example, make a charming, clean-cut appearance, while blue baptisia contrasts effectively with yellow 'Sun Gold' gaillardias. And in the shrubbery border, too, especially when it is in an all-green summer stage, the ivory spires of snakeroot are a splendid sight and should be interesting with *Clethra alnifolia,* the sweet pepperbush, or its variety, *rosea.*

Shasta daisies, one of the most useful and trouble-free of all early and mid-summer plants. GENEREUX PHOTO

FREE-WHEELING
DAISIES AND ASTERS

If you are fond of daisy flowers, it is probably because they have some nostalgic appeal for you. I know that explains their special attraction for me. I grew up in the country with open fields nearby, and my little sister and I often used to pick the white oxeye daisies and the black-eyed Susans for bouquets to bring to our appreciative mother—even when they were in a wilted state—and now my granddaughter brings bunches of daisies to me. I like them all, the common ones of roadside and meadow, and the sophisticated blossoms that are the result of the plant hunter's courage or the hybridizer's art.

In a border, or in a yard where flowers to enjoy and cut are grown mainly in odd spots or worked in along with shrubs, daisy plants are invaluable. They produce a massive effect, and the various kinds span the whole frost-free season, from April doronicum to November chrysanthemum. If your place is small, one or two daisy varieties selected for each season assure progressive color. If your border is both long and deep, many daisies can be used for massive effects of unrivaled brilliance. Singularly free of pest and disease, daisies do require more frequent division than many other perennials and more constant picking.

Daisy plants give strength to a garden. True, most, not all, lack the delicate charm of a columbine or an anemone, but like people of stalwart character but only moderate good looks, daisies have a vigor that endears them to all of us who have other things to do besides tending a garden. And daisies are grand to cut.

In general, they do best in full sun. In my experience, they are not particular about soil, but then I have grown them mainly for easy effects. Attention to soil preferences, as I shall indicate, will probably give you handsomer flowers. Most daisies come in yellow shades, a color that blends with all others, and gives a lift to almost any plant grouping.

Three for Spring

Of several species of leopardsbane, *Doronicum caucasicum* is the first hardy daisy to bloom, and the variety *magnificum,* alias 'Madame Mason', is the one you want. It grows to 2 feet, with single 2-inch April to May flowers, a lively yellow to put with spring pinks and blues, particularly nice with tulips. This variety is not so likely to disappear after bloom as most other species. As a precaution, though, mark the location and set plants with good summer foliage, as forget-me-nots, beside or in front of your doronicums. My plants grow back of white candytuft in the shade of a little rose tree. Unlike most daisies, doronicums grow well in heavy soil, either in sun or part shade, and sometimes produce a second crop if first flowers are promptly removed.

Opening in June, *Anthemis tinctoria* 'Moonlight' or 'Kelway's Yellow', the light and dark yellow marguerites, grow to 30 inches and are covered from June until October with 2-inch or larger flowers that rise above pungent ferny foliage. These daisies do have elegance despite their easy culture. In bouquets with pink roses or early blue delphiniums, they are particularly charming.

To face down delphiniums or other tall plants in the garden, the 1- to 3-foot fernlike pyrethrums or painted daisies, *Chrysanthemum coccineum,* red, pink, or white, are useful. I prefer the singles, especially 'Robinson's Rose', a medium shade, the flowers 3 inches across. The doubles strike me as ordinary, and I certainly would never grow pyrethrums in mixtures. First bloom comes in late May or June and continues into July; if plants are severely cut back afterward, a second blooming may occur in early fall.

The orange-scarlet *Lychnis x haageana* of the Pink family is striking with Shasta daisies and other white flowers. FITCH PHOTO

Summer Daisies: Coreopsis and Gaillardias

For durability and continuous production, for indifference to heat and drought, few perennials can match these two. Plant alternate groups of three at the end of your property for a sparkling accent there throughout the summer and an unfailing source of cut flowers. In fact, the spent flowers should be removed to keep more buds coming on. Again I prefer the singles, and taller varieties like coreopsis 'Gold Coin' to 3 feet. There is a new 6- to 8-inch dwarf 'Canary Bird' that might be another good edging plant, but I haven't grown it.

There is also a dwarf gaillardia, but it resembles the old familiar blanket flower and so is not for me, nor are the red-centered Portola Hybrids or any of the red varieties. It is the beautiful, clear gold 30-inch 'Yellow Queen' that I prefer. Like coreopsis, this gaillardia is undemanding and a joy to glimpse from your windows all through summer.

Shasta Daisies and Stokes-aster

Supposedly tender this far north, these plants have always prospered for me. The Shastas, *Chrysanthemum maximum,* come single and double. I particularly like the 2-foot single 'Alaska', which wants a good rich soil; it should be well mulched in winter. Shastas are effective with yellow daylilies, which bring out the yellow in the centers of the white daisies, and daylilies offer contrast to both plant form and flower form. Shastas are pretty for bouquets and also pleasant companions, indoors or out, for the purple cornflower-aster.

The *Stokesia* is less particular about soil, so long as it is well drained. The 4-inch lavender discs of 'Blue Star' appear through summer and until hard frost in autumn. This variety is notably hardy and a good substitute for the annual asters if these do not reciprocate your affection. If you don't know these two charming daisies, Shastas and Stokes-aster, do try a plant of each for a start. I'm sure you will be pleased. I should warn you, however, that stokesia is inclined to relax and sit back and looks best in small groups next to more moral and upright plants.

Three H's Plus Rudbeckia

Helenium, Helianthus, Heliopsis, and Rudbeckia are neither aristocratic nor elegant but comfortably undemanding, with a wealth of flowers for summer to autumn brilliance. These are no toy plants to be tucked in an inconspicuous spot; they are deep, glowing perennials for mass plantings among shrubs, for backgrounds in very wide borders, for screens along garages, or, as I have used them, for shields for the compost pits. Since any of the three will attain some 2-foot clumps of green growth early, they are well suited to this cover-up use.

Helenium or Helens-flower produces an abundance of pale yellow to mahogany-red daisies on plants 2 to 4 feet high. I have enjoyed the orange-tinted, bright yellow 'Riverton Beauty' and 'Chippersfield Orange' for years; 'Butterpat' is clear yellow, best of the self colors. All bloom from mid-August far into September. These energetic heleniums need division every other year at least, and every spring is better.

Of the perennial sunflowers, *Helianthus decapetalus florepleno,* a clear yellow, almost double, 4-foot variety, blooms from July to September. The sprays give the effect of small dahlias. In its place it is a useful plant but a rampant runner and can be a pest. It is for the outer reaches of a big property.

Helenium, interesting high-summer daisies, from pale yellow to orange and mahogany. GENEREUX PHOTO

Colorful from midsummer to fall, the false sunflower *Heliopsis scabra* grows 3 to 4 feet tall and produces brilliant wiry-stemmed daisy blooms for strong garden effect and fresh or dried bouquets. 'Gold Greenheart' is attractive with 3-inch, green-centered, buttercup yellow blooms; 'Incomparabilis' (a modest name!) is nearly double, a golden yellow with dark center.

All three of these summer-into-autumn growers need room, so it is wise to make their acquaintance with some diffidence. Start with a few plants of heleniums. You'll love bountiful summer baskets of them for the porch or for deep window ledges in a sunroom.

The rudbeckias or coneflowers, glorified black-eyed Susans, are coarse-growing plants but reliably hardy and tolerant of dryness and heat. They are just the perennials, in fact, for some sun-baked corner where the best of conditions do not prevail yet where space exists for increasing your cut-flower supply. The compact 2-foot 'Goldsturm' looks exactly like an improved Susan with 3- to 4-inch flowers from July into October. The 2-foot sturdy 'Gold Drop' is double, also 'September Gold'; I think the single 'Goldsturm' is the most attractive. Rudbeckia hybrids with ray flowers in various shades of red and purple-black discs, growing 2 to 4 feet high, are different and suggest new combinations. Two of the best and opulent are 'Earliest of All' and 'The King'.

MICHAELMAS DAISIES

Blooming at about the same time as many of the white and yellow daisy plants are the truly glorious Michaelmas daisies, hardy asters that introduce melting shades of pink, rose, lavender, and purple to the garden scene. Alone these asters produce lovely late-summer-to-early-autumn pictures. Also a few excellent asters come into bloom in midsummer. Descendants of the New England asters and New York asters of roadside and meadow and over the years hybridized with other species native from Georgia to Labrador, they have the same charm but with greater impact, for the massive plants are composed of much larger flowers and the color range is wider, with many deep rose, almost red, varieties. You can enjoy these hardy asters in a number of ways.

Ten Inches to Four Feet

The under-10-inch dwarfs make good edging plants if you prefer late bloom at your border's rim instead of spring concentration there. Since aster foliage is good, you can achieve a pleasant sequence by alternating one-color groupings of asters with plantings of May pinks, or you can achieve unusual September color with a completely fresh outline. 'Snowball' (early September) and 'Bonny Blue' would make a pretty sequence.

The semidwarf so-called Oregon asters are well suited to small gardens. Like most asters they are hardy and insect-free. The 15-inch or taller ones like 'Persian Rose', a marvelous shade, and 'Twilight', a deep purple, are nice together and might be planted in the bays of foundation evergreens to bring color there from mid-August into October. (Most late-summer doorway plantings have little color!)

For the center of the border or any spot suitable for 24- to 30-inch plants, by all means choose the distinguished *Aster frikartii* 'Wonder of Staffa'. Pre-eminent even among the most noteworthy asters, it blooms from late June until November frost. An enchanting lavender, this aster does well in

Aster frikartii, 'Wonder of Staffa', pre-eminent among daisy types. GENEREUX
PHOTO

light shade but in full sun it produces not just a fair showing of bloom but a rich, unfailing, long-season display of 2½-inch flowers. They are superb for cutting and delightful with pale pink roses. In a border 'Snow Flurry' is a nice contrast. The plant averages 24 to 30 inches and needs a loose soil with sand and peat added where there is heavy clay. It has no crown but dies down completely and in severe areas requires winter protection. If your place is too small for most of the daisies, I hope you will at least plant this frikartii wonder, for so it is.

Midborder asters work better if only three stems are allowed to each plant, these staked with inconspicuous bamboo. Fine growth producing cloudlike masses of small flowers then results, without using too much space. These are useful planted next to oriental poppies. There, one extra stem on each side is allowed each plant, and these stems are pinched back a few inches early in July so that a shorter, bushier spray is available to fill in when the poppy goes into retreat.

For the rear of a planting or as luxurious masses among shrubs, nothing is handsomer than 4-foot asters like the deep rose, 'Harrington's Pink', the lilac-pink 'Julia', 'Boningdale White', and dark 'Coombe Violet'. Many of the finest varieties grow only to 3 feet, like the pink 'Patricia Ballard', lavender 'Ada Ballard', deep violet 'Eventide', and 'Crimson Brocade' (such a lovely one). Any of these 3-foot varieties can be set to the rear of a narrow border. There I value them as early green backgrounds for island beds or strip borders that lack an important backdrop of evergreens or flowering shrubs. Let this type have four stems to a plant. These, though stiff, must still be staked. Pinching off 6 inches of growth in July results in more grace but in less height, of course, so in shaping your plants be guided by your purpose.

Companions and Culture

Good companions for Michaelmas daisies in September are early chrysanthemums and easy-from-seed dahlias of the Coltness Hybrid strain; these two planted with the hardy asters for background. They create a strong contrast of bold, shiny-foliaged dahlias with misty clouds of aster bloom. I also like the combination of marigold 'Yellow Supreme' with any of the "blue" asters.

Hardy asters have four requirements: full sun, plenty of room (crowding promotes mildew), adequate summer moisture (mulch plants by all means), and frequent division (in spring). Your average garden soil, spring-enriched along with the other perennials, will be just fine. You may need to divide some varieties yearly or in the second year—'Harrington's Pink' doesn't need it so often—rather than the third, which is usual práctice. If the growth gets too thick and centers get woody, plants decline and eventually disappear, so keep an eye out for this. When you do pull the clumps apart, throw away the hard centers and put three of the outside rooted shoots in one hole to form a clump. Avoid crowding. Like phlox, these asters are fresh-air fiends. If mildew shows, get out a fungicide, Benlate, Phaltan, or Flotox.

In vases, you will enjoy these easily arranged Michaelmas daisies. Late daylilies and dahlias go well with them. Buy your first aster plants; they do not come true from seed. A few plants will go far for you by the second year.

Whenever I think over all the daisies I have grown, I get excited. Each one I've had I want to urge you to plant, too. But what I really would suggest is that you find your way cautiously through the daisy maze since the majority grow rapidly, produce abundantly, and practically never die. And then I should add that chrysanthemums also are daisy plants and you must have some of these as well. I entice you with these in the next chapter.

A great bed of one kind of chrysanthemum, as these white ones, makes an effective display. TALOUMIS PHOTO

10

CHRYSANTHEMUMS
—THE FINAL BRILLIANCE

When New England maples flame red, orange, and gold and the wild grape vines hang great yellow curtains over trees and bushes along roadsides and byways, when the dogwoods and burning bushes around home and church turn a rich, rosy crimson, chrysanthemums offer their own glowing complementary hues as they carry garden color into the very teeth of winter. Bronze, copper, and tangerine varieties, reds verging on vermilion, along with many glowing yellows make one vibrant association when these same colors are brilliant overhead. Where crimson trees and shrubs predominate, pink, lavender, and purple hues with a yellow or two, and a few whites to set them off, make a lovely and appropriate picture.

Growers tell me that people are sharply divided in their color enthusiasms for chrysanthemums. If they want the golden group, they don't want the crimsons, and vice versa. I prefer the yellows myself—the Croesus golds my favorites—and I feel definitely that chrysanthemums belong to autumn. Brought to bloom in spring, they make me feel the world is even more out of wack than it obviously is. However, keep in mind that chrysanthemums can be two-season perennials. If you receive spring gifts of flowering plants or buy mums in bloom then, you can transfer them to an outdoor bed as soon as weather permits. First, pinch out the faded flowers along with a portion of the stem, reducing tops to 3 or 4 inches. Then as new growth forms, pinch that back so as to develop stocky, well-budded fall specimens that will give you a second bloom.

But before you start mail ordering and nursery visiting, let's have a look at the chrysanthemum plant and the flower forms at blooming time, since they vary considerably, and the type you select depends first of all on the role you want these late-season garden plants to play. Do you want chrysanthemums to bring fall color to the front of a border of evergreens and shrubs where bulbs made a bright edging in spring? Early bulbs and chrysanthemums are a fine garden twosome providing a brilliant early and a glowing late effect. Just place the bulbs with space left between the colonies for the insertion of single divisions from your overwintered mums or growers "green plants" that are offered by Park's in mid-July. Be sure the mums are set far enough forward from the shrubs to get plenty of sun.

Perhaps you value chrysanthemums as replacements for stretches of exhausted petunias or other annuals in your flower beds. A half-dozen well-budded plants will perk up your garden wonderfully. Because mums are so amenable to transplanting, you can lift them early in September from a vegetable row and set them just where they are needed for late-season color. The smaller kinds are easier to handle than the tall growers. Of course, the smaller kinds, the Cushions, can be grown along the edge of your perennial border. There they will make a tidy edging but take up green room for several months before providing bright early-fall color.

Or your primary interest may be in autumn flowers to cut for the house or to arrange for a flower show or to fill the church vases on *your* Sunday. The Spider mums are particularly effective for arrangements. Maybe you prefer to use mums, as I so often have (definitely the laziest way), as fall-purchased potted plants in bloom to set in urns on the front steps, beside a front walk, or on top of the ground in various strategic locations, where I can enjoy the blooms for weeks outdoors and then improvidently discard the plants or pass them on to more energetic friends.

DELIGHTFUL CUSHIONS

Like people, chrysanthemums come both short and tall. The Cushion mums that have so successfully responded to the modern hybridizer's attention are grand low plants with attractive foliage and moundlike growth 18 to 28 inches across, with flowers up to 3 inches wide on 9- to

Alternate Groupings of Cushion Mums for Edging

15-inch stems. I think of the Cushions as landscaping mums, nice for along paths, or facing down taller mums, or colorful surprises for an odd corner, but also attractive as pot plants.

On a terrace I have spaced out the Masterpiece Series of Cushions from Yoder's among young prostrate junipers that have not yet fulfilled their groundcover function. This series includes the full range of colors except blues and has required about as little attention as any garden plant I know. Set out 18 to 24 inches apart, after late-spring frosts, in well-drained locations *in full sun,* and kept watered in times of summer drought, they require only regular pinching back to encourage spreading and to avoid staking. To increase flowering I attend to the pinching when growth reaches about 4 inches, and I do this twice more as the little side branches stretch to 4 inches. (Our very curious little cat, Snug, enjoys the procedure and only just misses getting his own nose clipped.) Here in Connecticut and the Northern states checking of growth should stop soon after July 10. Gardeners in the Central states are advised to pinch on to July 20, and until August 1 in the South.

As for fertilizing, I found that the Cushions (as well as the taller Decoratives) responded well to a liquid dose of Miracle-Gro at planting time, with two doses later about a month apart. I was interested to hear from Mrs. Grace Mack, my neighbor and a professional chrysanthemum originator, that she also applies the liquid dose at the start; in her garden it is Ra-Pid-Gro. Her subsequent feedings are of dry fertilizer easily scattered around her plants through the spout of an old watering can, the nozzle removed, and the fertilizer then watered in, unless there is a convenient shower. Protected over winter, these Cushion plants come through safely, but unless divided they will grow taller the second year and have smaller blooms.

Here are some of the Cushions that have brightened my life and garden through September and until after the first *light* frosts. You will notice that they offer a variety of flower form, just as the taller garden chrysanthemums do, which we will consider next. Among the Cushions, I prize particularly the two large-flowered varieties, 'Classic', a lemon yellow, and 'Cloud 9', a superb ivory white. If you want to take the trouble to pinch off the side buds as they appear on these, you can get extra-big blooms. Mrs. Mack was the originator of 'Classic' and 'Cloud 9', also of 'Goldtone', and the white 'Penguin', and of the marvelous yellow 'Jackpot'. If you do not see all these listed in your favorite catalogues, you are very likely to find them as pot plants at local nurseries and wayside stands.

CUSHION CHRYSANTHEMUMS FOR BRIGHT LANDSCAPE EFFECTS

These varieties can be found in one or more catalogues.
Select them in the colors that complement your own autumn scene.

Name	Color	Bloom Time	Height in Inches	Type
Baby Tears	Pure white	Sept. 5	10	Button Pompon
Golden Cushion	Yellow, deeper center	Sept. 25	12	Daisy Bloom
Golden Jubilee	Bronze-gold	Sept. 1	15	Large Decorative
Gold Strike	Orange-yellow	Sept. 15	12	Pompon
Grandchild	Two-tone pink, deeper center	Sept. 20	12	Formal Pompon
Jackpot	Yellow (outstanding)	Oct. 1	9	Intermediate Decorative
Johnny Appleseed	Orange-bronze	Sept. 15	14	Intermediate Decorative
Lipstick	Bright red	Sept. 20	14	Small Decorative
Minnautumn	Red-bronze, profuse	Sept. 10	14	Intermediate Pompon
Powder River	Pure white	Sept. 25	18	Decorative
Ruby Mound	Crimson, large flowers	Sept. 20	14	Intermediate Decorative
Snowbound	White, pearly pink at first	Sept. 15	12	Pompon
Stardom	Pink	Sept. 20	12	Double Daisy
Yellow Starlet	Primrose yellow	Sept. 26	16	Spoon Type

Among the superb master-
piece chrysanthemums are
white 'Cloud 9', the yellow
'Starlet', and Jackpot'.

FLORIFEROUS SPRAY TYPES

Long favorites among gardeners are the taller chrysanthemums, up to 3 feet, that most of us have been growing for years and years. These are conveniently divided into Spray types—heavily clustered varieties that are sensibly allowed to develop all their 1½- to 3-inch flowers—and Standards or Disbuds. All but one bud is removed from these so as to produce large, 5-inch or so flowers, for cutting or exhibition. Since the very wide perennial border is attempted by few in this country today, the tall mums are usually grown now in display areas by themselves, or simply as background plants in narrow borders, say to a 4-foot width, where continuous color is not ex-pected. Suitable lower perennials of good foliage for the foreground of such a bed could be the smaller daylilies, astilbes, and hostas. Because these taller mums also do not resent transplanting, they are most satisfactory when grown in a vegetable garden row where space is not grudged for their long flowerless period. Carefully dug and transplanted in bud (string and stakes may be needed) on a sunless autumn day and then well watered, they do not miss a beat.

In September and October, this border of mixed chrysanthemums sparkles in the autumn light. TALOUMIS PHOTO

Rubellums and Koreans

But what to select from among the many possibilities of taller mums? Do you like the Spray types that produce fountains of bloom and need no disbudding? Hardly distinguished but valued for their huge bouquets for August and early September and their proven hardiness, the Rubellums are of this type and useful garden plants.

They grow to 18 inches, spread even wider, and are of airier appearance than the Cushions. Most of us who have gardened for many years have enjoyed the single salmon-pink 'Clara Curtis' outdoors. I am told that this also makes an excellent pot plant if dug in winter (that is, as soon as you *can* dig), potted, and forced into bloom in March in a cool, sunny, indoor location or in a greenhouse. 'Royal Command', to 2 feet and spreading to 30 inches, is the wine-red Rubellum.

The single and semidouble Koreans are also tall, rather loosely formed plants with handsome, mainly October flowers. Plants of these—and the Rubellums—are readily raised from seed, flowering five months after sowing. Seed comes only in mixture, but you can select and discard plants to get the colors you want after the first fall. Or you can buy plants sometimes simply listed as Singles. I think you will like the pale yellow 'Ceres', old-rose 'Daphne', the white daisylike 'North Star', and the pastel 'Peachtone'.

Spoons and Spiders

The Spoons are well named, for their petals really do look like narrow teaspoons. Mostly single, these chrysanthemums have elegance and are lovely in the garden or for cutting. However, they do not bloom early enough to escape frost in many locations. The compact, yellow 'Shining Light' and the orange-buff 'Starlet' with coral tubes, both but 18 inches high, are probably the earliest, usually in bloom by September 20. All the varieties are charming, I think, but 'Lemon Lace' doesn't open much before late September, and the red 'Firefly' not till October. The Spoons are reliably hardy, but bad weather may affect the petal form.

I have always been very fond of the Spoons, for I grew up near Dreer's Nursery in Riverton, New Jersey, where my good friend Eugene Michel discovered a shaggy new form among his experimental plants, and this form evolved into the Spoons. Actually, he was breeding to improve Anemone types for the garden when this unexpected development occurred.

The Spiders or Fuji chrysanthemums, with their lightly rolled irregular petals, some reaching quite far out, are dear to flower arrangers but definitely late for garden use, not blooming much before the end of October.

Chrysanthemums combine well with other perennials, as fall asters, heliopsis, and yellow marguerites, also with dwarf dahlias and tuberous begonias.

The Spiders require considerable care, with special attention to disbudding; their large, exquisite, threadlike blooms are not yours just for the wishing. Winter the plants in a coldframe or, if you have a greenhouse, make the Spider chrysanthemums one of your exciting crops. 'Miss Atlanta' is a coral Spider you will like (which is an odd-sounding statement unless you know that it is mums we are discussing), and I also like the soft-yellow 'Sun Spider' that sometimes makes it by mid-September, and 'Pink Pagoda' for late in the month.

Buttons and Pompons

These are familiar old-fashioned garden types. The Buttons open mid- to late September and into early October. They appeal to those who care for the diminutive in flower forms, in this case blooms half an inch to an inch across, nice for corsage or boutonniere and, like the Pompons, of almost eternal life when cut for bouquets. The first Buttons I grew were late and tall, really not the greatest, and I don't find even one variety from my old lists on those of today. Newer ones like the silvery-rose 'Cameo', yellow 'Chiquita', golden orange 'Rustic', and 'Baby Tears', a white Cushion type, are far more delightful.

Pompons also occur among the Cushions, as in 'Goldtone', the bronze 'Minnautumn', white 'Penguin', and purple 'Tinker Bell'. The dainty round, tight blooms, so called for their resemblance to the French military ornament or *pompon,* are excellent for cutting in mid-September, and the 14-to-20-inch plants make tidy and effective growth in pots. They can also be attractive as tailored edgings for more loose-growing tall varieties. 'Copycat', which looks like an orange marigold, 'Sunset Pom', and the red 'Daredevil' are worth considering if you care for Pompons.

Elegant Standards or Disbuds

These important garden types include handsome varieties with smooth or shaggy flowers, quilled or straight petals. Many, if disbudded and reduced to four to six stems, produce blooms equal in size to the florist's "football" chrysanthemums. In your catalogues, you will see alluring color-plate collections of these. In many offerings each flower is named, and this is an economical way to buy the best in a full range of hues.

Be sure to note the Harvest Giants from Michigan, a group of standard varieties of beauty and excellence. Disbud and stake these if you want spectacular blooms of proven weather resistance for late September into early October. Consider the white 'Silver Song'; yellow 'Golden Promise'; rose-pink 'Touchdown', the largest of the group with semi-incurved blooms to 7½ inches across (but do you really crave such enormous flowers?), and the scarlet-bronze 'Indian Summer'.

CULTURE TOWARD PERFECTION

Chrysanthemums are true perennials, the same plants performing year after year, but unlike most plants in this category, the majority of mums must be divided every year or at least every other year if you expect quality bloom. Although the root system is small (not heavy like the peony's), about the time the flowers fade, the plants get busy sending out a mass of new roots, and from each one a spring shoot develops to crowd the planting. Inevitably flower quality declines.

Planting and Feeding

The thing to do is to lift plants in spring when growth is in evidence and pull the roots apart. Discard the worn-out centers and plant each outside rooted shoot *separately* at the proper distance for the variety—16 to 18 inches for the smaller Cushions; up to 24 inches for the big Decoratives. In any case, don't put three or four shoots in the same hole.

Full sun, good drainage, and reasonable fertility spell success with mums. Specialists advise improving average soil (I wonder if there is such a condition as average) by working into the top 6 to 8 inches a 2- to 4-inch layer of garden compost, or failing this, peatmoss or well-decayed manure. Then, to insure fertility, include one to two pounds of 5–10–5 or 4–12–4 fertilizer for each 100 square feet. Of course, you don't have to be so thorough, for mums will flourish though maybe not be of exhibition quality under the soil conditions that suit your other perennials.

Additional food during the growing season is worthwhile. More of the same fertilizer you worked into the soil at the start could be applied, a handful around a plant about July 15 and again August 15, or you could dose with your favorite liquid plant food, as I often do. Whatever fertilizer you use on your roses or other garden plants will benefit your mums, or follow specialists' advice for a 1–1–1 analysis, as 10–10–10 or 20–20–20. If plants bud early and the weather is very hot, apply a liquid fertilizer and soak the plants well. And if you set out plants offered by growers for mid-July, you will probably have to nurse them along, even shading them at first.

Since the number of blooms depends for the most part on the number of stems, increasing these means a more colorful plant. You do this by nipping off the soft growth, pinching it between thumb and forefinger. This influences height of growth, and lower plants are less subject to wind damage and also less likely to require staking.

As I have pointed out, repeated pinching improves the low Cushions. On the taller Spray types, wait until growth reaches 7 inches, and then repeat twice, as for the Cushions. With the tall Decoratives, on which you want very large flowers, pinch only once, at 7 inches. More stems will then develop, and clusters of flower buds appear on each. Remove all but one bud on each stem and you will be on your way to exhibition flowers. Furthermore, if you restrict growth to, say, five strong shoots, you will get even bigger flowers. All this is a little too much bother for me, a bush plant with average-sized flowers for the type suits me just fine, but then exhibiting does not appeal to me. I just want a colorful garden and plenty of bloom.

Winter Survival

Some varieties are better geared to this than others, so inherent cold resistance should be considered in your expectations. Various government

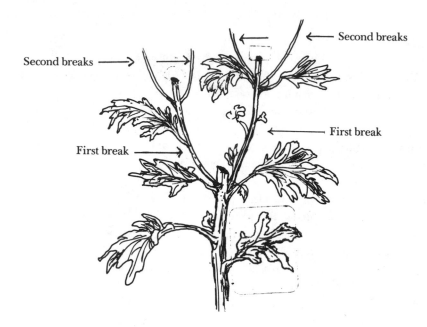

Second breaks →

Second breaks →

← Second breaks

First break →

← First break

Pinching Chrysanthemums

experimental stations are now working to this purpose. Minnesota has produced a number of varieties with Minn in the name, and Nebraska offers 'Quarterback', 'Stadium Queen', and 'Homecoming'. The Wyoming tests at Cheyenne have produced exceptionally hardy varieties, as would be expected from that cold-cold location. Eighteen inches high and as broad are the amber 'Inca', the white 'Powder River', and yellow 'Shoshone'. From the University of Nebraska comes the lavender 'Sachet', to make a pleasing color association with the Wyoming group. The state of Montana offers the subzero 'Blackfoot', 'Mountain Sunset', and 'Silver Run', the group called *C. montana*.

Spiders won't usually pull through outside, but some other mums you bought from the florist in bloom in September very likely will if you finally transfer them to a garden bed. Anyway, it is a good plan to select only the earlies for your garden if you live where the growing season is brief and frost comes soon, but choose some late September and October varieties if your garden grows where so long a pageant is possible in most years.

Planting and Wintering

Certainly mums need sunshine, for at least half the day, and a full day is much more desirable. Good drainage is always essential, particularly in its relation to winter hardiness. Plants that are alternately ice-locked and thawed rarely survive an average open winter.

After flowers fade and foliage succumbs to cold, but often it stays green until December, cut plants back to about 2 inches, unless they are transferred to a coldframe, where 3 to 5 inches is better. Then, unless you can count on a continuous snow cover after the ground is really frozen, not just touched by frost, spread a layer of evergreen boughs, maybe from your Christmas tree, over the outdoor plantings. Your purpose, of course, is to keep those plants cold and to avoid the dangerous condition of repeated freezing and thawing. Where the soil is heavy clay, some gardeners report good results from lifting plants and leaving the clumps *on top of the soil* for the winter. They are covered there, as for other plantings, but they do not suffer the heavy wetness of the clay. To be on the safe side, many enthusiasts make it a practice to lift one of each favorite kind and transfer it to a coldframe.

This is the method: After plants have flowered and well before a hard freeze, cut back the tall tops. Soak the roots well and transfer the plants to a coldframe. Water again after planting and each week thereafter until a hard freeze occurs. The idea is to encourage as much rooting as possible in the new location. Then cover lightly with oak or other leaves that curl after they fall or salt hay, and fasten down the glass of the frame. To avoid overheating by the sun, cover the glass. If you have a lath screen used for summer shading, place this on top.

From January on as warm middays occur, prop the glass up for short periods of ventilation. When in March examination reveals green growth, remove the leaf covering and the coldframe shade. By the first of April you can usually let the glass stay up all day and, as weather permits, all night, too. This hardens plants so they can face open conditions again. Separate and transfer your chrysanthemums back to the garden when new growth is a few inches high. This is fairly arduous business but a sure way to hold over certain exquisite but often tender ones like the Spoons, Spiders, and some other favorites.

Mrs. Mack reports that the safest wintering she ever had resulted from the use of polyethylene covering. She followed these directions from Thon's, who are experienced growers. "Transfer plants to a coldframe, cover with salt hay, and cover the hay with a polyethylene painter's dropcloth perforated with a few 1-inch holes to provide aeration. Close the coldframe, ventilate occasionally on warm days by slipping a 2-$\times$4-inch prop under the glass to hold it open at 2 inches."

Health Measures and Staking

So far we haven't thought much about insect and disease controls. You can spray every two weeks, as often advised, with a combination insecticide-miticide-fungicide, but I don't really think we average gardeners need to do this. I keep an eye out for aphids and rout them as required with a vigorous hose spray or an insecticide if necessary, and I certainly am alert to slugs, which can devour a young chrysanthemum plant in a single night. For some reason slugs have not been one of my problems until last year, when they finished off one small planting of mums very smartly. Thereafter saucers of beer placed among them insured a happy death for slugs and survival for my cherished plants.

If there is a complaint against chrysanthemums, it is that in some seasons and for some varieties an unattractive browning of the lower foliage occurs. This may be due to the effect on plant tissues of drought followed by wet spells; it may be caused by poor air circulation in overcrowded plantings, or it may be the result of a nematode attack. Attention to deep watering through rainless weeks, adequate spacing, and application of a deterrent fungicide dust like Orthocide will minimize or even eradicate this foliage trouble. Avoid overhead watering, provide mulch and, if you have reason to suspect nematodes, propagate by tip cuttings rather than crown division.

Most properly pruned plants require no staking, but some spray types will look better if they aren't allowed to sprawl. For these, you can use your tripod peony supports. With tall disbuds you may want to make them safe with a separate bamboo or wire stake for each stem. Fasten the props with some kind of plant tie.

With chrysanthemums, as with the other Big Four perennials, you can follow either course, plain or fancy. For simple garden pleasures you certainly don't have to make a big do about these richly rewarding autumn plants. Don't neglect them, but you don't need to coddle, either, whether you procure green plants in spring or gorgeous flowering plants in fall.

Now to get it all together, as the saying goes, look over this list of favorite Decoratives. Select these taller varieties in colors that will set off the rich reds or brilliant yellows of your own trees and shrubs.

TALLER SPRAY AND DISBUD CHRYSANTHEMUMS FOR GARDENS AND CUTTING

Name	Color	Height in Inches	Season	Description
Accolade	Silver lavender	24	Sept. 25	Large spray
Cherish	Rose to peach	24	Sept. 14	Cactus dahlia standard
Daredevil	Red to tangerine	18	Sept. 18	Small Pompon spray
Eventide	Lavender	20	Sept. 20	Quilled
Flamboyant	Bronze-scarlet	26	Aug. 25	Spray
French Vanilla	Cream-white	20	Sept. 23	Recurved decorative
Golden Promise	Intense yellow	26	Sept. 28	Small incurved disbud
Lightheart	Yellow to white	26	Sept. 20	Cactus dahlia standard
Orbit	Burnt orange	20	Sept. 20	Large spray spoon
Pumpkin	Golden-bronze	18	Sept. 21	Disbud
Quarterback	Rose-pink	26	Sept. 15	Huge incurved disbud
Red Headliner	Ruby red	24	Sept. 20	Spray, 3- to 4-inch flowers
Shining Light	Lemon-yellow	18	Sept. 20	Spoon spray
Silver Song	Ivory-white	24	Sept. 24	Large semi-incurved disbud
Stadium Queen	Red, golden reverse	30	Sept. 10	Huge disbud
Touchdown	Pink	26	Sept. 26	Semi-incurved disbud
Yellow Abundance	Buttercup yellow	22	Sept. 18	Huge decorative
Yellow Glow	Deep yellow	18	Sept. 1	Decorative

Alyssum saxatile citrinum overhanging a wall with lavender *Aubrieta* below.
GENEREUX PHOTO

11

GOOD EDGINGS
FOR GOOD LOOKS

When I plant a bed or border, I always decide first on the edging perennials, for neat edgings do wonders for plantings at any stage of season or weather. But before I select the plants, I like to make sure of maintaining the line with a controlled wood, metal, brick, or stone material. In my present garden, *treated* 2- by 4-inch wood headers (2- by 6-inch headers would raise the beds a little) were inserted along the straight edges before they were planted. A ⅛- by 4-inch steel band was fitted around my circular bed where a flexible material was essential. (A good substitute for steel, now that it has tripled in price, is a very thick, amber-colored plastic, Hortiscope Edging, which is available from some of the larger nurseries.) In other gardens I have inserted one or two rows, depending on space, of brick—broad side up—to edge beds. Bricks offer an excellent, low-upkeep device where there are adjacent lawn areas, since the mower can be pushed with one wheel along the bricks, and tedious hand clipping is avoided. If the edging plants sprawl a bit outside the bed, a little shearing won't hurt them, as mowing contributes to the neatness of the effect.

My landscape architect friend, Eloise Ray, also suggests that sections of flagstone, 8 by 12 inches and at least 2½ inches thick, can serve as neat edgings, if carefully laid so as not to look jagged. Pieces of flagstone 12 by 12 inches or 18 by 18 inches laid flat on the surface next to a bed not only receive the mower wheels but also serve as a narrow path when the adjoining grass is wet. Of course, all stone or brick edgings should be laid in well-tamped sand, gravel, or stone dust to a depth of at least 6 inches to prevent heaving and settling. Then for larger beds there are the more conspicuous but still suitable railroad ties that can be laid on the ground or dug in a little.

Most Reliable Edging Plants

First through many gardening years, the hardy evergreen candytuft, *Iberis,* remains my favorite. The 10-inch-high species, *Iberis sempervirens,* spreads to 18 inches and is just right for an informal planting of perennials where it can stretch at will among nearby plants. During the growing season this sturdy subshrub—it isn't a true perennial—has no shabby moments, while its six weeks of snowy spring bloom appear with yellow and cream narcissus and pink and blue hyacinths, as one of the first sweet enchantments of the gardening year. Just as the flowers fade I sternly shear the plants to encourage an abundance of new growth. I enjoy Gertrude Jekyll's remarks about this favorite plant of mine:

> Perhaps there is no white flower whose white is of such a pure and solid character as may be seen in some of these Candytufts. It is specially noticeable in *I. sempervirens,* where the white is of a curiously hard quality. White chalk is dim when set beside it, just as a white cat looks grimy in snow. This hard white can only be matched by some kinds of crockery; possibly its unity and absence of all gradation may be caused by the thick texture of the petals.

The 6-inch 'Little Gem' and 'Purity' are compact candytuft varieties with somewhat larger individual blooms. I prefer these for narrow borders and strip plantings. Then there are the supposedly twice-blooming candytufts, but their autumn showing has hardly been worthwhile in my experience. If part of your planting is struck by winter sun, you may need to spray the plants with an antidesiccant like Wiltpruf in late fall. I always do this to prevent browning of foliage; where my plants are on the shady side of the bed they don't require this.

With dependable foliage again in mind, I think of the almost evergreen coralbells, *Heuchera sanguinea.* The shapely geranium leaves and slender 1½- to 2-foot clouds of red, pink, or white bloom, and now chartreuse as well, have long been a delight in my gardens where foliage has been top

Iberis sempervirens, perennial candytuft, finest of all edging plants. FITCH PHOTO

quality throughout the season and plants show considerable shade toler-ance. In fact, for a strip border where you want continuity from sun to shade, these coralbells are an excellent choice. The deep-pink 18-inch variety 'Pluie de Feu', with bloom sprays opening from June well into August, has long been my choice, but you may prefer a white, pink, or green-white variety and a different height. 'French White' grows to 12 inches, 'Snow Cloud' to 30 inches. Heuchera is a plant that can safely be used in mixture since the colors blend well; also, it is easy from seed.

For a long edging by itself, catnip, *Nepeta mussinii,* is delightful. It makes a billowy, aromatic border, the gray-green foliage and spikes of lavender flowers a long delight. Each plant may spread to 18 inches and in bloom be 12 to 15 inches high. You can count on six to eight weeks of early-summer flowers and then, if you cut them off, intermittent bloom until frost. If you have visited English gardens, you know how this plant

is treasured there, but it is a quality edging for us, too. Nepeta thrives in
hot, dry, sunny places where the soil is sandy or only medium good. It
doesn't take well to continued dampness. For a strip border featuring
one or two strong-foliaged plants, like peonies or irises, along a flagstone
walk, it is particularly attractive. Snug is enamored of the leaves of this
plant, provided I crush them for him; otherwise, despite its name, he seems
not to notice it, for the aroma is, of course, not cast free on the air. Also,
he seems to like to play with the leaves rather than eat them, and so he
has a very gay tumbling time.

In my present garden where the beds hold a great collection of favorite
plants (maybe too great), I use the evergreen periwinkle, *Vinca minor* (not
the window-box variegated, *V. major*), as an edging plant to consolidate
the picture. If you have always thought of periwinkle as a groundcover,
try it as an edger; you will need to keep it trimmed narrow, but that's not
much of a chore, and it will flourish in both sun and shade. Let it bloom,
lavender or white, April into May, before you shape it.

Other Possibilities

For light shade, consider the clear, yellow primroses of the true English
type, *Primula vulgaris.* One small suburban garden I know is thus completely edged along evergreen and shrub borders as well as flower beds.
Behind the primroses are clumps of narcissus in many cream and white varieties. When other gardens are just waking up in April, this one appears in
full glory. And through division a few English primrose plants soon go a
long way. I like, too, to strengthen the picture with the lavender-blue Jacobs-ladder, *Polemonium reptans,* placed in bold clusters among the narcissus. In fact, this polemonium, with its fine ferny foliage, can qualify with
reservations for an informal edging in sun or shade. However, neither the
lightly fragrant April to May primroses nor the May to June polemoniums
have the foliage strength of candytuft and coralbells. Primrose plants tend
to work out of the soil, and the leaves lack the stamina for a sturdy edger.
The polemoniums die down after blooming and look shabby for a brief time
until they renew themselves. Anyway, I love them and so plant them in a
stretch where the edging is not conspicuous.

Now let me introduce you to the *true* geranium, not the familiar tender,
pelargonium pot plant, but a hardy perennial. I once planted the 18-inch
pink-lavender wild *Geranium maculatum* with lavender and white woods-
hyacinths for an April to May path edging. The effect was enchanting and
lovely for a whole month. The geranium performs much like the pole-

Hybrid primroses beside a wooden path in early spring. These are descended from *Primula veris*, the lovely yellow oxlip of Shakespeare's England. GEN-EREUX PHOTO

Close-up of a distinguished edging and groundcover plant, *Epimedium alpinum rubrum*. FITCH PHOTO

monium but prefers sunshine. After I cut down the flower sprays, the foliage gradually renewed itself, and stayed nice until frost. This geranium just isn't well enough known, yet a number of rather similar species and varieties are now available. Try 'Wargrave Pink' with 'Johnson Blue', a variety of *G. ibericum,* or the lavender *G. grandiflorum.* The effect will be charming and practically unique, for I never see this true geranium in gardens.

The forget-me-not, *Myosotis scorpioides,* brings the rare blue to my garden. Plants grow to 12 to 20 inches high in light shade and bloom profusely in May and June, lightly through summer. And how the forget-me-nots spread, reaching in to carpet the columbine bed and the bare ground under the azaleas. Furthermore, they are almost evergreen. By taking care to let some of them go to seed in June, I get a marvelous crop and find young plants springing up in unexpected places. In another garden, yellow primroses have been their pleasant companions.

For a long, one-plant edging, the so-called evergreen *Epimedium* is delightful. True, the leathery, heart-shaped foliage does last through winter, but I notice on my plants it is brown, not green. In light shade or sun and rather acid soil, the epimediums put on a fine May to June show. They grow 8 to 12 inches high and spread about as far but rather slowly. Lavender, red, white, or yellow, all the varieties are charming, I think, and once established quite undemanding. In my garden, I have combined the yellow variety *sulphureum* with the white *niveum*.

Certain violas are also worth considering. A few years ago I could not have recommended these charming perennial pansies for important edgers because they were not dependably heat-resistant. But last summer I grew the apricot 'Chantreyland', and from April to frost it was indefatigable. Because it was edging a long, oblong bed, I kept it pruned to neatness, but it could have been allowed to be a "weaver," in the manner of Christopher Lloyd's English violas that I described in the first chapter.

Finally, had you thought of strawberries, the Fraises des Bois types? In full sun, and they need that, plants are covered with white blossoms from May on, and there is a wealth of bright red berries from late June to frost, and conveniently no runners are produced on these upright growers. The dependable 8- by 12-inch plants are both pretty and unusual, and they will give your garden a "different" air.

Mixed Edgings for Long Lineups

So far I have been thinking of edging plants of one kind and, in general, my preference is for a one-color, one-variety lineup. However, sometimes I have inserted accent clumps of the double white April rockcress, *Arabis albida* 'Flore-pleno', in a long coralbell stretch, or used heuchera itself as an accent plant in an extended candytuft edging. Conveniently, the rockcress thrives in sun or shade and is particularly enjoyed because the flowers come so early. Trim plants back a little after they bloom.

Of course, there are a number of other flowering plants that measure up to my standard of fine foliage and prolonged bloom. Attractive and so easy to get abundantly from seed is a mixed edging of the old-fashioned, May-blooming, spicily fragrant clove pink, *Dianthus plumarius*. It requires full sun and prefers a limey soil. I worked wood ashes around mine in spring.

For lengthy borders a rhythm of your favorite dianthus in a repeated series would look lovely. You might select such low-growing, fine-foliaged plumarius varieties as the fringed pink 'Essex Witch', the double white

Dwarf fall aster, a charming miniature edging plant for summer's end.
TALOUMIS PHOTO

'Her Majesty', and 'Salmon Unique', all notably fragrant, or consider a series of Allwood pinks, as the white 'Blanche' and red 'Ian'. A series looks best if composed of uneven numbers, say two or three varieties, of five or more plants each to a stretch, and the series repeated at least three times. With long lines to fill in, the gardener who is fond of variety may quite rightly prefer to add the yellow perennial alyssum, *Alyssum saxatile,* and the purple Rockcress, *Aubrieta deltoides,* both easy from seed, and perhaps others.

The Cushion chrysanthemums are also good for edgings, and I think they have been overlooked for this purpose. Their clean foliage makes an excellent, though not narrow stretch, and plants produce a wealth of September bloom, while most other edging plants are colorful only in spring. The Cushions can be used alone in groups of three or five by color or, as with the pinks, they can be interrupted by spring accent plants of candytuft or coralbells. Groups of low-growing white 'Baby Tears' or 'White Prom', yellow 'Pixie Cushion' and pink 'Stardom' would make a pretty early-autumn picture. Or you might select the sturdy 'Minnwhite', 'Minnyellow', and orange-red 'Minnautumn'. All these are low-growing and spreading. (A longer list of Cushions is given in Chapter 10.)

Dwarf asters can be used in the same way. For September emphasis, I think of the golden-centered 'Snowball', 'Bonnie Blue', and the rosy-violet 'Romany' all no higher than 10 inches. These could be planted alternately in groups of three to make an interesting fall brightener for an end-of-season border.

You must, of course, decide what you want your edging plants to do for you and your garden. If you haven't much space but have a passion for many different plants, as I have, alas, you may decide that, although the one-kind lineup would perhaps be more effective, it wouldn't please you as such, so have a conglomeration if you wish. After all, your garden is for *you!*

A well-grown specimen fern, like this cinnamon, can be an arresting feature in the garden or as an accent elsewhere. TALOUMIS PHOTO

12

THE FASCINATING FERNS

My enthusiasm for ferns increases with the years—and also in with my broader acquaintance. They are invaluable plants, certainly perennial though lacking any flowers, producing sporangia instead. The royal and the cinnamon ferns do send up fruiting sprays that are decorative, and the plume-shaped spore clusters of the tall ostrich fern hold over winter. I like to plant ferns close by in my garden, since their fronds and their manner of growth delight me in the near view. I suppose my favorite fern is the hardy maidenhair, with its many small bright green parasols elevated on short ebony stems.

With bleedinghearts and Virginia bluebells, the maidenhair fern completes a small, elegant association. Indeed, ferns always seem to have exactly proper companions, so I plant narcissus colonies between the great clumps of Christmas ferns that edge the terrace and, in a tree well near enough to be looked down into, I enjoy a pleasing association of osmundas—royal, cinnamon, and interrupted. At the edge of the well a beguiling little cluster of pale green lacy New York fern creeps shallowly in a crevice between two great joining tree trunks. There I encourage it with trowelsful of rich soil and frequent watering to help it cling to what is surely a precarious perch.

My new neighbors, blessed with a New England gray stone wall, often called a fence here, plan a border of the taller ferns for background, with a foreground of very early spring bulbs that will bloom before the overhead shade gets heavy there. These bulbs will be followed by annual impatiens plants. Thus a charming garden is created but of lowest possible care, with ferns the chosen perennial.

If you don't know ferns and want to, as I certainly hope you do, have a look at Gordon Foster's *Ferns to Know and Grow* (New York: Hawthorn Books, 1971). It is a richly illustrated book and will help you get acquainted with these beautiful and useful plants. As for culture, ferns are so easy you can be sure of success without much study. In general, they thrive in light, in open shade, rather than in sun; and they require a soil rich in humus, the kind you find in the woods. Or you can prepare the fern bed at home by mixing in your own compost or the peatmoss you can buy by the bale. Plenty of water is absolutely essential, especially in dry weather. Ferns that turn brown early if roots dry out stay green well into autumn when moisture is plentiful.

A Dozen of My Favorite Ferns

These can be used in somewhat the same way as the herbaceous perennials. I offer common names before the botanical in case like me you find the botanical names almost impossible to conquer. However, you need them for ordering so as to get just what you want. (Some excellent fern nurseries are listed under Where to Buy at the end of this book.)

Bulblet Bladder Fern, *Cystopteris bulbifera.* This deciduous fern grows 1½ to more than 2 feet tall and likes a shaded situation. The narrow, tapering fronds, with pinkish stems and yellow-green pinnae, are pretty with rocks and a useful accompaniment for perennials that require a sweet, not acid, condition. Showing up in spring a month or more after the earlies like the maidenhair, it is a charming success with babysbreath, pinks, flax, delphiniums, and gasplant, all of which prefer lime in the soil.

Christmas Fern, *Polystichum acrostichoides.* Indispensable and evergreen to midwinter, this neat crown grower is 15 to 30 inches tall. It spreads slowly in open shade and is a fine companion for daffodils, perhaps with hardy candytuft to edge a bed. I could never have a garden without Christmas ferns.

Cinnamon Fern, *Osmunda cinnamomea.* Tall, handsome, and deciduous, this fern could grow to 5 feet, though it has not surpassed 4 for me. A na-

Typical uncoiling fiddle-
heads of native ferns in the
early spring, probably one
of the osmunda species.
TALOUMIS PHOTO

Royal fern in May, with
yew, viburnum, hosta epi-
medium. TALOUMIS PHOTO

tive, it needs an open location; rich, acid soil, and plenty of moisture. It makes a fine accent plant, its cinnamon stick rising like a flower from the depths of my tree well.

Goldie's Fern, *Dryopteris goldiana.* This 2- to 4-foot deciduous fern of tropical appearance has dark, yellow-green, oval fronds lighter underneath. It thrives in shade, in rich humus, neutral to slightly acid, and like most ferns requires a lot of moisture. Palmlike, it associates well with small shrubs.

Japanese Gray or **Painted Fern,** *Athyrium goeringianum.* (What a terrible name for such a lovely fern!) This one is difficult to locate today but worth a search. I don't know even one mail-order source, but you may be able to find it in a nursery, as I did. My own plant cost five dollars but is so beautiful I couldn't resist it. Gray-green with silvery markings, 1½ to 2 feet tall, it is deciduous. I grow it in open shade near the maidenhair ferns. They are a charming contrast. This Japanese fern spreads slowly, making a clump rather than a whorl. It likes leafmold on the acid side.

Lady Fern, *Athyrium filix-femina.* Growing 1 to 3 feet tall, this deciduous fern tolerates full sun, although it thrives also in part shade and is found in dry to wet woodland. Fronds are yellow-green, brownish in time, and finely cut. The plant is a creeper and on that account has many uses as a filler among strong growers like the daylilies.

Maidenhair Fern, *Adiantum pedatum.* Surely this *is* my favorite fern. Of early appearance, its dainty light-to-medium-green fronds look charming with spring wildflowers and early perennials like columbine, doronicum, and forget-me-nots. Deciduous, its creeping roots fan out in dense shade in rich leafmold. Moisture is important, but so is secure drainage. If you can have only two ferns, I'd say this one and the Christmas fern.

Royal Fern, *Osmunda regalis.* Charming for a strip or path planting and a good companion in wide beds with the cinnamon fern. The royal produces brown spore clusters that look like flowers rising from the center of the vase form. Native to swampy places, it accepts drier locations in acid soil, and is a handsome deciduous fern for light to deep shade and charming with Japanese iris and astilbes.

Silvery Glade Fern or **Spleenwort,** *Athyrium thelypteroides.* The great yellow-to-bright-silvery-green fronds changing to summer dark green and late-summer russet green are 3 feet tall and 7 inches wide. If deeply mulched with rotted leaves, this fern makes a good background garden subject and endures considerable sunshine, provided the soil is kept damp.

Wood Ferns. There are three excellent ones for garden use:

American maidenhair in woods soil with rhododendron. TALOUMIS PHOTO

Japanese painted fern, *Athyrium goeringianum pictum,* hardy in our Eastern and Central states. TALOUMIS PHOTO

Evergreen Wood Fern (Intermediate Shield), *Dryopteris intermedia.* The deeply cut, dark-green, prickly fronds come up late, so this is a good fern to plant with early bulbs whose departure will then be agreeably "shielded." It likes partial shade, plenty of moisture, and a soil rich in humus. It grows about 1½ to 2½ feet tall.

Leather Wood Fern (Marginal Shield), *D. marginalis.* Growing 1 to 3 feet tall, this blue-green evergreen has a lovely vase form. The fronds are of firm texture with fruit dots underneath along the margins of the leaflets. It prefers shade but is adaptable to part shade if planted in rich woods soil. It shows up late and so can be a cover-up for your departing tulips.

Toothed Wood Fern, *D. spinulosa.* Growing 1 to 2 feet tall, this fern is interesting for its two kinds of fronds, the sterile evergreen and the deciduous fertile ones. The circular clumps are lighter green than those of *D. intermedia.* It will look lovely in your rock garden.

I have never planted ferns in a mixed border, even though I do consider them as one kind of perennial. I have found them attractive and useful cover plants in my woodland settings where such wildflowers as trilliums, mayapples, Dutchmans-breeches, and wild ginger don't look like much after their two-week, early-spring festival. In my present garden, ferns please me particularly with bleedinghearts, various columbines, violets, wild geraniums, and a few Jack-in-the-pulpits.

Like other strong clumpy perennials, ferns can be used to the fore of a planting of shrubs edged with bulbs. When judiciously placed, the early ferns, like maidenhair, can cover up the slow demise of bulb foliage. In informal plantings, you can count on those that emerge late, like the evergreen wood ferns, to conceal the early-summer disappearance of such perennials as bleedinghearts, tradescantia, and poppies. Of course, you will like the pictures that ferns make with your forget-me-nots, small phlox, Jacobs-ladder, primroses, and veronicas.

In rock gardens that are almost always planted primarily for spring, the fragile bladder ferns uncurl early croziers late in March before those of other ferns, and thus can conceal the shabbiness of winter aconites, snow-drops, and February crocuses as these go out of bloom. The small ebony spleenwort and the maidenhair spleenwort, the tiny polypody that creeps over logs and rocks, the walking fern, and the small woodsias make summer green and lovely in a rock garden when the forget-me-nots, primroses, arabis, alyssum, pinks, leopardsbane, small iris, creeping phlox, Jacobs-ladder, and violas no longer offer color there.

Ferns for Your Rock Garden

Common Polypody, *Polypodium virginianum.* A charming evergreen creeper, not above 10 inches, this flourishes in light shade on moderate dry leafmold. It will grow over your rocks.

Ebony Spleenwort, *Asplenium platyneuron.* An up to 20-inch evergreen with narrow, dark-green fronds forming a crown, this grows best in a lightly shaded spot. It will be a nice companion for your wild blue phlox and white sweet woodruff.

Maidenhair Spleenwort, *A. trichomanes.* Evergreen and less than 6 inches, this one likes a limey soil and plenty of moisture. Good between rocks at the base of your slope perhaps.

Fragile Bladder Fern, *Cystopteris fragilis.* Deciduous, and less than 12 inches high, this likes shade and needs moisture. Let the deeply toothed green plants spread through your rock garden for late March coverage there.

Rusty Woodsia, *Woodsia ilvensis.* This light-green to gray-green, up-to-6-inch fern is deciduous and tolerant of open shade or alternate sunshine. It's just right for a spot where light comes through an open-foliaged tree like the locust. Rusty in the name describes the underside of the fronds, and also the condition of the plant if it suffers drought.

Walking Fern, *Camptosorus rhizophyllus.* Often the companion of the maidenhair spleenwort, this small medium-green evergreen, under 12 inches, with tapering and tip-rooting fronds, grows in shade or shifting sunshine and prefers a limestone situation.

Ferns are plants of quiet beauty, delicate textures, and intriguing greens. Once planted they are not forever needing to be divided and moved about. Do get to know their infinite variety. Particularly if yours is a garden in shade, plant ferns freely; in time, you may find them just as fascinating as the flowering perennials. I have.

On a snowy winter day my own small Eden is serenely pleasing. BUKOVCIK

13

IN PRAISE OF SMALL GARDENS
AND SMALLER PERENNIALS

To enjoy a small garden to the utmost, you must first have had a big garden or a big planted place with great lawn stretches and flower borders
that finally became too much for you. That's what happened to me. When
the autumn leaf cleanup cost more than two hundred dollars, I faced the
need for a change—and with what anguish! Now at the end of little more
than a year in my small garden, I cannot praise it enough! When you ex-
change acres for square feet, you move into an entirely new world of gardening, where every close-by plant is enjoyed to the fullest and the seasons pass by quietly instead of harshly, with their inexorable demands for
you to be always up and doing.

Here winter is deeply peaceful, with no snowplow worries; spring is filled
with the near-at-hand fragrance of hyacinths and other scented favorites;
early on summer mornings, after half an hour of work, I can sit on the
shaded terrace with Snug and simply enjoy; in autumn the leaves are a
matter of bushel baskets, not tonnage. Snug scampers among them as I
sweep the brick walks, both of us excited by the brisk air and the hint of
frost.

Primary Decisions

To make the most of your own small allotted space, you have first to come to some hard decisions. What plants from your broad experience are absolutely essential to you in your narrower sphere? I had a dreadful time eliminating old favorites. Finally I came to this: a two- or three-pronged white birch, a fringetree, a white dogwood, some deciduous azaleas and a small crabapple (both to be brought from the old place), the fragrant summersweet, a winter honeysuckle, carlesii viburnums, a climbing hydrangea, clematis vines, and a very few evergreens. Then I knew I could not do without many favorite perennials, some ferns, and winter-into-spring bulbs. Space for annuals cause me no concern; I care least for these and would use them in only a few places as I needed fillers among the bulbs. There would be no room for big lilacs and forsythias, no rampant wisteria vine; I sighed as I crossed this off. What it came down to was a certain amount of one-of-eaching, instead of the broad expanses of the same plant that I had always preferred.

If you can further reduce your necessities, perhaps you will get better effects than I have. Anyway, the smaller the garden the more personal it becomes, and if but one plant of the purple roof iris, one plant of the pink gasplant, and only one bleedingheart pleases you, then enjoy it and forget the great stretches you once had in the *near* pleasure of every observable part of your small new kingdom. Contemplation inches away of a 'Little Cherub' daylily on a mid-May afternoon or gazing down from your breakfast window on Christmas-roses in full bloom in the snow are among the special pleasures afforded by the small garden.

Essential Design

The small garden does not come off very well if it is randomly planted. Perhaps the simplest scheme for a backyard is based on an all-round border (as wide as space permits), with a center of grass or stone chips accented by a well for one shade tree—a honeylocust perhaps.

My own so-satisfactory design is patterned and formal. I have always admired the garden plots of Williamsburg and so, after consultation with my landscape architect, Eloise Ray (and I consider the advice of L.A.'s essential for any garden, and especially for a small one), the plan you see in these illustrations evolved. A 3-foot, 6-inch picket fence assures privacy, and

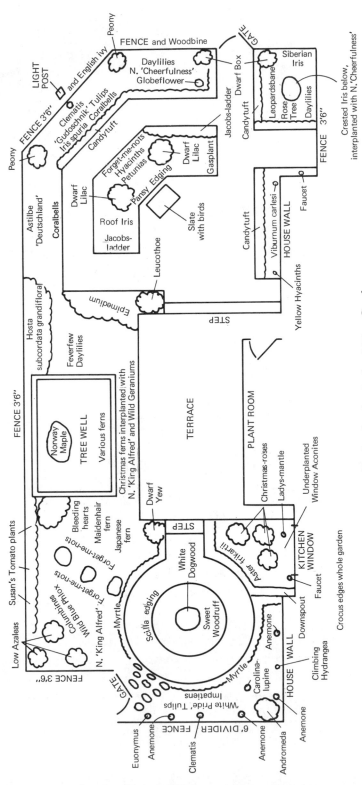

Design for the Author's New Garden

Following the plan made by Eloise Ray, L.A., the right side of the garden measures 20 by 21 feet, beds edged with firring strips, paths indicated but not yet laid. This and subsequent photos of my new garden by Bukovcik.

Brick replaces the white stones that couldn't be kept clean in winter. Petunias, pansies, impatiens, and finally potted chrysanthemums have followed spring bulbs. Two small standard lilacs give height to the long bed. The terrace with the winter houseplants is now shaded by the rolled-down awning.

wide paths of brick in the colonial manner give direction. (I tried the less expensive white stone chips first, but they became a mess of debris in winter and couldn't be swept.)

The bisecting terrace adjacent to the house takes up considerable central space. At the end of it a tree well supported by railroad ties encloses a great four-trunk, high-pruned Norway maple. (Not my favorite garden tree, but it was there.) The well turned out to be a fine moist location for various

To the left of the terrace a round design is indicated for an area 16 by 20 feet. Metal edging outlines the circular bed.

In the round garden sweet woodruff blooms under the dogwood; impatiens follows the spring tulips; pots of early yellow chrysanthemums are set about. Clematis and euonymus vines will soon cover the "divider." On the far right, "Reed's gate" leads to my neighbor's garden. The staring window will be less conspicuous when the climbing hydrangea grows around it.

ferns—royal, cinnamon, lady, and others. To the right of the terrace a square area 20 by 21 feet, even with so much brick, held a surprising number of perennials plus two small, standard lilac trees; a standard rose, 'The Fairy'; a leucothoe; a pair of dwarf boxwoods for each side of the gate, and two espaliered carlesii viburnums. When a small garden has a house wall for one boundary, this can be used to great advantage for climbing plants and perhaps an ornamental plaque, as here.

To the left of the terrace a white dogwood rises from a round mass of sweet woodruff in the center of a circular brick walk. The garden measures 16 by 20 feet. In the corners are deciduous azaleas, an andromeda, a dwarf yew beside the steps, a winter honeysuckle shrub, ferns, and various perennials. The two garden sections add up to about 750 square feet. Actually, either section could make a pleasing pocket garden by itself. Some 350 bulbs were tucked in everywhere in both garden plots.

A small sloping semicircular area outside the fence on the west holds certain of my indispensables: a two-pronged white birch, a Sargent crabapple, two summersweet shrubs, several laurels, more deciduous azaleas, and some viburnums, all bedded with pachysandra and mulched with wood chips.

Plants for the Small Garden

I admit I have crowded things a bit, but still the effect is pleasing, and I haven't had to give up many favorite perennials. Emphasis has been on those of enduring foliage except for one great bleedingheart that associates so charmingly with two maidenhair ferns. When the bleedingheart has finished blooming in June, I cut it down and, to avoid an unsightly gap, I place over the crown a large inverted flower pot and on top of this a 'Fluffy Ruffles' fern from the window garden. Any little open spaces in a small garden can serve thus as outdoor quarters for houseplants, especially if small new perennials leave sizable openings among them the first year.

In the small garden edging plants that hold their good looks are essential. Here dwarf candytuft, coralbells, and epimedium edge one plot with the early crocus 'Striped Beauty' lining them next to the paths. In the other plot, clipped blue periwinkle gives a charming finish with the yellow *Crocus susianus*.

The background against fence and wall is mainly hybrid clematis vines with one euonymus and four 'Queen Charlotte' anemones. There is no room in this small garden for great hollyhocks, fall asters, heleniums, and other big growers, despite my affection for all of them. Foliage of phlox, oriental poppies, and delphinium does not endure, so these plants are omitted. Chrysanthemums are used as fall-bought pot plants, since I cannot spare them year-round growing space. Otherwise the reliable Big Four are represented by two peonies, a few irises though no germanicas, and a number of daylilies. Hostas are here: the handsome *Hosta subcordata grandiflora,* an improved August-lily blooming well into September. Perhaps valued almost more than all the rest in a corner plot under my breakfast window are three

Feverfew, *Chrysanthemum
parthenium,* with little
white pompons, a friendly
plant for the intimate
garden. FITCH PHOTO

Our kitten, Snug, and I
enjoy the terrace with
mutual satisfaction on a
cool summer morning.

The terrace in summer is a
pleasant place to rest, and
rest is possible when a
garden is small enough for
easy care.

View from inside. The
oblong garden is decorated
with my familiar ceramic
pigeons, and a lamppost
just beyond the fence
illuminates a curving area
of my indispensable shrubs.

Christmas-roses (last year they bloomed in late January and February despite three snow storms) and one plant of ladys-mantle (Alchemilla). These are underplanted with golden winter aconites (Eranthis) that bloom early with the hellebores. Later, Stokes-aster opens in front, and the bed measures only about 3 by 5 feet.

Because a garden is small, it does not mean that it should contain only medium-height or low plants, which would result in a monotonous level of bloom. A few vertical or pyramidal plants placed as accents can give scale and perspective. I think of astilbe, dictamnus, liatris, lythrum, lupine, and thermopsis for this purpose. White varieties are especially good in the small garden that adjoins a terrace or screened porch, where their cool beauty will be enjoyed on moonlit nights or under soft artificial lighting. The white and quite fragrant phlox 'Miss Lingard' would be welcome there on a warm evening.

The possibilities of design and planting are considerable, even for a limited space. Your own small garden could be quite different from mine, less formal perhaps. Of course, it should include *your* favorite plants, but the design, I think, should, like mine, be related to your house and continue the main or secondary axis. A glimpse of a garden from the front door and down the length of a hall is always pleasing.

One interesting small garden, overlooked from a raised terrace, was composed of an informal pattern of groundcovers, easy to care for and virtually weed-free—epimedium, myrtle, plumbago, thyme, and sweet woodruff. A large boulder made a handsome focal point with ferns beside it. For shadows and height there was an airy, open-branched, small-flowered cherry tree.

The low-growing primroses, *Primula denticulata* and *P. polyantha*, various violets, white hardy candytuft, and arabis could be included in such a plan. Other groundcovers are the hardy, succulent sedums. Most of them are far too rampageous for even a large garden, but there are a few delightful and thoroughly civilized ones. *Sedum ewersii* (1 inch) has gray-blue leaves and purple-pink flowers in late summer. *S. spurium* (6 inches) has shining, rich green leaves and pink or white flowers. *S. dasyphyllum* (2 inches) threads tiny gray beads of leaves into a dense mat and then completely conceals them, in June, under a cushion of white or blush flowers. And *S. nevii* (4 inches) lifts dainty three-spoked parasols of rose-pink on slender handles in early June. This last species is an annual or biennial but self-sows freely in damp, acid soil. It is native to the mountains of Virginia.

Ornaments for the small garden need to be in scale and really kept to a minimum. My ceramic pigeons, which Dorothy Riester sculptured years ago for my other garden, have a central spot made important by a section of flagstone. A Grecian plaque on one wall will eventually be set off by the long reach of espaliered viburnums, and a tall black colonial lamp illumines our evening hours.

Satisfaction plus—that is the result of a well-designed small garden planted with your own well-chosen "best favorite" plants.

PERENNIALS FOR YOUR SMALL GARDEN

Name Botanical and Common	Height	Color	Season	Remarks
Achillea ptarmica 'The Pearl' Yarrow	1½'	White	June-Sept.	Carefree; excellent for garden or cutting; ferny foliage; small fluffy blooms filler for bouquets. Sun.
Alyssum saxatile citrinum	1'	Pale yellow	Apr.-May	Lovely edging plant. Sun.
Anemone japonica Windflower	2-3'	Pink, white	Sept.-Oct.	Among best for early autumn in half to light shade. 'September Charm' silvery pink.
Aquilegia, McKana Hybrids Columbine	2½'	Pink, purple, red, yellow, white	May-July	Large, long-spurred blooms, beautiful in garden or to cut. Light shade.
Arabis alpina Rockcress	6"	White	Apr.-May	For sun or light shade; prune to keep tidy, charming, not always reliable.
Aster frikartii	2-2½'	Large violet-blue fragrant flowers	July-Oct.	'Wonder of Staffa' lovely for sun or light shade.

Name Botanical and Common	Height	Color	Season	Remarks
Astilbe hybrids	18″-3′	White, pink, red	June-Aug.	Pest-free, dependable, fine in shade.
Baptisia australis	2-3′	Fine blue, pea-shaped flowers	June	Excellent lasting foliage; needs 18″ space.
Chrysanthemum, garden (see Chapter 10)	1-3′	All but blue	Sept.-Dec.	Cushion and tall types. Sun. If purchased in bud in pots, garden space is saved.
parthenium Feverfew	1½′	White	June-Oct.	Rampant, self-sower, tiny daisy blooms, sun or shade, nice to cut.
Convallaria majalis Lily-of-the-valley	8″	White	May	Fragrant, open shade, groundcover.
Dianthus, pinks *caryophyllus plumarius*	1-1½′ 1′	Red, pink, or white	June-Sept. May	Lime and full sun essential; fragrant; pretty edgers.
Dicentra eximia Plumy bleedingheart	1½′	Pink	May-Oct.	Good groundcover, sun or shade, persistent foliage.

spectabilis Common bleedingheart	2-3'	Pink	Apr.-June	Handsome, but summer disappearance must be concealed. Light shade, nice with ferns.
Dictamnus Gasplant	2½'	White or pink	June	Sun or light shade, fine foliage, rich soil, avoid transplanting.
Doronicum hybrids Leopardsbane	2'	Yellow	Apr.-May	Good spring yellow; dormant in summer; open shade.
Epimedium Bishops-cap	9"	White, yellow, red, lavender	May-June	Indispensable for edging or groundcover in sun or light shade; excellent foliage.
Eupatorium coelestinum Mistflower, Hardy Ageratum	1-2'	Deep lavender	Aug.-Sept.	Flat panicles of small, closely set tubular flowers in profusion, on strong stems, making a good mass of color.
Geranium maculatum Species geranium	1½'	Pink-lavender	May-June	Nice with ferns, cut down after bloom, soon renews. Also many fine hybrids, for sun.

Name Botanical and Common	Height	Color	Season	Remarks
Helleborus niger Christmas-rose	1'	Pink-white	Jan.-May	Sun in winter, light shade in summer. Evergreen. Twelve weeks of bloom, indispensable; avoid summer drought.
Hemerocallis hybrids Daylily	1½-4'	Yellow, orange, pink, cream, green tones	May-Oct.	Summer essential, fine foliage and flowers. Full light or sun.
Heuchera sanguinea Coralbells	1½-2'	Rose, white	June-Aug.	Excellent for edging, enduring foliage. Sun or very light shade. Some fine hybrids.
Hosta (Funkia) Plantain-lily	1-3'	White, lavender, purple	July-Sept.	Handsome foliage; improved August lily, *H. subcordata grandiflora*, my favorite.
Iberis 'Little Gem' or 'Purity' Candytuft	10"	White	May	Neat and compact, fine for edging. Shade or sun. Evergreen.

Iris (see Chapter 5)	3"-4'	All colors but true blue	May-July	A clump or two of tall growers effective; smaller kinds have many uses.
cristata Crested iris	3-4"	Lavender, white	May-June	Shade. Charming groundcover under my rose tree.
germanica German iris	2-3½'	White, yellow, lavender, purple	May-June	Good foliage, needs borer protection; lower types usually in better scale.
sibirica Siberian iris	2-3'	Purple, white	June	Grassy foliage; perhaps one plant for accent; clumps need a lot of space.
tectorum Roof iris	1'	Lavender, white	May-June	On thatched roofs of China; good scale for small place.
Myosotis scorpioides (palustris) Forget-me-not	1-1½'	Blue	Apr.-Sept.	Perennial type, wonderful spreader by seeding from just a few plants, for semishade.
Paeonia albiflora (lactiflora) Peony (see Chapter 4)	2-3'	Red, pink, white	May-June	Singles and low-growing Herbaceous Hybrids in good scale for smaller plantings. All need a few hours of sun; fine enduring foliage.

Name Botanical and Common	Height	Color	Season	Remarks
Phlox divaricata Wild Blue Phlox	1′	Lavender, white	May	Indispensable groundcover for shade, lovely with ferns.
Platycodon grandiflora Balloon-flower	1-2′	Purple, white	June-Oct.	Sun or fairly deep shade, fine foliage, good concealer, shows up late.
Polemonium reptans Jacobs-ladder	1′	Lavender-blue	May-June	Edging plant, pretty but dies down for several weeks, then renews.
Stokesia Stokes-aster	1-1½′	Lavender, white	July-Aug.	Fine foliage, lasting cut flower.
Thermopsis caroliniana Carolina-lupine	3-4′	Yellow	June-July	Pealike flowers in spikes; robust for background; sun or light shade; good accent plant.
Tiarella cordifolia Foamflower	1′	White	Apr.-July	Light to deep shade and moisture; choice, fine groundcover.

Trollius europaeus Globeflower	2'	Yellow	May-July	Charming buttercup blooms in light shade or sun; good in spring groupings; lasting foliage.
Vinca minor Myrtle, Periwinkle	3"	Lavender or white	Apr.-May	Glossy, trailing groundcover and carpet for bulb flowers; or use as clipped edging plant.
Viola cornuta Tufted Pansy	6"	Yellow, white, purple, apricot	Apr.-Oct.	Perennial pansy, not always heat-resistant, charming.
odorata Sweet violet	6"	Purple, white	Apr.-May; fall repeat.	'Royal Robe' and 'White Czar' fine fragrance.

Astilbe in a predominantly shady garden in early July. GOTTSCHO-SCHLEISNER
PHOTO

14

WHERE SHADE PREVAILS

Sometimes I think I almost prefer a garden in the shade, particularly through hot summer weeks. There's something soothing about the long shadows and the cooler temperatures; they invite me to the garden when the uninhibited sunlight rejects me. Of course, I'm not denying that I enjoy the sun-demanding flowers—chrysanthemums, tall bearded irises, phlox, most peonies, and delphiniums. But I certainly can't pity you if you have only the opportunities of shade. Just look at the perennials you can enjoy— astilbes, balloon-flowers, bleedinghearts, coralbells, Christmas-roses, Carolina-lupines, daylilies, globeflowers, and hostas—to name only a few that have gratified me in shaded situations.

Your Kind of Shade

But in my eagerness to convince you of your shaded opportunities among perennials, I am rushing things. Let's first have a look at the kind of shade your place offers and how you can handle it to advantage. If it is really dense the year round, perhaps due to old evergreens, I can't make any quick suggestions, for certain drastic measures, probably of tree removal and heavy pruning, are indicated. Here I just want to stress the opportunities of *light shade*. Deep-rooted late-leafing deciduous trees like ash and honey-locust provide this. Bare in winter and admitting shifting sunshine in summer, they provide a "livable" shade for you, your house, and your garden. Study the light through the day under your big trees so as to plant to best advantage. In early spring a wealth of bulbs can grow there; in summer you can enjoy a multitude of perennials. I certainly have, and for me perennials have also flourised under apple trees and birches and pin oaks.

Probably like most of us you have areas of half shade, half sun—that is, four to five hours of either morning or afternoon sunshine or even a fully light situation without direct sun. In either place you can succeed with almost any perennial you like, but the sun lovers will not bloom as freely as in full sunshine; others, really preferring shade, will do better there than in the sun.

Some Helpful Practices

In any case, if you will accept the fact that perennial plantings in the shade must be handled differently from those in the sun, you will be on your way to garden pleasure rather than the frustration you may have experienced before you faced this fact. Aside from a wise choice of material, certain practices will also contribute to the well-being of a shaded garden. I keep my trees pruned high and open to let the light through.

Then I have found that more food and water are necessary for shaded plants; furthermore, in untended areas, the soil under trees may very well be compacted. Loosen it with a spading fork, work in plenty of humus, either commercial or from your own compost pile, and add some horticultural lime if the surface has a greenish tinge, indicating too much acidity. Then apply a "complete" fertilizer, as a 5–10–5 in spring and perhaps twice more during the growing season. In shade, you have to feed more than for sunny plantings, because the greedy tree roots are going to take some of what you offer. Sometimes in spring I give a high phosphorus instead of a general fertilizer because phosphorus promotes bloom.

Keep your shaded plantings well watered. If tree foliage is at all lush, it will prevent light rain from penetrating, and heavy rains may simply flood without moistening too-dry flower beds beneath. Furthermore, summer rains can hardly be depended on, so have plenty of hose and sprinklers at hand for your shaded beds. Deep, long watering almost every other week will keep them in health and increase bloom.

A 2- to 3-inch mulch spread over shaded beds is also helpful, for it conserves moisture and keeps roots cool. I have used various kinds of mulch depending on availability, and these are discussed in Chapter 16.

So to assure success with your shaded perennials, prune your trees high and open if they are dense; loosen the soil, and improve it with humus, and fertilize in spring and maybe again in summer; water deeply through dry spells, and mulch. You see, shade is only one factor; a rich, open soil and adequate moisture are others.

Keep in mind that shade gardening can't be just by rule. Experiment. Try some of your favorites, even if you have always thought they had to have full sun. Don't give them up until you are sure. Peonies, for example, have done well for me with only a few early sunny hours, and Chinese delphinium (not the great tall hybrids, though) have been very satisfactory.

Winter into Spring

Perhaps my greatest treasure for light to fairly deep shade has been the Christmas-rose, with its white-pink January to May blooms that are undaunted by snow, and its handsome 1-foot spread of evergreen foliage. Christmas ferns and a sprinkling of little yellow winter aconites are a charming association with Christmas-roses.

Then for April to May in a broad sweep under a deep-rooted, late-leafing tree, or in a narrow planting along a shrubbery boundary that should include the marvelously fragrant winter honeysuckle shrub, you are sure to enjoy my favorite grouping of tall pink bleedinghearts; Virginia bluebells; yellow globeflowers and leopardsbane; white, yellow, and lavender columbines; yellow cowslips; with underplantings of blue self-sowing forget-me-nots, and early narcissus.

Cinnamon, interrupted, and maidenhair, or other ferns can be set so as to conceal the summer retreat of the bleedinghearts and bluebells, and the ferns also give interest to the border when the flowering time has past. Depending on the size of your spring border, you may want to add blue brunnera, with its May to June flowers and large summery leaves or the bold-foliaged pink-flowering bergenia that blooms in May. You might even care to use it alone in front of shrubs, for it has a shrubby look and will tolerate quite deep shade if it has moist to wet soil. Then an edging of evergreen candytuft in white flower makes an impeccably neat year-round edging for any spring planting.

As I have said, peonies can also be yours if a few hours of morning sun can be provided. From late May into June the single and double flowers are a joy, and their enduring foliage is a cause for thanksgiving in any planting. (Chapter 4 discusses peonies more fully.) And for spring, you will want a wealth of bulbs, especially the early narcissus, scillas, crocuses, grape-hyacinths, and true hyacinths. You can also have the small botanical tulips but not the big May-flowering kinds; they must have sun.

If you like irises, you need only forgo the tall bearded kinds that really are sun-demanding. In light shade these others will brighten your garden picture well into July: crested iris, slender iris, Siberian iris, and roof iris. (In Chapter 5 irises are described in detail.) If you are blessed with a brook or pond, the yellow flag iris and wild blue flag will look lovely in light shade along the edge, and the choice Japanese varieties will rivet attention wherever they bloom.

Spring into Summer

Before the July heat descends there are transitional perennials to grace your shaded garden. I really dote on the coralbells, with their airy pink or white panicles, and the plumy pink bleedingheart, smaller than the old-fashioned May one and with a longer blooming period, actually May into October. The June-flowering gasplant, white, rose, and purplish, holds its fine foliage to frost, and the yellow evening-primrose (*Oenothera*), Carolina-lupine, and perennial foxglove are colorful for separate clump plantings or in association with other perennials.

If blue is your favorite color and you want plenty of it, do consider brunnera, with its forget-me-not-like flowers in May–June. The Chinese form of delphinium will assuage your longing for this perennial, and the pea-shaped June flowers of baptisia, with its fine foliage, will be a June asset for the center of a border planting. The lavender-blue *Aster frikartii,* the only aster I've had luck with in light shade, never stops, June to frost. Various campanulas, lavender, purple, and white, carry on from June to October, and the purple balloon-flower (it comes in white, too) has bloomed profusely for me in quite deep shade. I wouldn't bother with phlox in shade; it always gets spindly and mildewed there for me.

For Summer

Now, if ever, the shaded plantings—strips, borders, or islands—come into their own with astilbes, daylilies, and hostas, plants that not only bloom luxuriously in shade, but also offer the finest possible foliage. I have strong feelings about good foliage and really grow few plants that don't provide it.

Coralbells and plumy
bleedingheart in a shaded
corner of the Hammond
Stroll Garden near North
Salem, N.Y. FITCH PHOTO

With good foliage and a few or no blooms, a garden keeps its looks. If foliage is weak and wan or disappears entirely—only about three such plants can count me their friend, the tall bleedinghearts, Virginia bluebells, and tradescantias—I rarely plant them.

But to return to summer in shade. Everyone doesn't know the astilbes (false spireas), I find, but surely everyone should, for they are "perfect" perennials. Varieties can be selected, 18 inches to 3 feet, for fragrant June-to-August steeples of bloom that rise from fine-cut feathery foliage. These perennials never seem to get anything, neither pest nor disease, but they will brown quickly if subjected to drought. The flourish in light shade (also in sun), in rich, moist soil, and look lovely with ferns and Japanese iris. Surprisingly they have also bloomed well for me in a dim corner under pine trees where once I set out some extras. Beautiful from spring emergence to fall crispness, the plants are decorative even out of bloom. I am fond of the whites, the 18-inche 'Avalanche' and somewhat taller 'Deutschland', the light-pink 'Peach Blossom' and deeper 'Rosy Veil', both to 2 feet. You may prefer 'Fanal', a fine, 18-inch carmine, or 'Red Sentinel', a good background astilbe to 30 inches. These are all fine to cut for fresh arrangements, for which they supply useful vertical flowers. To assure a good intake of water, split the woody stems as you would for shrubs. Astilbe blooms can also be dried for attractive winter bouquets.

The daylilies, so much flowers of our time (in my childhood we knew only the two species; today eight thousand hybrids) bloom from late May into September in luscious shades of cream, pink, yellow, and orange, with fountainous foliage that is valuable all on its own or as strong contrast to that of other perennials. True, bloom is heavier in full light or sun with some varieties, but I have had nothing to complain of even in fairly deep shade. (Chapter 6 tells *all* about this favorite.)

The hostas are also plants of today, the modern hybrids a far cry from our grandmothers' fragrant, white August-lily. One, 'Royal Standard', is a plant we get excited about here. In fact, in her amazement, Susan nearly fell over the ubiquitous Snug at the terrace door the morning she first spied the great umbel of bloom open in the shade of our big, high-pruned maple. We delayed breakfast for the count—fifty buds on the one cluster, and two more umbels showing up. August to September was the span of the flowers, a handsome sight above the green, heart-shaped leaves. This fragrant 'Royal Standard' is a variety of *Hosta subcordata grandiflora,* and both are superb plants for full or half shade. (I am informed that 'Royal Standard' also grows well in full sun.)

Hosta foliage varies from pale to deep green to blue-green. Some leaves have white markings and in deep shade are as decorative as flowers. Heights

All species of Hosta, when grown in moist, well-drained soil in shade or part shade, produce abundant, semi-glossy, markedly veined leaves all summer long. This one is *H. fortunei marginata.* GENEREUX PHOTO

vary from 1-foot dwarfs like *H. minor alba* to the 6-foot giant *H. fortunei robusta*. The 2-to-3-foot hostas are the most generally useful garden plants, and there are a number of these. If you enjoy collecting, and yours is a shaded place where you have had less pleasure in your plants than you should have had, you could have fun assembling these reliable hostas, some two dozen of them, including the fine newer hybrids.

Hostas are self-sufficient plants, staying healthy without spraying; even the tall ones require no staking. Small varieties make a good groundcover for an extensive site, nice accents, or edgings for the small garden. I liked the 12-inch white-bordered *H. minor alba* as an outline for a shaded bed. Other white-marked hostas, 'Thomas Hogg', *H. undulata variegata,* and *H. lancifolia albo-marginata,* are effective contrast plants in all-green settings, and you may like those with yellow markings like *H. fortunei aureo-maculata.* Except for the fragrant, white, evening flowers of the old-fashioned, 2-foot August-lily that grew with ferns and laurel by the terrace steps, I've never been enraptured by the lavender or white blooms of the other variegated ones; still, any florescence in *deep* shade is acceptable, I suppose.

Because there is some confusion in names, take care to read the catalogue descriptions carefully when you order. I have tended to use catalogue rather than the newest botanical nomenclature. Anyway, hostas are really great shade plants, not particular as to soil but demanding water in periods of dry weather. Space them generously, for they are exuberant growers that shouldn't need transplanting for years and years. The variegated types will have more pronounced markings in light than in deep shade.

These then are the three great plants for summer flowers in shade—astilbes, daylilies, and hostas—all three adding the great blessing of easy culture, all being completely pestfree. They have but one certain requirement, plenty of water, especially when they are forming buds.

Into Autumn

Chrysanthemums are not for growing in shaded places, but you can buy pots of well-budded plants, place them where you will, and these will give you weeks of flowers without sunshine. For direct planting in your shaded garden, there is the lavender mistflower, a rampant perennial, to grow where a big spread is possible. The deep blue aconite, 'Sparks Variety', growing 2 to 3 feet tall, is good for back-of-border use, so too the wind-flower or anemone, with its delicate air. It is about the same height and pleases me in front of a cream-colored yard divider. The silvery pink 'Sep-

Hostas are also long-lived, disease-free, and in mid- to late summer send up spikes of lavender or white flowers. One of the finest modern varieties, H. 'Royal Standard', has fragrant flowers.

tember Charm' is my favorite variety. Then there is at least one daisy type that doesn't require sun, 'Goldsturm' rudbeckia. This will bloom well for you from August to October if you plant it in a damp place.

In the Dictionary of Fine Perennials at the back of this book, you will find more shade plants, and these are plainly indicated for part or fairly deep shade, as I have experienced them. Then there are the sun *or* shade perennials that thrive in both situations but bloom more fully in the sun.

In *Successful Gardening in the Shade* (Garden City, N.Y.: Doubleday & Company, 1975), I wrote more fully of the many possibilities, not the problems, please note, of the many plants for shade. These include shrubs, flowering trees, annuals, and bulbs.

Lilyturf, *Liriope muscari*, with dark grasslike leaves and small lilac flowers in late summer, in a raised bed supported by railroad ties. FITCH PHOTO

THE BASICS
—DRAINAGE, SOIL,
COMPOST, FERTILIZERS

Whenever I read a dissertation on soils, I remember the story of the little girl who was telling her class about a book on gray squirrels. She concluded, "There is really more about gray squirrels in this book than I care to know." That's how I feel about all the heavy literature on soils. But fertilized soil is essential, and we have to know something, if not everything, about how to develop it if we are to have fine-blooming perennials.

But before soil preparation itself must come attention to drainage. If the area in which you plan to plant perennials stays wet longer than it should with puddles in evidence when other places have dried out after a heavy rain, you need to do something about drainage—and *before* you plant rather than afterward.

Recently I had an "afterward" situation on my hands. The contractor-designer who hauled in the soil to give me a level garden instead of a slope, simply didn't bother about drainage, so sections of the garden had to be dug about 2 feet deep and lengths of 4-inch plastic pipe laid to carry off the water that was drowning the perennials. Very few will tolerate constant dampness, which eventually causes death due to rotted roots.

Of course, I could avoid putting in drains by settling for a bog planting, but I don't want that in this small garden next my house. If you have a bog, you could enjoy a planting of marsh-marigolds, the osmunda ferns—cinnamon, interrupted, and royal—also the lady, toothed, sensitive, and wood ferns—but not too much else. But if your situation is only *somewhat* damp, have a look at the long list of plant possibilities on page 233.

If your whole place is poorly drained, I think you really have no choice but to install, or have installed by an *experienced* contractor, drainage tiles and pipes to carry off excess water and so leave you a healthy place with conditions that promote good gardening. This drainage improvement is not an inexpensive procedure but so basic you have to consider it seriously.

There's one more possible out: beds raised, say, to 15 inches or so above ground level. Such beds can be retained by redwood or flagstone sections, or the more elegant, and costly, brick. The area is first spread with a 2-inch layer of coarse gravel or crushed stone, then filled with well-enriched, crumbly soil. You can now grow just about any perennials you want in these raised beds with good drainage assured.

SOIL, FRIABLE AND FERTILE

Friable is an old-fashioned term that we old-time gardeners have used for years. Actually we could just as well say "crumbly," for that's what a friable soil is. When we talk about "good garden soil," we mean one that is both crumbly and fertile. To diagnose yours, pick up a handful and squeeze it. If the soil stays hard and firm, it isn't friable but too clayey (I struggled with such in Philadelphia); if your soil is of this kind, you can improve the texture with sand and compost, adding enough to get a crumbly consistency. On the other hand, if your sample is so crumbly it doesn't hold together, it probably has too much sand. Such a condition is improved by the addition of more topsoil and plenty of humus. However, *some* sand is needed to promote drainage and the openness that insures the necessary ventilation of plant roots.

About depth digging, you don't need to reach to China to prepare your perennial beds, nor to resort to the "double digging" favored by English gardeners. If the soil is spaded 10 to 12 inches (somewhat deeper for peonies), weeds and grass roots removed, and plenty of compost and fertilizer worked in, most plants are bound to prosper. Here is a more exact procedure that has worked well:

Spread 2 inches of peatmoss over the area to be planted.

Spread 2 inches of compost or humus or leafmold or a combination of these.

Sprinkle 1 cup long-lasting general fertilizer per square yard.

Sprinkle 1 cup superphosphate per square yard.

Work all this in to a depth of 8 to 10 inches.

The pH Factor

Don't be too concerned about this sweet-sour business. Certainly don't imitate the routine practice of some gardeners who follow spading with liming. The indiscriminate use of lime is dangerous policy, since lime is neither cure-all nor fertilizer but only a means of altering the pH. The term pH describes the sweet-sour condition of the soil, the way Fahrenheit readings indicate hot-cold degrees of temperature. Sometimes the pH of a soil is just fine as it is, and changing it means doing something you must later undo.

The pH scale runs from 0, extremely acid, to 14, extremely sweet or alkaline, 7 being neutral. Actually, perennials are tolerant of considerable variation. Most thrive under a slightly acid condition, as a 6.5 pH, or in a fairly neutral pH 7 soil, with toleration for slight variations either way. You can determine the pH of your own particular plot *only by test*. You can manage this yourself by means of a simple chemical home-testing kit you can buy through a seed catalogue or a garden-supply store, or you can send a soil sample to the laboratory of your state agricultural college. Your county agent will give you the address and supply mailing bags for the samples, with directions on how to take these. A small fee is usually charged for analysis and recommendations. For most home-ground soils, the test would give information on:

1. pH (sweet-sour bit)
2. Calcium (limestone)
3. Magnesium
4. Potash (K_2O)
5. Phosphorus (P_2O_5)
6. A quick textural examination (sandy, clayey, loamy, etc.)

In my state (Connecticut) the analysis is fed into a computer, and the print-out recommendations are mailed with an information sheet. With this in hand, you can tell just what fertilizer elements are needed to supplement your soil. If you find you need lime for a too-acid condition, apply it along with your spring fertilizer or late in autumn when other garden works slows down.

Humus

Humus is thoroughly decomposed organic or once-living matter—plants or animals. Humus improves a thin sandy soil by giving it bulk and some capacity for holding water. But the great value of humus lies in its supply of bacteria which, operating in the soil, make available to plant roots elements otherwise useless.

For gardens not yet on a self-running basis, either commercially available humus or peatmoss is excellent. Peatmoss corrects the mechanical ills of the soil and increases bacterial action. It supplies soil sponges for retaining water. In fact, it holds about ten times its dry weight in moisture. When beds are newly dug, add enough bulk to give the soil a crumbly consistency if a handful of it is squeezed.

Other sources of humus are the excellent shredded and pulverized manures where they are available. Well-rotted (that means two-year-old) horse or cow manure from a farm—a rarity today—is still perhaps the best soil conditioner there is. Leafmold, of course, is fine. In time, however, a garden can become self-sufficient and produce a large quantity of its own humus or compost.

About Compost

If you have even one tree, you have a source of fine, rich compost—the leaves that decompose; if you have many trees, you have an overwhelming source, as I well know. I used to have three big leaf piles going simultaneously. (More on mulching in Chapter 16.) On a small place, needing less, you can conceal a good-sized leaf pile behind a big forsythia or other shrub, and control it with a rampart of old boards. In due course, those leaves will rot into fine compost.

Manufacturers with our smaller places in mind now offer various neat devices for easy compost making. In catalogues, you will see descriptions of compost kits. One includes an "indestructible gridding for a small easily assembled and adjustable bin with twist fasteners and a supply of compost-making tablets" to reduce your garden wastes to a rich organic compost within weeks rather than months. This is convenient for a small garden that may have but one hiding place.

If you want a lot of compost, as I did, mark out a 4- by 6-foot or larger area in a well-drained spot; fence it with wire or boards. Into it throw grass clippings, leaves, pulled-up plants (both flower and vegetable but no diseased material), and soft clippings, but no woody twigs. Spread all this out evenly in a layer 4 to 6 inches thick. Then scatter a commercial starter or "activator" (according to directions) and spread a couple of inches of soil over all with a little fertilizer if you have some at hand. Repeat the layering to about 18 inches deep, then soak the pile thoroughly. (I used to set a fine sprinkler in the middle of my piles and let it run for hours or until the material was thoroughly moistened.) The water starts fermentation and so hastens decay. As you have more garden debris, repeat the layers. Now, whether you realize it or not, you are practicing good ecology.

Well-rotted compost—it is called humus in its final stage—improves the structure of the soil and, to a degree, also fertilizes it. Another fast way to obtain it is with a leaf shredder. Everyone who buys (or rents) an *electric* leaf shredder is vociferous in praise. Such a shredder is silent, as the gasoline motor-driven type is not, and it produces a most delectable fine-ground compost that doesn't blow or erode or mat. Throw into the shredder all kinds of garden debris in addition to leaves, even twigs, and what you will get is something you will think of as garden gold.

About Fertilizers

To keep your garden richly supplied with basic plant nutrients, you need to know something of plant requirements. They must have nitrogen to promote leaf and stem strength and to stimulate growth generally. When there is too much, they grow prodigiously, but in spindly fashion and are poor flower producers. Witness the too-thin delphinium plants with small florets of sickly bloom or the sappy growth of overfed phlox. Obviously, however, plants emphasizing leaf growth, such as baptisia, and most other plants in the enormous Pea Family, can do with a lot of nitrogen.

Phosphorus gives a steady push to flower and seed production. It is essential for good bloom and also develops early root growth. With too little phosphorus, foliage lacks color. With too much, it is sappy, lacking fiber, and so weak that plants require a lot of staking.

Potash, the third essential element, is the antitoxin among plant foods. It wards off disease, stabilizes growth, and intensifies color. It has been termed the catalyst that makes the other elements perform properly.

The amounts of these three basic elements are marked on the bags and containers of the various trademarked brands of "complete" plant foods in numbered series like 5–8–5, 4–12–4, 6–7–3, etc. The first number *always* represents the proportion of the nitrogen content, the second the phosphorus, and the third the potash. In addition, mention may be made of the presence of certain "trace elements"—iron, boron, and manganese—which in small quantities are also necessary to healthy plant life. Certain essential secondary elements—calcium, magnesium, and sulphur, supplied by limestone and superphosphate—should have been included in the initial preparation of the perennial beds. When buying a commercial plant food, *read the label carefully* and try to select a brand on which it is plainly indicated that some of the nitrogen is from organic or once-living material. These organic elements will be less quickly available and hence have a more lasting value than those that the greedy plant can consume all at once. For regular use, I am partial to a 6–8–5 plant food "with not less than 60 per cent of the nitrogen derived from organic sources," but I have, too, a purely chemical 4–12–4 mix for spring and summer stimulation. With this, plants need some rotted manure or organic bonemeal in fall as supplementary food.

Then there are the timed-release plant foods like Precise, favored by nurserymen. These *gradually* feed your plants. Some are effective for three to four months, others up to eight months, obviously great time-savers. If you select one of these, again read the label carefully to be sure your flowering perennials will get plenty of necessary phosphorus (the second number in the formula).

As a general thing, apply commercial plant foods to perennials about April 15 and again on May 15 in sufficient quantity slightly to obscure the soil. Do this just before you cultivate. After you have worked food in well, water deeply, unless you are lucky enough to catch a rain.

Avoid mixing plant foods with the soil in which seeds are to be sown. Also, if seedlings are transplanted, and not just thinned out, wait until growth has commenced before applying fertilizer. These all-purpose foods often act faster than such young plants can tolerate.

About Planting

Try to pick a time when it is sunless, cool, and damp, preferably early morning or evening. If you have a helper, make sure that he does not expose your plants to air or sun. I nearly had a fit one day when I had to leave my helper to answer the telephone. When I came back he had un-wrapped a dozen chrysanthemums and laid them out uncovered in the sun and air while waiting for me to place them. When I am planting or transplanting, I like a good big piece of wet burlap at hand to cover roots in case I am slow in making up my mind about placements. And if there is any possibility of drying out due to a long journey or delayed unpacking, I like to soak the roots for an hour or so in weak fertilizer solution before planting.

Give each plant a plenty-big hole so that roots will be encouraged to spread out and so stimulate growth. Take care not to plant too deep. Sometimes a previous soil line is indicated, sometimes not, so use your judgment, and do firm the soil well around each plant so that no dangerous air pockets remain. Water in the soil when you are finished, but don't puddle it.

Here then is all I know about soil and the other basics. I can only hope I haven't told you "more than *you* care to know."

16

PERENNIAL COMFORTS
—MULCH, WATER, SUPPORTS

Once on a garden tour I noticed a rather pretentious formal garden that somehow didn't quite come off. Pondering the difference between it and a much smaller, not so perfect, planting, I came to the conclusion that no one person cared very much for the big place, though it may have been a source of pride. In the jargon of the day, I suppose I could describe it as unloved. When our plants mean a lot to us, we are inevitably aware of their needs, actually their comforts. So it is that summer and winter mulches, proper watering, and a certain amount of staking for very tall or floppy growers receive our attention.

MULCHING FOR SUMMER PEACE OF MIND

A proper hot-weather mulch does wonders for your perennials. It keeps down weeds and conserves moisture so that roots are cool and plants are less likely to suffer drought. Thus it reduces your garden chores by eliminating weed pulling and watering. But a good mulch also adds to the attractiveness of your plantings. Where the mulch is applied after spring cleanup and fertilizing, I do enjoy the neat looks of my perennial beds; I even feel relaxed as I gaze upon them, and I must say relaxation has hardly been one of the experiences of gardening for me—though it should be, and I hope it can be for you.

Free Mulch Material

As I have explained in Chapter 15, you can produce good mulching material on your own place. A compost pile, even a small one, will supply you with fine, crumbly leafmold to serve as a mulch, and this is also richly nutritious. It can be worked back into beds to serve as plant food. In Chapter 15 you will see how to make compost right on your own place from your own plant materials. A layer of compost an inch or so deep makes a fine mulch.

Perhaps you have a stand of pine trees. The fallen needles make an excellent 2-to-3-inch mulch, slow to deteriorate and certainly attractive in appearance. To avoid a possible acid reaction where it wasn't wanted for perennials, I always brushed mine aside in spring, fertilized freely with a 5-10-5 all-purpose mixture, worked this in a little, and watered well before replacing the needles and adding to them as required.

Mulch Material to Buy

You can, of course, buy various excellent mulching materials. Town-maintenance crews and tree-pruning firms often sell their by-product of woodchips (rarely do they give them away). Spread about 2 inches deep, woodchips do a nice mulching job. But by all odds my favorites are the redwood or pinebark nuggets. They have an elegant, orderly appearance. I have used them in several sizes, depending on the size of the beds, spreading them an inch or so deep among the perennials. The bark breaks down slowly and permits good air and water circulation. For perennial plantings, nothing looks nicer or more natural.

Also recommended are stone chips, but I have never liked them for perennials, especially white stones, which appear positively garish. Grass clippings, salt hay, spoiled hay, and black polyethylene are mulches in their place, which is the vegetable or cutting garden perhaps, but not for our ornamental beds of perennials. Long ago I used peatmoss. At first it looked nice and later, worked into the soil, was a good source of humus, but I found it caking so hard that water ran off rather than through it, and strong wind always blew some of it away, too. The lumpy kind stays put longer and lets some water through, but even so, other kinds of mulch are better and more practical.

Compost is, of course, the most beneficial of all, since it not only serves the function of a mulch but also, worked into the soil, gradually improves structure and adds fertility.

MULCHING FOR WINTER PROTECTION

Don't provide cold-weather protection unless it is necessary. If you are new in an area, find out how your neighbors handle their plants. Winter coverings where they are not needed are not only a bother to apply but also can overheat your plants. Around Philadelphia and here in Connecticut near Long Island Sound and in many areas where gardens are hedged in considerably, very little may be needed. Indeed, for some years now I have not covered my garden at all, and my losses seem slight.

The aim in covering or mulching at this season is, of course, to prevent the alternate freezing and thawing of the soil that our fluctuating climate induces. The summer mulch is used to conserve moisture and insulate the soil against extreme heat, but the winter mulch is applied to keep the cold in and the frozen condition constant, the plants unstimulated by occasional midwinter warmth.

Persisting snow is a natural mulch. So, too, are leaves—and this is the one that most of us rely on.

With plants that maintain green tops like the foxglove, hollyhock, and primrose, coverings are drawn under, not over the tops. For these and woolly-leaved subjects like the mulleins, a layer of stones is excellent. Chrysanthemums with their green crowns require no covering whatever, and peonies, iris, oriental poppies, and delphinium, except in very cold sections, are better left uncovered except in their first year after planting. Daylilies never need a cover. All young plants, not far beyond the seedling stage, are mulched earlier than established perennials. This is to conserve autumn warmth and so prolong their growing stage. Early November is usually not too soon to protect them.

One perennial I find that needs special winter treatment to prevent sunburn is the hardy evergreen candytuft, which is really a little shrub. I spray

Wilt-Pruf or a similar antidesiccant on this fine edging plant wherever the winter sunshine strikes. In shaded areas this is unnecessary.

In spring the greater part of the mulch is removed just as the forsythias bloom while the final amount is lifted as the flowers appear on the Norway maple trees. No exact dates can be set, since the end of winter differs not only with localities but also with the years. Late in March is the time most of us have a winter-underwear feeling about mulches. Then it is time to poke underneath leaves or mulch and see what goes on. Very likely coverings can be loosened a little to aerate the awakening plants. Mulches left too long in place force abnormal growth, but if spring fever gets your ambition in operation too early, you may invite a touch of frostbite for your perennials by removing winter protection while spring is still much too far behind.

Many leaves naturally collect, however, and catch among the crowns of the plants in the perennial border (the tall tops are, of course, cut down before mulching). But more leaves usually have to be added to get a uniform distribution. Any leaves will do except those of the poplars and Norway maples that mat down like soggy rags and exclude all air from the plants while pressing dampness down upon them all winter long. Oak, birch, hickory, beech, linden, and most maples are fine. Indeed, any leaves that curl when they fall will do, while those that lie flat will not. Leaves may be collected in baskets or piled in a corner of the yard until needed in mid-December or later if a hard freeze has not occurred by that time. Then they are spread in place and a few evergreen boughs, perhaps the lopped-off Christmas-tree branches, are placed on top to hold them in place.

THE ART OF WATERING

Although mulching conserves moisture, there still are times of prolonged drought in summer that necessitate extra watering. When these occur, be thorough. (Even if your husband adores it and it soothes and quiets him in hot weather, don't give him the hose to play with in the evening.) Nothing is worse for a garden than a regular evening sprinkle. It encourages surface instead of deep rooting of perennials and is an out-and-out invitation to a number of blights and diseases because foliage then goes into the darkness wet, and fungus spores can thus make a field day of the night. Morning and late afternoon are the best times to water, but not nearer than two hours to sunset. For me 5:00 P.M. is always the cutoff hour. Blazing midday and early afternoon are not good. But if you are doing the job thoroughly, it will not matter if the sun shines on the foliage at the same time that the sprinkler is running. But watering with a sprinkler is secondary. What is required, especially in periods of prolonged drought, is deep watering.

The best way to soak roots deeply, of course, is not to use a sprinkler but to draw a slow-running hose among peonies or phlox or into the midst of the border. If the nozzle is laid on a narrow board, this will prevent washing.

Let the water run about an hour in each area. You will be surprised if you examine the soil in less time to see how little of it has been reached. At least 3 inches is your goal. Or you can take a big juice can, punch holes in the bottom, and insert it a little in a bed where there is room and the soil is soft enough to receive it. Let the hose run in this. As the can fills, water seeps deep into the soil. You can also measure what your sprinklers are supplying by setting a can under the outside drip and timing the inch fill. You will discover that not much is accomplished in half an hour.

Sometimes, of course, you will need to use a sprinkler that projects a fine mist over some distance. This overhead method, taking the place of rainfall, covers a wide section of garden without puddling soil and without requiring much attention from you. And it does afford great refreshment to plant tops on a hot day. Various kinds of sprinklers are available. I have a couple of old metal rings that are so useful for watering right in a flower bed. I also like the fan sprinklers that rise up and bow low as they deliver the welcome mist across the garden from one set of beds to another, and those swinging sprays cover an area in the same complete way. If the pressure is kept low, the distance covered is less, and loss by evaporation is slight; a considerable area can be watered before the next move. Sprinkler watering is the easiest but also the most wasteful because of loss through evaporation as the fan of water is cast high in the air.

Early in the evening set the sprinklers in place for their *early*-morning work. Then it's easy to turn the faucets on without getting feet wet running around in the wet grass.

Incidentally, if the autumn tends to be dry, give your garden a thorough final soaking in late October or early November. Then plant roots will go into the winter plump and healthy. Perennials left thirsty in autumn are always likely to winterkill.

STAKES AND OTHER SUPPORTS

Good looks in a garden depend to a great extent on tidiness. This is particularly true of small plots. In these no amount of handsome individual flowers will give a good effect if scattered about are supine plants that should be perpendicular rather than prone. One source of support for medium-height plants that tend to sprawl—platycodon, veronica, coreopsis, gaillardia, achillea, and the like—would be lengths of twiggy growth cut to the right size and set *early* among them so that, as the plants develop, they arrange themselves naturally over their supports and these are eventually hidden. You can have a convenient source of just the right kind of twiggy branches if you will plant, for the purpose, in some out-of-the-way corner, a couple of bushes of California privet and allow them to grow unpruned.

For single-stemmed perennials, I use assorted lengths of bamboo and wire fastened with that invaluable little device, the Twistem. Natural color bamboo is less expensive than that dyed green, but the green ones are worth the difference because they show less. Galvanized iron wire one-eighth inch in diameter and in 2- to 6-foot lengths I like even better, because it is narrow yet very strong. When there are many separate stems as in mature plants of foxglove or delphinium, I clip a separate wire support to each. This is a beautifully neat and strong arrangement, especially for a windy site.

Available also are wire stakes with a nickel-plated twisted-wire device at the top. Push the stake into the soil close to the plant, then guide the stalk into the twist by turning the stake. Tall stems are thus well anchored.

For bunchy plants—peonies and the taller chrysanthemums—I like the double-ring Model Peony Trellis of tripod type. Some gardeners use this also for large delphinium, oriental poppy clumps, meadowrue, and salvia. Thrust among the plants early, the tripod is soon covered by new growth. Two kinds of double-ring supports have been available, one with the top ring adjustable. I prefer the type with both rings stationary because it wears better. Mine now have eight years of double duty to their credit. In April they are thrust deeply around each clump of peonies. In late June, they are transferred for the summer to those chrysanthemums destined for prolific autumn display. With either full-grown plant they are blessedly invisible, and that's what good supports should be.

Today originators, mindful of our smaller places and lower dwellings, are producing plants that are of lower stature than they used to be. You can now obtain an 18-inch phlox, as 'Pinafore Pink', and some Blackmore and

Langdon hybrid delphiniums are only 3 to 4 feet high, as compared to the standard 6-to-8-foot hybrids. There are Cushion chrysanthemums that reach only to 12 or 15 inches.

Pinching back the stems to 4 to 6 inches on these and various other plants in spring—hardy asters, helenium, boltonia, and other daisy types—results in shorter growth and smaller flowers though more of them, and these shorter stems may not need staking. To get larger blooms and stronger stalks, thin out phlox, even young plants, to four or five stems. On mature plants, you will be reducing the usual ten to twelve stalks considerably; plants will be healthier and the larger flowers will be more effective, and also rewarding for exhibition.

Disbudding is another means to larger blooms, with peonies the classic example. Remove the two side buds in each cluster of three, and the remaining center one will develop into a handsome exhibition specimen. For general garden effect, however, let your peonies be!

17

IF YOU WANT MORE
—SEEDS, CUTTINGS, DIVISIONS

Growing perennials from seed has taken on new importance now that plants have become so very expensive due to labor costs and other aspects of inflation. Three fine columbine plants may cost you four to five dollars; a packet of seed will yield a dozen or so plants, relieving you of less than seventy-five cents. The saving results, of course, from your own energetic efforts.

Plants to Purchase

However, since some fine *varieties* of perennials do not come true from seed (that is, their seedlings do not exactly duplicate the hybrid parents), and also since some perennials take forever to reach blooming size—most of them two years—you may want to start with plants. These would be worth buying, I think, in the exact named variety you desire or have seen in a nursery: aconite, anemone, babysbreath, chrysanthemum, daylily, delphinium, gasplant, hardy aster, hardy candytuft, iris, oriental poppy, and peony. If you are in no great hurry and enjoy growing plants from seed, you could confidently sow—and get a big crop for little money—certain *species* that do exactly reproduce themselves. I think of babysbreath (*Gypsophila paniculata*), baptisia (*Baptisia australis*), bleedingheart (*Dicentra spectabilis*), gasplant (*Dictamnus fraxinella*), and mertensia (*Mertensia virginica*). If you already have some of these varieties or species in your garden but want more, or a generous friend is willing to share with you, you can obtain divisions or start root cuttings that cost nothing.

If you are buying plants, you don't need quantities of each. Three or more, depending on space, will suffice of delphinium, iris, anemone, gasplant, mertensia, and aconite. One each is enough of the named varieties of Christmas-rose, chrysanthemum, aster, babysbreath, and bleedingheart, since all of these soon lend themselves to simple means of home propagation. And, of course, with the more expensive kinds of peony and oriental poppy, one each is plenty, especially if you are not familiar with the variety.

Biennials

You will want to start most biennials from seed—alpine forget-me-nots, campanulas, foxgloves, sweet William, perhaps others. Biennials are the puzzlers in our gardens. Sometimes they seem to behave more like annuals because many of them produce an early, if sparse, fall crop of flowers from prompt spring sowings. Often they tend to be perennial, living on from year to year or else appearing to, because they propagate themselves by self-sowing. The definition of a biennial as a plant that "sown one year, flowers and dies the next" is only moderately helpful. A good approach is to treat as biennial those plants that *give the best results* when they are sown one year and harvested the next. On the whole, biennials are more trouble than either annuals or perennials.

But biennials include unusually lovely plants that seem to bloom just when we need them most. Foxgloves, for example, bring early height in June while the delphiniums are only making up their minds. Sweet William is colorful when the rest of the garden is recovering from its first spring spurt and has not yet gathered strength for summer. Nothing surpasses Canterbury bells for June drama, while the alpine forget me-not produces a marvelous blue cloud. So *you* have to decide how worthwhile biennials are for you, and, of course, you can buy plants if you don't want to bother with seeds.

MULTITUDES FROM SEED

Make sowings of the various biennials and perennials you are propagating at approximately the same time they would sow themselves, if nature were permitted her own course. Make exceptions of delphiniums that develop more satisfactorily if sowing is delayed until the midsummer heat is past, also Korean chrysanthemums, which behave practically like annuals. Of these two you want fresh seed, and unless you are using your own, it cannot be purchased before late July. As for the rest, sow the spring-flowering alyssum, arabis, columbine, hardy candytuft, and primrose, preferably in May and June; the early summer campanulas, coralbells, foxgloves, lupines, meadowrue, pyrethrum, and thermopsis before the end of July; and the aconite, gaillardia, platycodon, salvia, scabiosa, Shasta daisy, stokesia, and other summer- and fall-blooming perennials between mid-July and mid-August.

Coldframe or Open Bed

Make your sowings either in a coldframe or in the open near a hedge or wall. Keep in mind that your success depends on a *constant* supply of moisture, protection from wind and strong sunshine, and a loose soil that will neither bake out nor drain rapidly. Prepare the top inch of soil with particular care. Finely pulverized humus or compost will improve texture; sand should be liberally added if the soil is heavy. Unmilled sphagnum moss is good or a sterile commercial medium containing peatmoss and vermiculite or perlite. Or use the compressed peat pellet called One-Step or Jiffy 7. Soak the pellets in water and they will expand considerably. They contain everything, all the necessary food, and conveniently, the "pots" of young plants can be set directly in the garden so there is no transplanting shock.

Sow the seeds evenly and press them lightly into the material you are using. Then water gently. I use the houseplant syringe or my quart bottle sprayer for this purpose. Finally, cover with a thin layer of soil or other medium, and never for a minute thereafter neglect the need for even moisture. Sowings are easily protected from glare and drying wind, and also from drowning in a heavy rain, by a lath shade, old window shade, a length of cheesecloth, or polyethylene supported by sturdy plant stakes.

Meanwhile, unless you are using the One-Step pellets, prepare a second bed or another coldframe section to receive the seedlings as soon as they are of a size to handle conveniently. Use plenty of humus in this second bed but no chemical fertilizers. Space the plants according to their natures from 3 inches for hardy candytuft to 9 inches for foxgloves. Provide protection from the sun for the first week after transplanting and, to eliminate weeds, cultivate carefully by hand. Many perennials, certainly, may be propagated in several ways, depending on your preference and convenience.

Of course, you must have a coldframe. Even if your garden is small, gardening without one is like cooking without electric appliances. You can do it, but it's more work and less fun. In its basic form a coldframe is simply a box without top and bottom. For bottom it has the soil; for top, a piece of glass. In a sunny spot this wooden frame is inserted into the ground so that the front rests about 10 inches above soil level and the rear twenty. Thus a sloping top surface is provided to catch sunshine. For cold protection the box is banked with several inches of soil on the outside and, in extreme weather, burlap bags or a piece of blanket or carpet are thrown over the glass at night to keep in the warmth the sun afforded during the day.

My first coldframe was simply a wooden grocery box inserted into the soil near the kitchen door where the sun would warm it quickly and I could examine it constantly. It was amazing the crops I grew there, using a cheap adjustable window screen as a sunshade in the heat. Late in March I'd start a crop of Chinese delphiniums. When these were moved in May, I might put in cuttings of 'Miss Lingard' phlox, followed by a sowing of some long-spurred columbines; these remained until the next spring. Thus that little makeshift structure was put to use every month of the year.

Other Uses

Besides a spot for plant propagation, frames also offer safe winter quarters for tender plants like Spider chrysanthemums and other precarious winterers that are moved there after they bloom. Cuttings and seedlings still too small for outside wintering can likewise be stored there during the cold months. And I like an extra frame too for a permanent crop. I particularly enjoyed a small duplex built in a sun-drenched corner by my study steps. Here I had a planting of *Iris stylosa* and sweet violets—very nice for midwinter and early-spring picking.

Without a coldframe you can still raise many perennials from seed or cutting. A somewhat raised bed in a light, but not sunny, protected spot outdoors near a faucet or within reach of the hose will do. Or a box of well-prepared soil makes a nice nursery. After sowing, cover with a piece of burlap to keep the soil from drying out. Water right through this until germination occurs. But at the sign of the first green shoot, whisk away the

Useful materials for starting seeds: LEFT: plastic flat with compartments; FRONT LEFT: dry Jiffy peat pots; TOP CENTER: after soaking; TOP RIGHT: small plastic "greenhouse." Shasta daisy seeds in the dish are large enough to place three or four to a pot. FITCH PHOTO

Shasta daisy seedlings several weeks after planting in Jiffy pots. The whole pot is later planted in the ground and disintegrates there. FITCH PHOTO

burlap, for plants have been known to get their young necks broken when they poked them through burlap weave. You cannot regulate conditions so well in the open and, of course, you cannot sow so early or protect plants so late. So do have a coldframe, even a makeshift one like my own early love.

If you want detailed plant-by-plant advice, do turn to *The Complete Book of Growing Plants from Seed* by Elda Haring (New York: Hawthorn Books, 1967). Written by an experienced home gardener, it is a mine of helpful information. Also, in the Index of Park's seed catalogue you will find symbols indicating germination time, bloom time, and cultural notes, including the time to sow.

To avoid transplanting shock, bare-root daylilies are first soaked in a weak fertilizer solution in which Rootone powder has been dissolved. At LOWER RIGHT, a potted plant. FITCH PHOTO

MULTIPLY BY DIVISION

After heleniums, Shasta daisies, and most chrysanthemums have grown in your garden for only a year you can lift the plants with a spading fork in spring, and carefully pull, pry, or cut them into a number of divisions. These, set out separately, give you new plants of a size equal to the parents' by summer or fall. Phlox, iris, and columbine can be divided by the third year.

When you lift some plants, a hard, woody center will appear. Discard this, resetting only the younger outer sections. But don't make the divisions too small, or the next year your garden will have a very meager look. Experience will reveal each plant's rate of development. You will discover that a well-grown phlox can usually be separated into thirds, while every small piece of rooted chrysanthemum has the capacity for equaling its mature parent within the one growing season.

And you will find that spring- and summer-flowering plants like iris, phlox, columbine, and primrose are best divided after a rain in late August or September. Deal with them as soon as the heat has sufficiently waned for you to attack the business comfortably but while at least a month or more of growing weather remains before frost. This allows divided plants to anchor themselves in their new locations. Plan spring division for chrysanthemums, hardy asters, aconites, and other fall-flowering plants. Some perennials— peony, gypsophila, bleedingheart, lupine, gasplant, anemone, and Christmas-rose—you will not disturb for years and years, since these flourish only after they have been thoroughly acclimated to your garden.

MORE FROM CUTTINGS

From Stem Sections

Another method of increase is by cuttings—stem or root. In early summer, when the second growth of rockcress, hardy candytuft, phlox, or pinks is well advanced, just go through the plantings with a razor blade. Exactly beneath the point where a leaf emerges, cut the stems off. Of course, leave several eyes or points of growth below the cut so that the older plant can sprout again. This treatment does not harm developed perennials. It only makes them thick and branching.

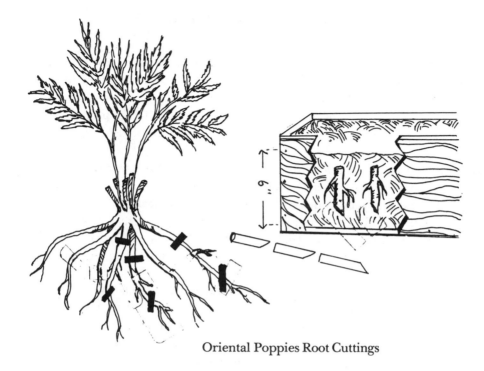

Oriental Poppies Root Cuttings

Next, from the cut sections you have taken, remove the lower leaves and any incipient flowers at the top. Then insert the bare stems an inch or so of their approximately 3-inch lengths in a box of moist sand set in the shade or in your shaded coldframe. In this way you can quickly and easily obtain a large crop of one variety. I have had 'Miss Lingard' phlox root in less than three weeks in August and with little attention from me. If you want to obtain economically an edging of one kind, like hardy candytuft, for instance, try this method of increase after your three or more purchased plants are established.

From Root Pieces

The root cutting is a good way to extend your stock of bleedingheart, phlox, sea-lavender, babysbreath, anemone, and oriental poppy. In late August or September, lift the plant you wish to propagate and select roots of approximately lead-pencil size. Cut these into 3-inch pieces and lay the sections horizontally in rows in your coldframe. Space them about 3 inches apart, and firm over them a 1- to 2-inch layer of sand or sand and peatmoss mixed. Leave the frame open until after freezing weather. Then close and shade it until warm middays occur in February. Begin to ventilate for progressively longer periods as the spring season advances. Water from April on as the soil requires it. By May you will have a fine, lusty crop of complete plants to move to permanent quarters.

So it is that big crops can be obtained at little expense but, I'd say, with big labor. But obtaining plants from the start by seed, division, or cutting is interesting, and you may well find propagation the most rewarding aspect of your perennial experience.

18

FOR PEST-
AND DISEASE-FREE PERENNIALS

Garden controls in my estimation are an unmitigated nuisance, but without some attention to them, your perennials might be a real mess—that is, if you grow certain ones that are not exactly care-free. These include the giant delphiniums (not *D. chinense,* which seems to be immune), anemones, bearded iris (for sure), chrysanthemums (maybe), hollyhocks, monkshood, peonies (maybe, but not mine), and phlox. Now, some of those you are bound to want despite the problems, but there is a multitude that in my experience never get anything. I think right off of astilbes, bleedinghearts, coralbells, daylilies, hellebores, hostas, violas, and, of course, ferns. In fact, my care-free list is so long that I am giving it to you separately on page 236.

To begin with, plants that are physically content are more likely to resist trouble because they are strong. Place your perennials according to their preference, sun-lovers in sun, shade-demanders in shade; prepare soil properly though not exhaustingly, being mindful that some perennials favor a sweet soil, some acid (but see Chapter 15 about this); and water adequately so that plants don't faint in drought and stems harden then so that later they can't take up water. Free air circulation also promotes health and is good insurance against blackspot, mildew, and rust. Crowded plantings are inevitably prone to these troubles. Garden sanitation is essential, especially for iris beds, so get rid of disease-ridden stalks, yellow leaves, and weed accumulation. Anyway, keep in mind that common sense will prove more beneficial than complete reliance on chemicals. With such a program my own dealings with trouble have certainly been limited.

However, to avoid the dreadful intricacies of pest and disease and still be on the safe side, you could regularly apply an all-purpose material that is both insecticide and fungicide, as Ortho Rose & Floral Dust (from a squeeze duster), or Spectracide Rose and Flower Spray (from a spray can). For insects, work into the soil a granular systemic as Isotox or Spectracide. The Spectracide container also indicates that it is a control for black spot and powdery mildew. Then if you have to deal sternly with disease, dust with Orthocide Garden Fungicide or use it as a soil drench.

INSECT PESTS—SUCKERS AND CHEWERS

I suppose everyone is familiar with aphids, that most common insect. They deform and destroy by sucking out the plant juices. Black, green, red, or white, you may find aphids clustering on new growth, making it sticky with their honeydew secretions. Usually aphids are not too difficult to get rid of. A strong hose spray can often clear out the black colonies in the shoots of chrysanthemums, the white ones on the undersides of columbine foliage. If hosing isn't adequate, spray with Malathion or an all-purpose combination with Malathion in it.

The red-spider and two-spotted mites likewise debilitate plants by sucking. And they are almost invisible without a magnifying glass. However, mites will proclaim their presence if you know what to look for—thickening of leaves, cupping, curling, and brittleness of leaves with tiny webs underneath, and finally, a general yellowing of foliage. Attacks can occur as soon as leaves begin to develop and are most persistent when air is hot and ground is dry. A good hose drenching helps to *some* extent because it dampens the atmosphere and mites do not thrive when it is cool and moist. Hosing from below also breaks the webs. Phlox, hollyhocks, delphinium, and the hardy evergreen candytuft (Iberis) are favorite abodes. You may have to take specific measures—such as spraying with Kelthane or working the granular Spectracide lightly into the soil—to control mites.

Other insects may harm by chewing even to the point of skeletonizing foliage. They are destroyed when they eat foliage that is covered with something poisonous to them. Japanese beetles are the worst, and you can hardly protect flowers from them, only leaves, since an opening blossom presents a continually *fresh* surface for attack. When plants, such as hollyhocks or rose mallows, need protection, spray with Malathion or Sevin at emerging time and keep on spraying as you have to, to save your plants. Or omit hollyhocks for a few years. Japanese beetles eventually leave a locality, you know. Although I have none here now, I once lived in the primary "beetle belt" near the New Jersey nursery to which they were first introduced. If you can bear it (I can't), you can dispatch *a few beetles* by picking them off and dropping them into a can of water topped with kerosene, or set out Japanese beetle traps.

Borers or caterpillars that work inside stems are likewise chewers and are very hard to deal with. Sometimes they can be caught working and destroyed on the spot. A dust or spray on their favorite eating place, the bearded iris, is the best protection; it is a *special* attention that must be provided if you expect any pleasure from the beautiful big-bearded irises. (See Chapter 5 for details of treatment.)

Occasionally trouble originates in the soil, as when cutworms attack the columbines or other seedlings just after you have set them out. And slugs, which are slimy snails without shells, may feed at night on your chrysanthemums, leaving riddled leaves as evidence or no leaves at all, just bare, limp stalks and slimy trails. You can use a pellet preparation like Bug-Geta for snails and slugs, or simply place saucers of beer among the plants at night to insure a happy death for all who come.

Ants may cause trouble, not on peony buds, from which they disappear when the flower opens, but in flower beds, where their busy hills are objectionable. The granular Spectracide is excellent for controlling these soil-borne enemies, including the grubs of Japanese beetles. Indirectly it deters moles by destroying the grubs on which they feed.

If you grow columbines, I am afraid you will know the leafminer that makes labyrinthine tunnels in the leaves. Eggs are laid *inside* the foliage, and the emerging larvae feed voraciously. Sometimes tunnels run together to make a blotch. Unchecked, leafminers defoliate and hence destroy leaves and plants. Dust or spray with Malathion or Sevin, as soon as new leaves are up, then once a week for three weeks. This catches the adult insects before they lay eggs. After eggs hatch it's too late, for the larvae have the protection of the leaf surfaces. I prefer to work a systemic insecticide containing Di-Syston lightly into the soil around the plants about May 1 at the rate indicated on the container, and water it in. The poison is absorbed throughout the vascular system of the plant, and all parts are protected. The residual effect continues for months. I have found systemics a much easier way to handle leafminers than either dusting or spraying. If you see tiny white flies flitting around your plants, apply your all-purpose spray or dust or use pyrethrum; it controls all the stages of this pest.

SOME PLANT DISEASES

It would be pleasant if at this point I could end this sad account with the assurance that not all perennials get all the pests, nor even some of them, every year—which is, indeed, a comforting as well as a true thought. I must add, however, that there are fungus diseases that must sometimes be dealt with. Three kinds are most common: mildew, leaf blights of many kinds, and rusts.

Mildew sometimes covers chrysanthemum, delphinium, fall aster, and especially phlox, with a white, powdery coating when July and August days are damp and muggy. You can clean it up by spraying with Phaltan or dusting with Flotox, or a combination spray containing one of these. Apply preventative spray or dust at the end of summer. Crowded, damp, or sunless plantings, or those too close to wall or fence where the air does not move, are the most prone to attack, or gardens regularly watered in the early evening so that foliage goes into the night wet. Cut down and burn all plant tops in fall as a control measure, and plant mildew-resistant varieties if these are available.

Various leaf blights and spots may mar, curl, and disfigure foliage. In spring, if buds have blackened and fail to open on your peonies, plants are probably suffering from a fungus known as botrytis blight. In summer, botrytis shows on peonies as blotched discolorations on leaves and stems; in winter, hard black blisters may be visible on stalks you have neglected to cut down. Botrytis may also attack your anemones and chrysanthemums, though this is not usual. The prevention of botrytis is sanitation, air circulation, and plenty of sun; the cure may be a use of the fungicidal spray Phaltan or Benlate every two weeks, starting when the spring points emerge until the foliage is about a foot high. But don't do this unless you must. (My peonies don't get botrytis.)

When humidity is high, unsightly leafspots may mar the foliage of chrysanthemums, delphiniums, and monkshood; for these, proper conditions are the best with prevention applications of a fungicidal spray only if trouble gets ahead of you.

Rust may appear as reddish, black, or yellow blisters on your hollyhocks, lupines, or meadowrue, usually on the underside of leaves. The same treatment with Benlate every two weeks is indicated, with steady hand-picking of infected leaves and destruction of tops when the flowering season is over, and, please, no stalks on the compost heap; get rid of them.

EQUIPMENT AND MATERIALS

A duster or sprayer is an almost essential piece of equipment for garden doctoring unless you are using systemics. I prefer dusting to spraying, and I really enjoy using my midget duster. There are other types, of course. If you have only a few perennials to guard, you can use an aerosol can filled with an all-purpose mixture. If you have a good many plants (and, incidentally, climbing vines), you may prefer the hose-and-bottle-type sprayer. You put the lethal dose in the bottle in the amount directed and turn on the hose. The water passing through the bottle dilutes as it sprays.

I think that systemics are the controls of the future, since they can be applied regardless of weather, and they last a long time. Today there are excellent insecticide and fungicide types, and like many other gardeners, I have discovered that the insecticide systemics also have fungicidal action, although this is not advertised. Also, I have it on good authority that since systemics in their cruise through the plant structure do not reach the nectaries of the flowers, they are not injurious to beneficial insects.

If you are an environmentalist and want to avoid the use of chemicals, you may want to depend partly or entirely on nature, introducing to your garden the natural enemies of destructive insects. Ladybugs do a big job on aphids and mites, and ladybugs can be bought in packages of ten thousand adults. The larvae of lacewings take a terrific toll of many sucking insects, and lacewing eggs are sold in vials you can purchase by mail from insect farms. We have long respected the praying mantis, which attacks not only aphids but also beetles and caterpillars, and egg cases of the praying mantis can also be purchased. (To get rid of Japanese beetle grubs, introduce milky-disease spores available in garden centers and from some special firms; see Where to Buy Natural Controls at the end of this chapter.)

If you depend on chemical controls, don't overdo it. Powerful broad-spectrum materials may not be required in your almost-clean garden. Maybe dusting with sulphur will clean up the mildew on your phlox. When you do apply chemicals, read the labels carefully and follow instructions for safety and good results. With some sprays you need to use a spreader or sticker; be sure it is a kind that won't clog your sprayer.

Insecticides, Fungicides, and Slug Controls

In this discussion the trade names of the preparations that you will find at your dealers are given in italics following the name of the chemical.

Malathion (*Malathion*) or methoxychlor (*Marlate*), a substitute for DDT. These are considered broad-spectrum pesticides for aphids, leaf-miners, leaf hoppers, Japanese beetles, iris borers, and thrips (not spider mites). Used alone, Malathion gives protection for only three to four days. Methoxychlor protects for twelve to sixteen days. With either one you may have to repeat until the last batch of trouble has hatched.

Carbaryl (*Sevin* or *Isotox Insect Spray* or *Rose and Floral Spray*, this also a fungicide), spray or dust for leaf-chewers, Japanese beetles, iris borers, and leafminers.

Diazinon (*Spectracide*), a broad-spectrum granular material for use in the soil to control grubs, or as a wettable powder for dusting, or as an emulsifiable liquid in a can for a foliage spray; *Spectracide Rose and Flower Spray* also a disease control.

Dicofol (*Kelthane*), a specific for mites.

Di-Syston (*Noculate* or *Ortho Systemic Rose & Flower Care*), 8–12–4, granular systemic insecticides for leafminer and other sucking insects.

Mesurol (*Slug-Geta* or *Bug-Geta*), a snail and slug bait, or put out shallow saucers of beer at night; beer is lethal.

Meta-Systox (*Isotox Insect Spray*), with systemic action to control chewing and sucking insects.

Fungicides

Benomyl (*Benlate*), a new systemic-fungicide spray, excellent *preventative* and control for mildew on phlox, blackspot on delphinium.

Captan (*Orthocide*), spray, dust, or soil drench for a broad range of diseases; this can be combined with most insecticides as a spray; effective for early blights.

Folpet (*Phaltan*), a spray for powdery mildew and blackspot on phlox. You will see it listed on the label of your all-purpose spray for roses, and it will do a good job on perennials, too.

CONTROL CHART

Problems and "Cures" at a Glance

If plants are prone to both pests and disease, apply preventive materials that control both; consider systemics. Recommended products are available at this time, but all are subject, of course, to government control.

Plant and Ailment	Cause	Control
Aconitum (Monkshood) Dark spots on leaves may run together; some withering	Leafspot, a fungus disease, where humidity is high	Cut off infected leaves, stems, etc., as necessary. Prevention best. Spray early with Orthocide or Phaltan; repeat every two weeks.
Labyrinthine tunneling of leaves	Leafminers working in foliage	Spray or dust new leaves with Malathion or Sevin; or apply a systemic, Isotox or Spectracide.
Althaea rosea (Hollyhock) Curling foliage, webbed underneath, rusty blisters	Aphids; spider-mites, rust	Apply an all-purpose spray or dust to control both insects and fungus, as Ortho Rose and Floral Dust or Spectracide Rose and Flower Spray.
Holes in leaves	Japanese beetles	Dust or spray with Malathion or Sevin. Omit hollyhocks for a time in areas of severe infestation; beetles move on eventually.

Plant and Ailment	Cause	Control
Anemone japonica Chewed look to foliage and flowers	Long, dark, or striped beetles	Spray or dust with Malathion.
Aquilegia (Columbine) Labyrinthia markings on foliage	Leafminers inside foliage	Spray or dust early with Malathion or Sevin to control both; or apply Isotox as a systemic spray or granules in soil.
Pale insect clusters on underside of leaves	Aphids	
Chrysanthemum (see Chapter 10) Lower leaves turn dry and brown	Weather factor or nematode attack	Water deeply in dry spells and apply a mulch; avoid over-head sprinkling; re-move badly affected plants. If brown wedges indicate nema-todes, start cuttings, avoid divisions.
Leaf tips curling, covered with black insects	Aphids	First try strong hosing; if no cleanup, spray or dust with Malathion or Sevin.
Brown spots on foliage	Leaf blight	Spray or dust with Phaltan or Orthocide for both fungus troubles.
White coating	Mildew	For this alone, dust with sulfur (Flotox).

Plant and Ailment	Cause	Control
Chewed leaves, slimy trails	Slugs chewing at night	Scatter Slug-Geta late in day or put out saucers of beer in which slugs will perish.
Delphinium (see Chapter 8) Distorted leaf and stem growth and blackened flower stalks	Cyclamen mites	Destroy worst plants; spray others every two weeks in spring, possibly also in late summer, before trouble shows, with Kelthane. Or apply Benlate, a systemic fungicide that controls mildew and blackspot.
Leaves curl down	Red aphids on underside	Try strong hose spray; if inadequate, spray or dust with Malathion, Spectracide, or pyrethrum.
Blackening and rotting of whole plant	Crown rot	Serious; remove whole plant; sterilize soil with a fumigant.
Dark spotting of leaves	Blackspot	Remove infected leaves. See as for *Aconitum* above.
White coating of leaves from midsummer on	Powdery mildew	Dust weekly with Folpet or Phaltan, midsummer on, or Benlate for everything.

Plant and Ailment	Cause	Control
Chewed leaves, slimy trails	Slugs chewing at night, especially on lower leaves	Scatter Slug-Geta or put out saucers of beer at night; it destroys them.
Discolored leaves, silvery streaks	Almost invisible thrips	Spray with Malathion or Cygon; repeat at two-week intervals if necessary.
Hardy Aster; white coating	Powdery mildew	A muggy-weather ailment; avoid late-day overhead watering. Dust with Flotox or Phaltan.
Iberis (Hardy Candytuft) Leaves turning yellow, gray, or brown	Spider-mites in hot, muggy weather	Strong hose spray to break underneath webs; if necessary, spray weekly with Kelthane.
Iris (tall bearded) (see Chapter 5) Pierced ragged spots on foliage, water-soaked look	Borer, a pale caterpillar working between leaves in spring and then down into rhizome; eggs winter in old leaves and debris	First, sanitation! Dust or spray new leaves with Methoxyclor or Sevin at 3 inches and repeat until buds form. Remove borers you see by piercing leaf with a knife, or sever leaves below point of attack.
Leaves rotting at ground line, foul odor when pulled off	Bacterial root rot, caused by winter injury or tunneling borers	Where much damage, try a soil drench of Captan or lift roots, cut out borers and decay. Dust with a fungicide like Orthocide.

Plant and Ailment	Cause	Control
Paeonia (Peony) (see Chapter 4) Grayish mold at base, toppling over young stems or just bud blasting while buds are small	Botrytis blight	First, sanitation. Cut off and destroy affected buds and stems. Remove all and destroy open flowers before they shatter. Spray with Phaltan or Benlate as shoots appear; repeat until buds form.
Insects crawling on partly opened buds	Ants	They disappear when flowers open, no damage.
Phlox Browning of lower foliage	Probably drought	Water deeply in dry weather.
Moldy white appearance of leaves	Powdery mildew	Dust repeatedly with Flotox or spray or dust with Phaltan.
Yellowing of leaves	Spider-mites	Try strong hose spray; apply Kelthane if necessary.

WHERE TO BUY NATURAL CONTROLS

W. Atlee Burpee Co.   Ladybugs, praying mantis
Hunting Park at 18th
Philadelphia, Pa. 19132

Lakeview   Praying mantis egg clusters
Box 69
Limerick, Pa. 19468

Pyramid Nursery   Ladybugs, praying mantis cases
Box 5274
Reno, Nevada 89503

Fairfax Laboratories   "Doom" milky spore
Clinton Corners, N.Y.
12514

Geo. W. Park Seed Co., Inc.   Ladybugs, praying mantis eggs
Greenwood, S.C. 29647

Romil Acres   Milky disease spores
68 Genesee Street
Greene, New York 13778

The Vitova Co., Inc.   Lacewings
Biological Control Division
P. O. Box 745
Rialto, Calif. 92376

World Garden Products   "Doom" (also milky disease spores)
World Building   Ladybugs
First and Seaview Avenues
East Norwalk, Conn.
06855

WHAT TO DO WHEN

Month-by-month Suggestions for the Dedicated

January

The works of a person that builds begin immediately
to decay; while those of him who plants begin directly
to improve. In this, planting promises a more lasting
pleasure than building.

—William Shenstone

Make a New Year's resolution to plan better and so to work less in your
garden. If you attempted too much last year, cut down. Gardens are not
meant to be an endurance test but a joy.

Chrysanthemum. On warm unseasonable middays lift the coldframe glass
for short periods for ventilation.

Helleborus (Christmas- and Lenten-rose). Cut generous bouquets from
the white and pink flowers of *Helleborus niger* plants. If you have *H. foetidus,* pick at least one handsome green inflorescence.

Convallaria (lily-of-the-valley). If you have an abundance of these, lift a clump or two, pot them, gradually introduce to heat indoors and then to sun. This will result in fragrant flowering in the house.

Make the acquaintance of some of the newer perennials this month. Study a general catalogue like Wayside Gardens, which is exceptionally well illustrated in color. Then obtain and read a few special catalogues on peony, iris, daylily, and chrysanthemum. Many catalogues are sent free on request. A fee is usually charged for the more richly illustrated ones. If you are an experienced gardener, select a trial few of the newer varieties in your favorite plant group.

Buy or make some wooden seed flats. A good easily handled size is 12 by 12 inches.

February

Out of the bosom of the Air,
   Out of the cloud-folds of her garments shaken,
Over the woodlands brown and bare,
   Over the harvest-fields forsaken,
     Silent, and soft, and slow
     Descends the snow.
     —Henry Wadsworth Longfellow, *Snow-Flakes*

Chrysanthemum. Continue to ventilate coldframes for longer periods as weather permits.

Astilbe, Iberis, Primula, Dicentra. Dig a clump of any of these some pleasant day, pot them, and urge them with sunshine, water, and warmth to put on an out-of-season indoor show.

Work and rework your garden plans this month. It's a very pleasant fireside occupation.

Get your orders in early to insure prompt delivery of choice material. Remember to include, too, fertilizers, mulching material, spray equipment, stakes, plant ties, tools if you need them, and various oddments. It's so much easier to start equipped than to have to await some necessary item just when you need it most. Order your sundries as locally as possible to save delivery costs, but buy your plants where the exact variety you want is obtainable. Substitutions are seldom satisfactory to the particular gardener, especially when it's a matter of color.

Don't overlook the season's novelties, but don't go all out for them either. The acquaintance of a few each year makes gardening that much more interesting.

Save your wood ashes. Either add them to the compost where they will speed humus decomposition or collect them until spring when, scattered on the garden, they will supply potash. To keep their fertilizing value intact when stored separately, place them under cover. You want them "unleached"—that is, unweathered.

Think about a metal bin for compost, very useful for a small garden.

March

Who loves a garden still his Eden keeps,
Perennial pleasures plants, and wholesome harvests reaps.
—Amos Bronson Alcott

Sow seeds of annuals indoors four to six weeks before the last killing frost in your area so as to have plants of a size to transfer outdoors. Of course, perennial seeds can be planted outdoors as soon as the earth is warm and workable. Remember: Do not apply any fertilizer until growth is well advanced.

Chrysanthemum. When you discover green leaves under the mulch in the coldframe, remove the mulch and the coldframe shade. But keep the glass down except during the warm part of the day.

Iris. Examine these and other perennials for signs of heaving. Particularly if your garden has not been mulched, you will need to go over plantings and firm back roots dislodged by frost. If you have had borer trouble, dust with Sevin this month if new growth is well out of the ground, or apply a systemic insecticide.

Late this month poke around a bit and see what goes on under the winter mulch. If green growth appears, loosen mulches to aerate plants. It's not time yet for removal unless the season is unusually advanced.

April

A gush of bird-song, a patter of dew,
A cloud, and a rainbow's warning,
Suddenly sunshine and perfect blue—
An April day in the morning.
—Harriet Prescott Spofford, *April*

Iris. Clean out plantings by hand as early as possible. Burn old leaves and all debris in which the eggs of the iris borer may lie. Dust a second time unless you are using a systemic. Check Control Chart, page 207.

Peony. If *previously* buds have blackened, dust or spray with Phaltan or Zineb to deter possible botrytis blight. Repeat until buds appear. If plants have been healthy before, no spraying is necessary. Set the double-ring tripod supports around the plants before heavy growth makes the task a real chore. Apply a trowelful of wood ashes and one of a commercial fertilizer. Triple these amounts for enormous plants.

Chrysanthemum. Lift all but the Cushion varieties (divide these in alternate years), discard centers of taller types and plant fresh single-rooted sections at distances depending on size. "Space plants two thirds their height" is a good old rule.

Hardy Asters. Lift and divide most asters each spring. Discard woody centers. Plant three young, well-rooted shoots together to form a new clump. Provide fresh soil with bonemeal and humus or select a new site.

Daisies. Divide heleniums and Shastas the second year into many small sections that will equal the parents in the one growing season.

Delphinium. Fertilize established plants. Transfer youngsters from cold-frame to permanent quarters early this month.

Viola cornuta. Sow this now. It does not care for summer heat.

Remove the greater part of the winter mulch when forsythia blooms. Clean up the remainder or work it into the soil as buds appear on maple trees.

About midmonth apply to all established perennials a balanced commercial plant food in sufficient quantity slightly to obscure the soil. Rake in lightly and water well. (But don't keep so busy with routine that you miss the miracle of spring!)

Set dry, twiggy growth, cut from privet or other shrubby material among low-branching perennials like achillea, gaillardia, and coreopsis. These plants will soon hide their excellent supports.

Divide fall-flowering perennials at this time.

Scatter your hoard of wood ashes lightly over the perennial beds in any available amount, particularly on delphinium and pinks.

May

—For I hold that the best purpose of a garden
is to give delight and to give refreshment of
mind, to soothe, to refine, and to lift up the
heart in a spirit of praise and thankfulness.
It is certain that those who practise gardening
in the best ways find it to be so.
—Gertrude Jekyll

Iris. Make the acquaintance of the small and intermediate irises, the Siberians, and others. They are worth knowing. If the season is dry, give all iris plantings a thorough soaking to improve flower quality. If, last year, borers attacked, dust plants again with Sevin, unless flower buds are well advanced. Cut off any punctured leaves well below noticeable points of attack. Burn these and any debris gathered from around plantings.

Peony. Remove the side buds from each group of three if size rather than quantity is your aim. Otherwise let them all develop. Don't worry over the harmless ants on the buds.

Delphinium. Stake your fast-growing plants before a storm breaks off the lovely spires. They look best with a separate support for each flower stalk.

Phlox. To achieve unusual size, pinch out all but four or five stems of each mature clump.

Chrysanthemum. When divided single plants have six leaves, pinch out the tops to induce branching. Pinch back branches as each of these develops six leaves. Get rid of any aphids with a strong hose spray.

Columbines. Before foliage shows labyrinth markings indicating leaf-miners, spray or dust with Malathion or Sevin. Rout aphids with a strong hose spray.

Late this month or early next, make sowings of spring-flowering perennials for next spring's bloom—arabis, alyssum, columbine, forget-me-not, iberis, and primrose.

Around the fifteenth, apply the second dose of balanced plant food to all established perennials.

If you are considering changes that must wait until fall, write yourself a garden note or two and tuck it into the appropriate spot. I use the broad-topped Perfect Labels for this. In September I find such reminders to myself as "Move these daylilies to roomier quarters" or "Don't dig here. Remember your mertensia," or "This salmon phlox requests paler companions." It's a useful scheme.

If bleedinghearts are to be divided in August, mark their location now so you can find them later when the foliage has died down and disappeared.

Keep notes of any color clashes. Later you can improve the situation perhaps by introducing some gray-foliaged plants among the offenders.

June

Delphiniums have come to call
In mass against my garden wall;
  Lifting a torch of lapis flame
  As lovely as their lyric name.
Their presence holds my eyes in thrall.
          —Anne Lloyd

Iris. Remove at the ground line all stalks carrying faded flowers. Keep orientals well soaked. Hand-weed clumps as they require. Make a list of any new iris you have seen this year and want next.

Hardy Candytuft. Prune plants back after flowering to induce thick new growth.

Chrysanthemum. Place around the tall, huskier varieties the tripod supports no longer needed by the peonies. Fertilize lightly the middle of the month. Keep pinching side growth back.

Hollyhocks. Apply deterrent in Japanese-beetle-infested areas. If problem is serious, better to omit hollyhocks for a few years.

Columbine. Sow seeds every other year for a multitude of fine-blooming plants.

Edging Plants. Take stem cuttings of rockcress, hardy candytuft, dwarf phlox, and pinks when second growth starts. Also, consider: Are the edges of your garden fine enough, or should they be improved?

Peony. Select new varieties while they are in flower, but delay delivery and planting until autumn.

Phlox. Be prompt about snipping off faded flowers. Then you will have a long blooming season and no unwanted seedlings.

Hardy Asters. To keep them tractable in the border, pinch out all but three to four shoots in each clump.

Digitalis (Foxglove). Sow seeds thinly this month.

Dianthus barbatus (Sweet William). Sow this month in an open but protected seed bed or coldframe.

Early this month after some cultivation and fertilizing, apply a summer mulch to discourage weeds and conserve moisture and to promote good looks.

Fork over the material in your compost pile and soak it with a slow-running hose for a whole day. Be sure to leave a "saucer" on top to catch rainwater.

Sow now, for early-summer bloom next year, seeds of perennial coralbells, lupines, pinks, meadowrue, thermopsis, and pyrethrum.

July

Nothing in human affairs is worth any great anxiety.
—Plato

If the weather is very hot, don't read this for a while. Just sit and fan. Remember, gardening is primarily for fun. Doubtless your borders can survive a little neglect at this time.

Iberis (Hardy Candytuft). Be alert about spraying, especially if the weather is hot and dry. You won't see the red-spider, but a yellowed plant usually means he's been seriously at work on his favorite.

Phlox. Spray for spider-mites and mildew, and give deep soakings if there is little rain.

Flax. Remove at ground line some of the hardening older shoots that have flowered freely. This will induce new growth.

Hollyhocks. Watch out for red-spider and rust, and spray as necessary.

Helleborus (Christmas- or Lenten-rose). Deep summer soakings are to its liking through dry spells.

Chrysanthemum. Guard against mildew by dusting or spraying, and soak if there is drought. Fertilize midmonth. Stop pinching back early varieties by the fifteenth, later ones by the thirtieth.

Hemerocallis (Daylily) and **Hosta.** Water well in dry weather or bloom may be meager.

Delphinium. If the weather is damp and muggy, be faithful about dusting or spraying to deter mildew and blight. Don't let annuals crowd these plants when they are cut back and small after flowering. Allow a two-week rest after flowering, then fertilize.

Biennials. Most of them can be sown late this month or early next. Time this for a cool spell after a rain.

Hardy Asters. Stake early, particularly if you are allowing only a few tall shoots for each plant.

Violas. Cut back sharply, water deeply, and mulch. Maybe they will prove perennial for you.

Fork over the compost pile and soak it well.

If the weather is dry, soak sections of the garden thoroughly and progressively until each section has been moistened six inches deep. Use the overhead sprinkler, only occasionally and never at night, to cleanse and refresh plant tops.

This is usually a bad pest and disease month, especially for powdery mildew if the weather is muggy. Be watchful, and spray to deter rather than to eradicate. See Control Chart, page 207.

Protect the corners of your garden from careless steps or a dragging hose by short right-angle sections of 12-inch wire fencing. The hardware man will cut them to your specification. These short bits of fencing also help in the re-education of dogs and children whose short-cut habits need changing.

August

This is the very dead of summer. I am not sure that I ever heard just that phrase before. . . . Surely, it describes at least the impression that August creates as she slumbers, replete and satisfied. Spring was a fever and autumn will be a regret, but this is the month too aware of its own successful achievement to be more than barely sentient. . . . If Nature is ever purely *vegetative*, it is now.

—Joseph Wood Krutch

Iris. If foliage rots at base, lift plants, cut out decay from rhizomes; cover with Orthocide.

Aconite. Keep well soaked.

Chrysanthemum. Soak deeply if rainfall is slight. This will help check leaf browning. Stake as growth indicates. Three bambo lengths bound by green raffia will do a neat job for tall plants.

Phlox. Increase your supply by taking stem cuttings of some favorite varieties. Cut two thirds back those that have bloomed heavily. They will soon get to work again.

Delphinium. Sow fresh seed (shaken up in packet with Semesan) some cool day this month. Use a deep flat and keep it in a cool garage or shed until germination is evident.

Hardy Asters. Don't let them suffer drought.

Helleborus (Christmas- or Lenten-rose). How about making a planting of these this month or next? They will complete your flowering year and seem like a miracle when they are in full flower in winter.

Edging Plants. Consider sowing mixed *Dianthus plumarius* for a great supply of fragrant edging plants.

Digitalis (Foxglove). Space six-week-old June-sown plants 10 inches apart in row or coldframe. Be careful they do not suffer dryness.

After a rain, during a relatively cool spell, sow seeds of the summer- and fall-flowering perennials—aconite, gaillardia, platycodon, salvia, scabiosa, Shasta daisy, and stokesia.

Turn over and soak the compost pile once this month.

Take root cuttings this month or next of babysbreath, anemone, phlox, sea-lavender, and oriental poppy as the new foliage develops.

September

The morrow was a bright September morn;
The earth was beautiful as if new-born;
There was that nameless splendor everywhere,
That wild exhilaration in the air,
Which makes the passers in the city street
Congratulate each other as they meet.
—Henry Wadsworth Longfellow

Iris. Divide and reset crowded clumps. Cut tops halfway back. Plant small divisions of bearded varieties 1 inch deep and 15 inches apart. Face rhizomes in the same direction. Set three single pieces of Siberians three inches apart to form one clump. Water regularly if dry weather follows transplanting.

Biennials. Transfer open sowings to rows in a protected reserve bed. Separate coldframe seedlings to stand 4 to 8 inches apart, according to variety.

Primrose. Separate into small but not too tiny divisions or they will disappear

Anemone. Don't be alarmed if your first-year plants aren't flowering much. They incline to be backward about coming forward until they are well established in your garden.

Phlox. About every third or fourth year, divide big clumps into thirds.

Peony. Divide and reset any failing old plants or set out new ones the last two weeks this month. Remember: A place in the sun, good drainage, and only 2 inches of soil over the crowns. Don't disturb healthy, established plants.

Oriental Poppy. Set out new plants and divide and reset very thick old ones. You can also take root cuttings now.

Delphinium. Place your new seedlings 4 inches apart in a coldframe. Use equal thirds of leafmold, topsoil, and sand.

Chrysanthemum. If you wish to transfer well-budded plants to the border, wait for cloudy weather. Then soak plants the day before and daily for several days after moving. They will bloom on without an indication of resentment. Stake any inclined to be floppy.

Heuchera (Coralbells). Perhaps you can edge a whole bed by dividing several of your large, established clumps. Separate by pulling gently apart. From the taproot, cut only those sections with some fine roots of their own.

Start a compost pile or buy a small metal adjustable bin with tablets for making compost in a small area.

If your order of lily bulbs has not come, place stakes among your perennials to indicate proper bulb placement. When some lilies are already present but there are others yet to go in, perhaps next month, mark present locations with wire stakes and future ones with bamboo. Stakes left in place over winter are also a safe guide to early cultivation of perennials if late hardy plants or bulbs must be worked around.

October

There is no season when such pleasant and
sunny spots may be lighted on, and produce
so pleasant an effect on the feelings, as
now in October.

—Nathaniel Hawthorne

Peony. Cut off and burn all foliage. Work in a trowelful of bonemeal per plant.

Chrysanthemum. As soon as flowering ceases, cut back tops and lift stock plants of doubtfully hardy varieties. Place these in an open coldframe and water once a week until a hard freeze occurs.

Visit a chrysanthemum nursery or any fair-sized private collection and make your list of varieties for next year.

If you plan to mulch the borders with leaves, collect in a corner of the shrubbery border or in baskets all you will need of the type that curl when they fall—oak, birch, beech, red or sugar maple, etc. Avoid soggy mulches made by poplar or Norway maple leaves.

Should there be little rainfall this month, as sometimes occurs, soak your perennials deeply about the third week. Plants that have suffered drought incline to winterkill. Let yours go dormant in good condition.

Early this month is a grand time to redo a badly designed planting or one overcrowded by the maturity of its plants. Sometimes I do sections year by year—edging and foreground one autumn, center or rear another. Lift out all plants. Separate those requiring it. Throw away poor varieties or those past their prime. Dig deeply. Work compost and bonemeal into the soil. Reset plants. The weather usually favors you, and the work is fun. Ensuing satisfaction, tremendous!

November

Take winter as you find him, and he turns out to be a thoroughly honest fellow, with no nonsense about him, and tolerating none in you, which is a greater comfort in the long run.

—James Russell Lowell

Iris. After a hard freeze, mulch new plantings lightly the first year. Only in subzero sections continue this practice in subsequent years.

Chrysanthemum. After freezing weather, mulch all plants. After mulching those in the frame, put down the glass and shade it. You may not need to do this until next month.

Early this month, mulch lightly all young plants just beyond the seedling stage. Do not cover adults until after the first hard freeze.

Plant inconspicuously a few bushes of California privet as a source of next year's twiggy supports for coreopsis, gaillardia, stokesia, veronica, etc.

December

Announced by all the trumpets of the sky,
Arrives the snow, and, driving o'er the fields,
Seems nowhere to alight: the white air
Hides hills and woods, the river, and the heaven,
And veils the farm-house at the garden's end.
The sled and traveller stopped, the courier's feet
Delayed, all friends shut out, the housemates sit
Around the radiant fireplace, enclosed
In a tumultuous privacy of storm.
                              —Ralph Waldo Emerson

After the first hard freeze—not simply a touch of frost—mulch perennials to keep them cold and unstimulated by occasional midwinter warmth. Pull the mulching material under, not over, green-topped plants. After the first year, leave uncovered peonies, irises, oriental poppies, and delphinium (except in very cold sections). Daylilies never need a cover.

For your garden-mad friends, remember that an order for some choice perennial plants is a very fine present.

Merry Christmas and Good Gardening next year!

PLANTS
FOR SPECIAL PURPOSES

A RAINBOW OF COLORS

The colors of most perennials blend well in a border or other planting. Only a few clash violently, as orange poppies and rose-pink peonies. Where drifts of one color are likely to affront drifts of another, plant between them pale yellow flowers, like 'Primrose Drift' iris. Oddly, yellows are better peacemakers than whites, which may make too emphatic accents. Or set the clashing colors somewhat apart with drifts of babysbreath between or plants in foliage not in blooom at the same time, as fall asters.

Check the varieties listed in the various chapters of this book, in the Dictionary (page 237), and note also the descriptions in the catalogues from which you are ordering. If it's a melon-pink daylily you want, don't get confused by the multitude of choices and find yourself next spring with something in the raspberry department. Wayside Gardens' catalogue in full color is helpful; also catalogues of specialists like Schreiner's for iris; Smirnow for peonies; Wild for peonies, irises, and daylilies; Conard-Pyle and Sunnyslope for chrysanthemums. (Addresses are given under Where to Buy at the back of this book.)

WHITE

Althaea (Hollyhock)
Anemone japonica (Windflower)
Chrysanthemum (Chrysanthemum)
Chrysanthemum maximum (Shasta Daisy)
Cimicifuga (Snakeroot)
Dictamnus albus (Gasplant)
Digitalis (Foxglove)
Gypsophila (Babysbreath)

Hardy *Aster* (Michaelmas Daisy)
Hosta, or Funkia (Plantain-lily, or August-lily)
Iberis sempervirens (Hardy Candytuft)
Iris (Iris)
Paeonia (Peony)
Papaver orientale (Oriental Poppy)
Phlox (Phlox)

"TRUE" BLUE

Baptisia australis (False Indigo)
Brunnera (Forget-me-not Anchusa)
Delphinium (Larkspur)
Gentiana (Gentian)
Linum (Flax)
Lupinus (Lupine) (some species)
Mertensia (Virginia Bluebells)

Myosotis (Forget-me-not)
Plumbago (Leadwort)
Pulmonaria (Lungwort)
Salvia pitcheri (Meadow Sage)
Veronica longifolia subsessilis (Speedwell)
V. spicata ('Crater Lake Blue')

LAVENDER AND PURPLE

Aconitum (Monkshood)
Aquilegia (Columbine)
Aster (Michaelmas Daisy)
Aster frikartii (Summer Aster)
Campanula (Bellflower)
Chrysanthemum (Chrysanthemum)
Delphinium (Larkspur)

Echinops (Globe Thistle)
Eupatorium coelestinum (Mistflower)
Geranium maculatum—and some other species—(Cranesbill)
Hemerocallis 'Luxury Lace' (Daylily)
Iris (Iris)

Lavandula (Lavender)
Limonium latifolium (Sea-lavender)
Liriope (Lilyturf)
Lupinus (Lupine)
Phlox (Phlox)

Platycodon (Balloon-flower)
Polemonium (Jacobs-ladder)
Stachys (Betony)
Stokesia (Cornflower-aster)
Veronica (Speedwell)

PINK AND ROSE

Althaea (Hollyhock)
Aquilegia (Columbine)
Aster (Michaelmas Daisy)
Bergenia (Bergenia)
Campanula medium (Bellflower)
Chrysanthemum (Chrysanthemum)
Dianthus (Pinks)
Dicentra (Bleedingheart)
Dictamnus (Gasplant)
Hemerocallis (Daylily)

Hibiscus (Rose-mallow)
Lupinus (Lupine)
Monarda (Beebalm)
Paeonia (Peony)
Papaver orientale (Oriental Poppy)
Phlox (Phlox)
Physostegia (False Dragonhead)
Primula (Primrose)
Veronica spicata rosea (Speedwell)

YELLOW

Achillea (Yarrow)
Adonis (Pheasant's-eye, Adonis)
Althaea (Hollyhock)
Alyssum saxatile (Basket-of-gold)
Anthemis tinctoria (Golden Marguerite)
Chrysanthemum (Chrysanthemum)
Coreopsis (Tickseed)
Digitalis (Foxglove)
Doronicum (Leopardsbane)
Gaillardia (Blanket-flower)
Geum (Avens)

Helenium (Helens-flower)
Helianthus (Sunflower)
Heliopsis (False Sunflower)
Hemerocallis (Daylily)
Hypericum (St. Johnswort)
Iris (Iris)
Oenothera (Sundrops)
Primula (Primrose)
Rudbeckia (Coneflower)
Thalictrum glaucum (Meadow-rue)
Thermopsis (Carolina-lupine)

ORANGE AND RUST

Chrysanthemum
  (Chrysanthemum)
Gaillardia (Blanket-flower)
Geum (Avens)
Helenium (Helens-flower)
Hemerocallis (Daylily)

Penstemon (Beard-tongue)
Physalis (Chinese Lantern-plant)
Rudbeckia (Coneflower)
Tritoma (Red-hot Poker)
Trollius (Globeflower)

CERISE AND RED

Althaea (Hollyhock)
Centranthus (Jupiters-beard)
Chrysanthemum
  (Chrysanthemum)
Dianthus (Pinks and Sweet
  William)
Gaillardia (Blanket-flower)
Lychnis (Campion)

Lythrum (Loosestrife)
Monarda (Beebalm)
Paeonia (Peony)
Papaver orientale (Oriental
  Poppy)
Penstemon (Beard-tongue)
Phlox (Phlox)
Pyrethrum (Painted Daisy)

BRIGHT PICTURES WITH LILIES

From June through August a series of lilies planted with your perennials of the month will give you exciting combinations of color and form. Lily bulbs, not usually available until October or November, can be ordered earlier and conveniently held until spring by some specialists, among them Blackthorne Gardens. Except for the shallow-rooted candidums (Madonna) and martagons, set lily bulbs 4 to 8 inches deep (measured from the base), and depending on their height—the 2-foot 'Pink Dawn' at 4 inches, the 5-foot 'Nutmegger' or taller kinds nearer 8 inches. Here is a beautiful series:

Late May to June, with baptisia, brunnera, columbines, iris, peonies, poppies.
  Coral Lily, *L. pumilum* (*L. tenuifolium*), scarlet, 24 to 30 inches.
  Golden Chalice Hybrids, yellow to apricot, 2 to 3 feet.

Mid to Late June, with baptisia, coralbells, lower-growing delphiniums, platycodon.

Madonna Lily (*L. candidum*), white, fragrant, 3 to 4 feet.

L. martagon album, to 3 feet, white, turkscap form, mid-June.

Midcentury Hybrids, including 'Joan Evans', 'Destiny', 'Enchantment', 'Prosperity', 'Cinnabar', rich coloring, yellow-to-red, late June, very easy.

June to July, with astilbe, daylilies, Italian bugloss, (*Anchusa italica*), phlox, sea-lavender, Shasta daisies, babysbreath, gaillardia, plumy bleeding-hearts, thermopsis.

Magic Pink Strain, June, *L. auratum* hybrid, pale pink, 3 to 4 feet.

'Connecticut Yankee', early July, apricot, 4 feet, long blooming;

'Nutmegger', late July, black-spotted yellow, 5 feet, very strong stems.

Regal Lily, *L. regale,* white within, pink without, spicy fragrance, 3 to 4 feet; also 'Royal Gold'; among best. *L. centifolium* is a splendid hybrid from *L. regale,* with looser form.

Aurelian and Midcentury Hybrids, 'Limelight', Moonlight Strain, chartreuse; 4 feet, late July.

'Pink Dawn', *L. speciosum roseum* hybrid, June into August, 2 feet.

'Bright Star', creamy white, apricot markings, July to August, 3 feet.

August to September, with anemones, chrysanthemums, daylilies, hardy asters, meadowrue, phlox.

'Allegra' (*L. auratum* variety), ruffled white, August, 4 to 5 feet.

Goldband Lily of Japan, (*L. a. platyphyllum*), fine scent, crimson-spotted white, 4 to 5 feet.

Imperial Gold Strain, white, crimson spotted, gold rays; Imperial Silver Strain, same without rays; Imperial Crimson Strain; all these for August, 4 to 5 feet.

'White Champion', (*L. speciosum album*), into September, 3 to 4 feet; and *L. s. rubrum,* "true pink lily," 3 to 4 feet.

PLANTS FOR FRAGRANCE

Fragrance is a blessing added to beauty in many perennial species and in some varieties. When the fine qualities of two varieties are equal, if one is scented, by all means select that one. A garden is lovelier too if some plants are included just for the aromatic quality of their foliage that crushed in the hand gives off a pleasant aroma. Especially in the night garden is fragrance desirable, as well as for all plantings that are near a terrace or beside frequently open doors or windows of the house. A breeze bearing the sweetness of garden heliotrope or the spiciness of pinks is delightful in the dining room, while a bouquet of lilies-of-the valley or of lemon-lilies in the hall is pleasant to come home to. Near the house let the white August hostas, 'Festiva Maxima' peonies, or 'Miss Lingard' phlox perfume each hour of contemplation and rest. Gardens having many fragrant flowers have proved a deep delight.

Artemisia   (Artemisia)
  abrotanum   (Southernwood) aromatic leaf
Asperula odorata   (Sweet Woodruff)
Astilbe   (False Spiraea) 'Avalanche', 'Deutschland'
Chrysanthemum   (Chrysanthemum)   (pungent foliage)
Convallaria majalis   (Lily-of-the-valley)
Dianthus   (Pinks)
  allwoodii
  caryophyllus (Carnations)
  plumarius (Grass Pinks)
Dictamnus albus   (Gasplant)   aromatic leaf
Hemerocallis   (Daylily)
  Species   *citrina*
          dumortieri
          flava
  Varieties   (all not easy to locate)
          Cool Waters
          Dawning
          Fond Caress
          Hyperion
          Lemon Lustre
          Midwest Majesty
          Vespers
Hosta subcordata grandiflora   (Fragrant Plantain-lily, August-lily)
Iris   (mostly blues)   (varieties hard to find)
  Great Lakes
  Missouri
  Pallida dalmatica 'Princess Beatrice'
Lavandula vera   (True Lavender)   aromatic leaf
Monarda didyma   (Beebalm)   aromatic leaf

Nepeta mussini (Catnip) aromatic leaf

Paeonia (Chinese Peony)

Bowl of Cream	Mrs. Franklin D. Roosevelt
Festiva Maxima	Philippe Rivoire
Mons. Jules Elie	Sarah Bernhardt
	Therese

Phlox (whites and pinks best)

Primula vulgaris (English Primrose)

Thymus citriodorus (Lemon Thyme) aromatic leaf

Valeriana officinalis (Garden Heliotrope)

Viola cornuta (Viola or Tufted Pansy)

Viola odorata and varieties (Sweet Violets)

PLANTS THAT BILLOW AND BLEND

Between clumps of rather solid perennials, as phlox or clusters of spire flowers like delphiniums, an airy cloud of one of these is effective, especially in the long line of a border. The very tall moundlike growers are also useful concealers as well as decorators. All are good to cut and also to dry.

Achillea ptarmica, 'The Pearl', 18 inches, white clouds, June to September, outstanding.

Bocconia cordata (*Macleaya*), (Plume-poppy), 6 to 8 feet, July to August, creamy pink clouds, good concealer for back of border use, a very big billow.

Chrysanthemum parthenium (Feverfew), 1 to 1½ feet, rampant bushy plant, small white daisy flowers, excellent with daylilies.

Eryngium amethystinum (Sea-holly), masses of bluish flowers in cylindrical heads surrounded by most decorative silvery bracts, on bluish stems to 2½ feet, July to August.

Eupatorium coelestinum (Mistflower, Hardy Ageratum), to 3 feet, good with chrysanthemums.

Gypsophila paniculata (Babysbreath), white 'Bristol Fairy', broad, 2-to-4-foot mounds of tiny white (or pink) flowers in vast profusion and veil-like effects in midsummer, and 'Pink Fairy' to 18 inches. Keep cut to encourage repeated bloom.

Limonium latifolium (Statice, Sea-lavender), 18 to 24 inches, feathery July to August panicles, 'Violetta', 'Collier's Pink', July to September.

Salvia pitcheri (Meadow Sage), 3 to 4 feet, August to September, one of the few true-blue garden plants, needs support.

Thalictrum aquilegifolium atropurpureum, to 3 feet, numerous delicate panicles of pale rosy lilac, delightful with *Iris germanica.* Also white and pink forms. *T. glaucum* (Meadowrue), 3 to 4 feet, July, ferny leaves, clouds of yellow flowers; *T. rochenbrunianum,* nice lavender mist for August to September.

FOLIAGE PEACEMAKERS

Arabis alpina   (Rockcress)
Alyssum saxatile   (Basket-of-gold)
Artemisia albula   (Silver King
  Artemisia)
Bocconia cordata   (Plume-poppy)
Centaurea cineraria   (Dusty
  Miller)
Cerastium tomentosum   (Snow-
  in-summer)

Dianthus allwoodii   (Garden
  Pinks)
  plumarius   (Grass Pinks)
Hosta fortunei   (Plantain-lily)
  sieboldiana, quite glaucous leaves
Stachys lanata   (Lambs-ears)
Veronica incana   (Woolly
  Speedwell)

DROUGHT- AND HEAT-RESISTANT PERENNIALS

Achillea   (Yarrow)
Betonica   (Betony)
Coreopsis   (Tickseed)
Dianthus barbatus   (Sweet
  William)
Gaillardia   (Blanket-flower)
Gypsophila   (Babysbreath)
Helianthus   (Sunflower)
Heliopsis   (False Sunflower)

Limonium   (Sea-lavender)
Nepeta   (Catnip)
Oenothera   (Sundrops)
Papaver   (Poppy)
  nudicaule   (Iceland)
  orientale   (oriental)
Rudbeckia   (Coneflower)
Silene maritima   (Catchfly)

PERENNIALS FOR RATHER WET PLACES
but not for areas of standing water that never drains

Asarum europaeum (Wild Ginger)

Asclepias incarnata (Swamp Milkweed)

Asperula odorata (Sweet Woodruff)

Aster novae-angliae (New England Aster)

Astilbe (False Spirea)

Bergenia cordifolia (Heartleaf Bergenia)

Caltha palustris (Marsh-marigold)

Cimicifuga racemosa (Snakeroot)

Eupatorium maculatum (Joe-Pye-weed)

Ferns

   Athyrium filix-femina (Lady Fern)

   Dryopteris spinulosa (Toothed Wood Fern)

   Onoclea sensibilis (Sensitive Fern)

   Osmunda cinnamomea (Cinnamon Fern)

   claytonia (Interrupted Fern)

   regalis (Royal Fern)

Helenium autumnale (Helens-flower)

Iris kaempferi (Japanese Iris)

Iris pseudacorus (Iris, Yellow Flag)

   versicolor (Iris, Blue Flag)

Lathyrus palustris (Marsh Pea)

Lilium canadense (Canada Lily)

   superbum (Turkscap Lily)

Lobelia cardinalis (Cardinal-flower)

Lysimachia clethroides (Japanese Loosestrife)

Monarda didyma (Beebalm)

Myosotis palustris (Forget-me-not)

Primula japonica (Japanese Primrose)

Ranunculus acris (Meadow Buttercup)

Trollius spp. (Globeflower)

Valeriana officinalis (Garden Heliotrope)

Viola blanda (Sweet White Violet)

   cucullata (Common Blue Violet)

PERENNIALS FOR THE SEASHORE

High winds, salt spray, and sandy soil epitomize the problems of seashore gardening. A screen of tall shrubs or tangled vines is important, as bayberry, high-bush blueberry, native juniper, bush honeysuckle, and catbrier. When they do prosper, however, the flowers are of unusual size and brilliance. If in winter lengths of burlap are fastened on uprights to make a temporary screen for well-mulched plants and if other untoward conditions are minimized, many perennials prove extremely tolerant, especially if they receive repeated additions of humus and manure. Patches of binding grass and rugosa roses planted beyond the flower bed areas help to prevent shifting of soil.

Althaea rosea   (Hollyhock)

Armeria maritimum and vars.
   (Thrift)

Aster novae-angliae, novi-belgii,
   and hybrids   (Michaelmas
   Daisy)

Chrysanthemum maximum
   (Shasta Daisy)

Centaurea cineraria   (Dusty
   Miller)

Dianthus   (Pinks)

Echinops   (Globe-thistle)
   Various species and 'Taplow
   Blue'

Erigeron ramosus   (Midsummer
   Daisy or Fleabane)

Eryngium amethystinum   (Sea-
   holly)

Eupatorium coelestinum   (Mistflower, Hardy Ageratum)

Gaillardia   (Blanket-flower)

Gypsophila paniculata   (Babysbreath)

Hemerocallis hybrids   (Daylily)

Heuchera   (Coralbells)

Iris,   Bearded and Siberian

Limonium latifolium and *L.*
   sinuatum   (Sea-lavender)

Linum   (Flax)

Lychnis coronaria   (Rose
   Campion)

Lythrum salicaria   (Loosestrife)

Monarda didyma, many forms
   (Beebalm)

Rudbeckia   (Coneflower)

Sedum spectabile   (Showy
   Stonecrop)

Senecio cineraria   (Silvery
   Groundsel)

Silene maritima   (Catchfly)

Veronica maritima or *V. longifolia
   subsessilis*   (Speedwell)

Yucca filamentosa   (Adams-
   needle)

FOR THE CITY

Alyssum saxatile   (Basket-of-gold)

Armeria maritima   (Common
   Thrift)

Brunnera (*Anchusa myosotidiflora*)
   (Forget-me-not Anchusa)

Chrysanthemum

Convallaria majalis   (Lily-of-the-
   valley)

Dianthus barbatus   (Sweet
   William)

Dicentra spectabilis (Bleeding-heart)

Dictamnus fraxinella (Gasplant)

Eupatorium coelestinum (Hardy Ageratum)

Gaillardia (Blanket-flower)

Gypsophila (Babysbreath)

Hemerocallis (Daylily)

Hesperis matronalis (Sweet Rocket)

Heuchera (Coralbells)

Hosta (August-lily, Plantain-lily)

Iberis sempervirens (Hardy Candytuft)

Iris, Bearded (if in full sun)

Liatris (Gayfeather)

Mertensia (Virginia Bluebells)

Monarda (Beebalm or Bergamot)

Phlox subulata (Moss-pink)

divaricata (Blue Phlox)

Platycodon (Chinese Balloon-flower)

Plumbago larpentae (*ceratostigma plumbaginoides*) (Lead-wort)

Sedum spectabile (Showy Stonecrop)

Tradescantia virginiana (Spider Plant)

Viola (Tufted Pansy)

LONGEST-BLOOMING PERENNIALS

Plants that stay in flower for six weeks to three months are certainly a joy, and there are many such perennials. If you grow these, you will have almost constant color, provided, of course, that you keep cutting off the faded flowers so that the plants will keep on trying to set seed and thus produce more flowers.

Achillea (Yarrow)

Aster frikartii

Astilbe (False Spirea)

Coreopsis (Tickseed)

Dicentra eximia (Fringed Bleed-ingheart)

Gaillardia (Blanket-flower)

Helleborus niger (Christmas-rose)

Heuchera (Coralbells)

Nepeta (Catnip)

Oenothera spp. (Sundrops)

Physostegia (False Dragonhead)

Veronica spp. (Speedwell)

Viola cornuta (Tufted Pansy)

Viola tricolor (Pansy)

PLANTS MOST LIKELY TO CARE FOR THEMSELVES

Of course, this doesn't mean that they need no care at all, as some advertisements would have you believe, but they are relatively undemanding and less likely to be troubled by pest or disease. Many are not distinguished or even refined growers, but they are sturdy. Some, however, such as the bleedinghearts, are the loveliest possible garden flowers, while such perennials as baptisia, gasplant, and hosta have an enduringly fine plant form with consistent attractiveness from spring to fall. Hybrid delphinium, bearded iris, phlox, and chrysanthemum are not included. For reasons that you may happily never discover for yourself, I omit them from this list of essentially reliable plants. I also see no reason to prejudice you against plants that, under *your* conditions, might easily be the joy of your garden.

Astilbe   (False Spirea)

Baptisia   (False Indigo)

Chrysanthemum maximum
    (Shasta Daisy)

Convallaria   (Lily-of-the-valley)

Coreopsis   (Tickseed)

Delphinium   (Chinese type only)

Dianthus   (Pinks)

Dicentra   (Bleedingheart)

Dictamnus   (Gasplant)

Doronicum   (Leopardsbane)

Eupatorium   (Mistflower)

Gaillardia   (Blanket-flower)

Gypsophila   (Babysbreath)

Helenium   (Helens-flower)

Heliopsis   (Orange-sunflower)

Helleborus niger   (Christmas-rose)

Hemerocallis   (Daylily)

Hesperis   (Sweet Rocket)

Heuchera   (Coralbells)

Hosta   (Plantain-lily, August-
    lily)

Iris sibirica   (Siberian Iris)

Linum perenne   (Flax)

Monarda   (Beebalm)

Papaver orientale   (Oriental
    Poppy)

Phlox subulata   (Moss-pink)

Physostegia   (False Dragonhead)

Polemonium reptans   (Jacobs-
    ladder)

Primula   (Primrose)

Pyrethrum   (Painted Daisy)

Salvia azurea   (Blue Sage)

Thalictrum   (Meadowrue)

Thermopsis   (Carolina-lupine)

Valeriana   (Garden Heliotrope)

Veronica   (Speedwell)

Viola   (Violet)

DICTIONARY OF FINE PERENNIALS

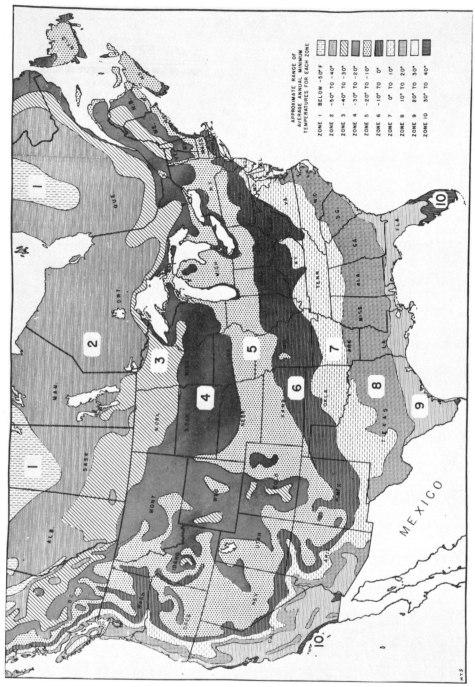

THE ZONES OF PLANT HARDINESS

This map, prepared by the U. S. Department of Agriculture, shows hardiness Zones 2 through 10, each representing an area of winter hardiness for plants. Of course, the zones do not represent hard-and-fast conditions; areas in adjacent zones must also be taken into consideration, as well as mini-climates, particularly in hilly or mountainous areas. The adaptability of a plant is also influenced by its location in a zone, as to sunlight, rainfall, and soil composition as well as zone temperatures. If allowances are made for these inevitable variations, planting by zone can be extremely helpful, a guide to satisfaction and success. In the Dictionary of Fine Perennials that follows, zone numbers indicate where the various plants can be successfully grown.

Name	Height	Description, Culture, Zones	Remarks
Achillea filipendulina (ak-il-LEE-a) Fernleaf Yarrow 'Coronation Gold'	3'	Large, flat bright yellow flowers, June-Aug. Carefree plants for full sun. Zones 3-8.	All excellent for fresh or dried bouquets or in garden.
ptarmica 'The Pearl' Sneezewort 'Snowball' 'Angels Breath'	1½' 15" 2'	Small fluffy white blooms, June-Sept.; pretty filler for bouquets or in gardens with blue delphiniums. Zones 3-8.	
Aconitum carmichaelii fischeri (ak-o-NY-tum) Azure Monkshood	5'	Purplish blue or white helmet flowers, Aug.-Sept.; may grow taller, depends on conditions; good foliage. Prefers light shade and rich soil, doesn't care for moving about or drought. Zones 2-7.	Nice with anemones; 3-ft. 'Sparks Variety', darker blue, blooms well into Sept. Aconites poisonous if taken internally.
Adonis vernalis (ad-O-nis) Pheasants-eye	15"	Yellow flowers, almost 3" across, Mar.-Apr. Woods soil. Sow seeds in fall. Zones 3-8.	One of the most welcome earlies, nice with snowdrops.
Ageratum, Hardy (see *Eupatorium*)			

Name	Height	Description, Culture, Zones	Remarks
Ajuga reptans (aj-OO-ga) Bugleweed	3-4″	Purple, blue, white flowers, May-June; glossy evergreen or semi-evergreen foliage. Light to deep shade. Zones 2-8.	Fast useful spreader. Also with variegated leaves (not my favorite).
Alkanet (see *Anchusa*)			
Althaea rosea (al-THEE-a) Hollyhock	8′	White, pink, red, yellow, lavender, purple, single, double, plain or fringed; flowers on tall stalks rising from low, hairy clumps; needs staking. July-Aug. Full sun, plenty of room. Cut back after bloom. Zones 3-8.	Best in shrub border or with a fence for background; avoid in Japanese beetle areas.
Alyssum saxatile citrinum (al-LISS-um) Basket-of-gold	1′	Pale yellow, Apr.-May. Zones 3-8.	Lovely edging plant.
Anchusa azurea (an-KOO-sa) Alkanet, Bugloss	3-5′	'Dropmore' deep blue; 'Opal' pale blue. June-Aug. For full sun or light shade. Cut back after bloom to encourage second flowering. Zones 3-8.	Good tall blues for border.

Anemone japonica (an-EM-o-nee) Japanese Anemone	2-3'	Rose, white, single or double; Sept.-Oct.; stems rise from a 12-in. mound. All half to light shade. Zones 5-8.	Among best for autumn. 'September Charm' lovely silvery pink. Endures city atmosphere.
pulsatilla Pasque-flower	9-12"	Purple flowers, Apr.-May. Zones 5-7. Likes lime	Enchanting for edging or rock garden.
vitifolia Grape-leaved Anemone	2½'	Pink, Aug.-Oct. Similar to *A. japonica* but hardier, withstanding severe winters; spreads rapidly in rich soil. Zones 4-8.	
Anthemis tinctoria (AN-them-is) Golden Marguerite	2½'	Light and dark yellow flowers, June-Oct., above pungent ferny foliage. Full sun. Zones 3-8.	Fine to cut; 'Moonlight' and 'Kelway Yellow' excellent varieties.
Aquilegia caerulea (ak-wil-EE-jia) Colorado Columbine	1½'	Lavender, May-June, native. All columbines prefer light soil and open shade. Zones 3-8 for all.	Rocky Mountain columbine, dainty, airy plants; charming to cut.
chrysantha Golden Columbine	2½'	Yellow, May-July, native.	Bushy, floriferous species.
flabellata nana alba Dwarf Fan Columbine	6-8"	White flowers, blue-gray foliage, May-June.	Dwarf for edging.
McKana Giant Hybrids	3'	Pink, purple, red, yellow, white; May-June.	Large, long-spurred bloom.
Spring Song Hybrids	2½'	Same as above with more petals.	Effect of doubleness.

Name	Height	Description, Culture, Zones	Remarks
Arabis albida (AR-a-bis) Rockcress	6"	Apr.-May, small, white, fragrant flowers. Light shade. Zones 3-8.	Keep tidy by pruning back straggling growth; pretty edger, especially nice with violas in rock garden; not always reliable.
Armeria maritima (ar-MEER-ia) Thrift, Sea-pink	1'	Evergreen narrow leaves and spherical clusters of deep pink flowers in early summer. Full sun and dry situations. Zones 4-8.	Divide in early spring. Other species and hybrids available.
Artemisia albula (ar-tem-IS-ia)	3'	Gray foliage. Prefers poor, dry soil but accommodates to border life in full sun. Zones 4-8.	Good mist plant for "peacemaking." Foliage pleasantly pungent.
Aruncus sylvester (a-RUNK-us) Goatsbeard	4'	Large, plumy white panicles, June-July, native. Best in moist situation. Zones 4-9.	Fernlike effect, handsome background plant or along a stream.
Asperula odorata (as-PER-u-la) Sweet Woodruff	6-8"	White May-June flowers, used in May wine. Moist shaded areas. Acid soil. Zones 4-9.	Charming leaves in whorled tiers; small bulbs can grow amid foliage.

Aster, Hardy (AS-ter) Michaelmas Daisies (see Chapter 9 for varieties)	1-5'	Lavender, purple, pink, white, ray flowers; Sept. to frost. Prefers full sun, plenty of room, summer moisture, spring division about every second year. Zones 4-8.	Essential fall accents in full sun, dwarf and giant, lacy effect.
frikartii	2-2½'	Large, single lavender flowers, late June to frost. Full sun to light shade; one of the very best for long bloom. Zones 5-8.	'Wonder of Staffa' is the aster I have grown best in shade, but some dwarf and semidwarf types could be worth trying there for early autumn color.
Astilbe Hybrids (as-TIL-be) False Spirea	1½-3'	White, pink, red spires; June-Aug. Light to quite deep shade; rich moist soil, must not get dry. Zones 4-8.	Marvelous pest-free plants, dependable bloomers, enduring ferny foliage, my first choice for shade. Fine to cut, split stems as you do shrubs. Dry flowers for winter bouquets.
Aubrieta deltoides (au-BREE-ta) Purple Rockcress	3-6"	Apr.-June mat of red-purple flowers; for sun with good drainage. Zones 4-9.	Nice for edging where it thrives as on Pacific Coast. Shear back after flowering with hopes of a second bloom.

Name	Height	Description, Culture, Zones	Remarks
August-lily (see *Hosta*) Babysbreath (see *Gypsophila*) Balloon-flower (see *Platycodon*)			
Baptisia australis (bap-TIZ-ia) False Indigo	3-4'	Spikes of blue, pea-shaped flowers in May-June; full sun or light shade; rarely needs division; pick to prevent seeding. Zones 3-8.	Lasting foliage, good blue for center border accent; needs plenty of space, to 18 in. or more.
Basket-of-gold (see *Alyssum*) Beebalm (see *Monarda*) Bellflower (see *Campanula*) Bergamot (see *Monarda*)			
Bergenia cordifolia (ber-GEN-ia)	12-20"	Pink or white panicles, May. Open to deep shade, moist to wet soil. Zones 4-8.	Handsome dark green fleshy rosettes of foliage; impressive, good for fore-front of shrubs, making large clumps.

Betony (see *Stachys*)			
Bishops-hat (see *Epimedium*)			
Blanket-flower (see *Gaillardia*)			
Bleedingheart (see *Dicentra*)			
Bluebell (see *Campanula*)			
Boltonia asteroides (bowl-TOE-nia)	3-5'	Full sun or light shade, a fast, rampant, white daisy type. Zones 3-8.	White 'Snowbank' excellent. Also a dwarf form 2½ ft.
latisquama	3-4'	Pink or lavender. Zones 3-8.	
Brunnera macrophylla (*Anchusa myosotidiflora*) (BRUNN-er-a) Forget-me-not Anchusa	1½'	Blue, May-June. Open shade to sun, deep moist soil. Zones 3-8.	Fine true-blue forget-me-not flowers; large spreading plants, coarse leaves.
Bugloss (see *Anchusa*)			
Caltha palustris (KAL-tha) Marsh-marigold	12-15"	Yellow buttercups in Apr. followed by big spreading leaves, native. Moist ground or shallow water; light to deep shade. Zones 3-6.	Fine early color in swamp area. Disappears in summer.

Name	Height	Description, Culture, Zones	Remarks
Campanula lactiflora (kam-PAN-ew-la) Milky Bellflower	4'	Pale blue or milk-white flowers in panicles, July-Aug. Often 100 flowers per stem. Zones 5-7.	Needs staking and rich soil.
latifolia	4'	Purple-blue bells on tall spikes, a white form, and a vivid deep blue, June-July. Zones 4-8.	Needs no staking. Var. *macrantha* to 5 ft.
medium Canterbury Bell	1½-3'	Lavender, pink, or white bells large and in few-flowered panicles. June-July. Zones 4-9.	This species is a biennial, but comes readily from seed.
persicifolia Peach-leaved Bellflower	3'	Large, open bells, violet or white on short spikes in June-July. Zones 5-8.	Divide every fourth year. A long-lived, hardy plant. 'Telham Beauty' fine.
pyramidalis Chimney Bellflower	5'	Clear blue and white flowers in tall spikes, profuse bloomer when well grown. Winter protection in coldframe. Zones 5-7.	Also a biennial but worth the trouble of sowing seed every year and special care. Needs staking.
rotundifolia Bluebell, Harebell	15-18"	Nodding bright blue flowers, wiry stems, June-frost. Easy from seed; semishade; plant among rocks for a blue cascade. Zones 4-8.	Spreads readily; the bluebells of Scotland, naturalized in this country.

Campion (see *Lychnis*)			
Canada Phlox (see *Phlox divaricata*)			
Candytuft (see *Iberis*)			
Canterbury Bell (see *Campanula*)			
Carnation (see *Dianthus*)			
Carolina-lupine (see *Thermopsis*)			
Catchfly (see *Lychnis*)			
Catnip (see *Nepeta*)			
Cerastium tomentosum (ser-ASS-tium) Snow-in-summer	6″	Rapidly spreading procumbent plant with downy silvery leaves and small white flowers from late May through June. Light sandy soil and sun. Zones 3-7.	Fine on a rock wall, but hard to eradicate.
Ceratostigma plumbaginoides Plumbago larpentae (ser-at-OS-tig-ma) Leadwort	6″	Dark blue, Aug.-Sept. Part shade or sun. Zones 6-9.	Not the greatest, though color is good. (Terrible new name!) Late to appear in spring, but increases fast.
Christmas-rose (see *Helleborus*)			

Name	Height	Description, Culture, Zones	Remarks
Chrysanthemum, Garden (kris-ANTH-em-um) (see Chapter 10)	1-3'	All colors but blue; Sept.-Dec. Zones 4-8.	Fall indispensables, cushion and tall.
coccineum Pyrethrum	1-3'	Pink, red, or white June-July flowers; full sun, rich soil, plenty of water. Zones 4-8.	Fine daisy flowers single or double for cutting.
maximum Shasta Daisy	1-2'	White; June-Nov. Zones 4-8.	Superb to set off brightly colored plants and for cutting.
parthenium Feverfew	1½'	White and yellow flowers, pungent leaves; June-Oct. Zones 3-6.	Rampant self-sower, tiny daisy blooms, nice bouquet filler.
Chrysogonum virginianum (kris-OG-o-num) Goldenstar	6-10"	Yellow flowers, Apr.-June; native. Partial shade, rich, moist soil. Zones 6-7.	Not reliably hardy, worth chancing for lovely, long golden bloom.
Cimicifuga racemosa (sim-i-SIFF-ew-ga) Snakeroot	4-5'	White wands; July-Sept.; very showy, native. Sun or shade, moist soil. Zones 3-9.	Lovely with hemlocks and gray stone walls; also with old-fashioned tawny daylilies.

Name	Height		
Columbine (see *Aquilegia*)			
Coneflower (see *Rudbeckia*)			
Convallaria majalis (kon-val-AIR-ia) Lily-of-the-valley	8"	White, very fragrant flowers; May-June, native. Open shade to partial sun; in deep shade, no bloom. Zones 2-6.	I simply remove tops in early fall if spider-mites attack; needs heavy fertilizing and much water.
Coralbells (see *Heuchera*)			
Coreopsis grandiflora (ko-ree-OP-sis)	2-3'	Full sun, endurance of heat and drought. Rather sparse leaves. Zones 4-9.	Good cut flowers. Tall single 'Gold Coin' attractive.
Cowslip (see *Primula*)			
Cranesbill (see *Geranium*)			
Daylily (see *Hemerocallis*)			

Name	Height	Description, Culture, Zones	Remarks
Delphinium (del-FIN-ium) Larkspur (see Chapter 8)		Finest blues, also purple, lavender, pink, yellow, white; require full sun; rich, well-drained soil, some lime. Zones 3-7, in cooler sections.	Giants may not be perennial in warm areas. Select lower growers for less favorable climates and for smaller gardens and strip plantings.
cheilanthum formosum Garland Larkspur	2-4'	June-Sept., light and dark blue Bella-donna and Bellamosum Hybrids, also whites.	Tall types need staking; all benefit from summer mulch and no crowding. Where summers are hot, treat as biennials.
'Connecticut Yankee'	2½'	Bushy type, fine stamina; easy from seed.	
elatum Candle, Bee Larkspur	5-6'	Giant English and West Coast Hybrids for regions of cool summers.	
grandiflorum (chinense) Chinese or Siberian Larkspur	2'	Feathery bushy grower, flowers in open panicles, easy from late April sowings.	
Dianthus (dy-AN-thus) Pinks, Carnations	1-1½'	Flowers red, pink, white or mixed colors with clove scent on evergreen plants; requires full sun, good drainage, likes lime. Zones 4-7.	Sweet William, *D. barbatus*, 1-2' free-flowering biennial for mid- to late spring, self-sows. Others perennial.
allwoodii Perpetual Pinks	1-1½'	May-June, intermittent to fall; compact for edging. Zones 4-7.	

caryophyllus Border Carnation	1-1½'	June-Sept. Zones 6-7.	Plumy type, sun or shade, persistent foliage.
plumarius Cottage, Grass Pink	1'	May, excellent for edging. Zones 4-7.	
Dicentra eximia (dy-SEN-tra) Plumy Bleedingheart	1-1½'	Pink, May-Oct. Zones 4-8.	Handsome, but summer disappearance, light shade.
spectabilis Showy Bleedingheart	2-3'	Pink, May-June. Zones 4-8.	Generally recommended for full sun but has performed handsomely for me in light shade; flowers can be ignited without danger to plant. Long lived.
Dictamnus albus (dik-TAM-nus) Gasplant	2½'	White, also pink and purple varieties have showy racemes in June; good foliage. Open shade, rich loam, well-drained soil; avoid transplanting. Zones 3-8.	New Excelsior and Hyacinth Hybrids, pink, rose, yellow, red, etc., are biennial, and white may be. Fine verticals to set among daylilies and various low growers.
Digitalis purpurea (dij-it-AL-is) Foxglove	2½-3'	For June-July, full sun or light shade with moisture. Heavier shade in South. Zones 4-8 for all.	
ambigua Yellow Foxglove		Biennial or short-lived perennial.	
mertonensis Merton's Foxglove		Perennial, rose color.	

Name	Height	Description, Culture, Zones	Remarks
Doronicum caucasicum (do-RON-ik-um) Leopardsbane	2'	Yellow, Apr.-May. Light shade but tolerates full sun. Zones 4-8.	Good spring yellow; dormant in summer. Lovely with bleedingheart and mertensia.
Echinops exaltatus (EK-in-ops) Globe-thistle	3-4'	Purple, July-Sept. Light shade. Zones 3-10.	Coarse grower, very hardy, good for dried bouquets; 'Taplow Blue' best.
Epimedium alpinum rubrum (ep-i-MEE-dium) Bishops-hat	6-9"	Red, Apr.-May flowers; leaves richly colored in fall. Light shade; rich, acid soil. Zones 3-8 for all.	Choice, this small epimedium almost unknown, an excellent groundcover for large flower beds.
macranthum niveum	9"	Long-spurred white flowers; handsome leaves.	Aristocratic beauty.
pinnatum	8-12"	Yellow flowers.	Showy, pretty associated with rocks as edging; flowers before foliage in spring.
Eupatorium coelestinum (yew-pat-OR-ium) Hardy Ageratum, Mistflower	2-3'	Lavender flowers, Aug.-Oct., native. Full sun to light shade; moisture. Zones 3-8.	Weedy grower; plant where you want coverage. Useful fall color with chrysanthemums; nice to cut, good in wild garden.

Name	Height	Description	Remarks
False Dragonhead (see *Physostegia*) False Indigo (see *Baptisia*) False Spirea (see *Astilbe*)			
Ferns (see Chapter 12)		Woodsy, acid soil, semishade with moisture.	
Feverfew (see *Chrysanthemum parthenium*)			
Filipendula vulgaris (hexapetala) (fil-a-PEN-dew-la) Meadowsweet	1½'	Pink in bud, white clusters of double flowers on straight stems above low, ferny rosettes, July-Aug. Full sun or light shade. Zones 4-8.	Good cut flower; needs moisture. I've planted it in woodland.
Foamflower (see *Tiarella*) Forget-me-not (see *Myosotis*) Forget-me-not Anchusa (see *Brunnera*) Foxglove (see *Digitalis*)			

Name	Height	Description, Culture, Zones	Remarks
Fragaria hybrids (frag-AY-ria) Strawberry	8"	For ornamental use grow the Fraises des Bois European type. White spring flowers and red fruits in June-July. Full sun, plenty of water, and fertilizer. Zones 3-10.	A neat and charming edging plant. 'Charles V' is upright in habit without runners.
Funkia (see *Hosta*)			
Gaillardia (gay-LARD-ia) Blanket-flower	1-2'	Red-yellow; June-Nov. Mighty bloomer in full sun and average, not heavy, soil; tolerates drought. Zones 3-9, except Gulf Coast.	Drought-enduring, useful for long color in garden, fine to cut. 'Sun Dance' yellow-edged red dwarf; 'Yellow Queen' all yellow, no red, finest.
Garden Heliotrope (see *Valeriana*) Gasplant (see *Dictamnus*) Gayfeather (see *Liatris*)			

Geranium maculatum (jer-AY-nium) Cranesbill	1-1½'	Pink or lavender May-June flowers above finely cut leaves; full sun; average soil. Fine hybrids: 'Johnson's Blue' May-Aug.; 'Wargrave Pink' June-Sept.; 'Grandiflorum', lavender, May-June. Zones 4-8.	Not to be confused with the familiar pelargonium called geranium. This is pretty with ferns and *Scilla hispanica*.
Globe-thistle (see *Echinops*) Goatsbeard (see *Aruncus*) Golden Marguerite (see *Anthemis*) Goldenstar (see *Chrysogonum*)			
Gypsophila paniculata (gip-SOFF-ill-a) Baby'sbreath	2-4'	White; June-Oct. 'Bristol Fairy' to 2'. Zones 4-8.	For garden blending and bouquets; cut for repeat bloom. For edging or rock garden.
repens and var. *rosea*		Creeping; white, pink, June-Sept. All species like lime. Zones 4-8.	
Hardy Ageratum (see *Eupatorium*) Harebell (see *Campanula*)			
Helenium autumnale (he-EE-nium) Helen's-flower	1-4'	Yellow to red; Aug.-Sept. Zones 3-8.	Showy daisy form; divide every spring.

Name	Height	Description, Culture, Zones	Remarks
Helens-flower (see *Helenium*)			
Helianthus decapetalus var. *flore-pleno* (he-li-AN-thus) Sunflower	4'	Yellow; July-Sept. Zones 3-8.	Coarse plant, dahlia flower, rampant but useful.
Heliopsis scabra (he-li-OP-sis)	3-4'	Yellow, orange; July-Nov. Zones 3-9.	Strong, fine to cut.
Helleborus niger (hell-e-BOR-us) Christmas-rose (see Chapter 2)	1'	Pink-white; Jan.-May. Sun in winter; light shade in summer; protection from wind. Doesn't care for moving about; avoid drought in summer. Earlier bloom if near a wall. Zones 4-7.	Evergreen foliage; choice and essential. Slow to establish; among the finest of perennials.
orientalis Lenten-rose	1½'	Green to rose to purple; Apr.-May. Zones 4-7.	Foliage almost evergreen.

Hemerocallis (hem-er-o-CAL-is) Daylily (see Chapter 6)	1½-4'	Cream, green, pink, yellow, orange, May-Sept. Some 8,000 hybrids, marvelous gamut of heights and coloring. Light to fairly deep shade. Zones 3-10.	Summer essential, fine foliage and flowers. Not to be missed.
Hesperis matronalis (HES-per-is) Sweet Rocket	3-4'	Loose night-fragrant racemes, white or lavender; June-Sept. Any soil, any location, light to deep shade here. Zones 4-8.	Self-sowing biennial; start with a white and violet seed mixture.
Heuchera sanguinea (hew-KER-a) Coralbells	1½-2'	Rose, white, scarlet, chartreuse; June-Aug.; sun or light shade. Zones 4-9.	Very fine foliage, excellent edging plant, especially for a sun-to-shade border.
Hollyhock (see *Althaea*)			
Hosta species and hybrids (HOS-ta) August-lily, Funkia, Plantain-lily	1-3'	White, lavender, purple flowers, July-Sept.; handsome foliage, green, blue-green variegated. Light to fairly deep shade; rich soil and keep well watered. Zones 3-9.	August-lily, *H. subcordata grandiflora* to 2', white, fragrant, an old favorite, but many newer hybrids; low types good groundcover.

Name	Height	Description, Culture, Zones	Remarks
Iberis sempervirens (EYE-ber-is) Hardy Candytuft	10"	White, Apr.-June. Shade or sun; excellent for a sun-to-shade border. Zones 3-8.	Sprawling evergreen species, my favorite edging plant; requires winter antidesiccant protection if in sun, not in shade.
'Autumn Snow'	6"	White; Apr.-May, often again in fall.	Three varieties neat and compact; fine for formal edging. 'Purity' a little larger than the others; all evergreen.
'Little Gem'	6"	White; May.	
'Purity'	6"	White; May.	
Iris (EYE-ris) (see Chapter 5)			Many types and many sizes. Select according to season, site, zone, and purpose.
cristata Crested Iris	3-4"	Pale lavender, white, May-June, native. Part shade required. Zones 3-9.	Can be used as groundcover, choice.
germanica Bearded Iris	2-3½'	Various colors; May-June; full sun, good drainage; dwarf and giant types. Zones 3-8.	Beautiful but borer protection essential.
kaempferi Japanese Iris	3-5'	Pink, purple, white; June-July; light shade; moisture but not for bogs; prefers acid soil. Zones 5-8.	Handsome flat bloom, lovely with royal ferns.

sibirica Siberian Iris	2-3'	Purple, white, grassy foliage; June; light shade, deep planting; dependable; moisture. Prefers acid soil. Zones 3-8.	For accent clumps in wide borders.
spuria	3-4'	Moisture spring and summer. Plant deeper than the beardeds; sun. Zones 4-10.	Better in Southern gardens. Bloom after tall beardeds.
tectorum Roof Iris	1'	May-June; light shade. Zones 5-8.	Nice for small garden.
versicolor Blue Flag	2-3'	June-July, native; shade, wet soils. Zones 3-8.	Good to naturalize.
pseudacorus Yellow Flag	2-3'	May-June; wet places. Zones 5-10.	Pretty beside a pool.
Jacobs-ladder (see *Polemonium*)			
Kniphofia uvaria (ny-FO-fia) Red-hot Poker, Tritoma	3-4'	Yellow or orange, red-tipped conical flowers. Full sun in North, some shade in South. Zones 6-10.	Interesting accents; white and all-yellow varieties available. Dislikes being moved.
Larkspur (see *Delphinium*) Leopardsbane (see *Doronicum*)			

Name	Height	Description, Culture, Zones	Remarks
Liatris scariosa (ly-AY-tris) Tall Gayfeather	5-6'	Purple or white wands for accent in Sept. gardens; in full sun or light shade. Zones 3-8.	Interesting, rarely seen verticals for early fall. Does well in city gardens.
spicata Spike Gayfeather	3'	For small gardens and narrow borders.	
Lilyturf (see *Liriope*) Lily-of-the-valley (see *Convallaria*)			
Limonium latifolium (ly-MO-nium) Sea-lavender, Statice	1½-2'	Lavender; July-Aug. Zones 3-10.	Good for misting, for dried flower winter bouquets.
Linum perenne (LY-num) Flax	1½'	True blue or white for May-Aug., as wide as high; full sun, good drainage, some lime. Zones 4-8.	Lovely plant with delicate, airy panicles. Cut back shoots that have bloomed to induce a second flowering.
Liriope muscari (li-RYE-o-pee) Lilyturf	1-2'	Lilac or white flowers, July-Sept. Grassy evergreen foliage. Light shade, good in South. Zones 6-10.	Needs sheltered area, may not be hardy north of New York City.

Live Forever (see *Sedum*)			
Lupinus polyphyllus (loo-PY-nus) Blue Lupine	3'	Long spikes of pea flowers rising from clusters of large palmate-lobed leaves. Also white and shell-pink. June-July. Zones 3-7 (7-9 on West Coast).	All lupines like a somewhat acid soil, cool situation, and moisture. Can be grown from seed.
Russell Hybrids	3-5'	Have much denser spikes of larger flowers in a great range of colors but do not come true from seed. Propagate by cuttings taken with a bit of root.	
Lychnis chalcedonica (LIK-nis) Maltese Cross	2-3'	Clusters of scarlet flowers on erect stems; midsummer. Zones 3-8.	Eye-catching plants from Russia but long since naturalized in eastern U.S.A.
coronaria Rose Campion	2'	Sometimes biennial; gray, woolly leaves with rose-pink to crimson flowers; summer. Zones 3-8.	An old-time favorite in New England gardens.
x *haageana*	12"	Orange-scarlet flowers to 2" wide in terminal clusters on hairy-leaved stems. Quite showy. Dies down in fall to a semi-tuberous root. Zones 6-10.	Sandy soil in sun or light shade.
viscaria German Catchfly	1½'	Thick panicles of rich pink flowers in profusion. Variety 'Splendens' deservedly well-known. Zones 3-8.	All three species in the pink family, grown for several centuries. Need full sun.

Name	Height	Description, Culture, Zones	Remarks
Lythrum salicaria (LITH-rum) Purple Loosestrife	3'	Purple to pink flowers in whorls on long, leafy stems. June-Sept. Recent hybrids have denser spikes in brighter colors, e.g., 'Morden's Pink', and are often taller. Zones 3-8.	Needs moist but well-drained soil. Can make large patches of color.
Maltese Cross (see *Lychnis*) Marguerite (see *Anthemis*) Marsh-marigold (see *Caltha*) Meadowrue (see *Thalictrum*) Meadowsweet (see *Filipendula*)			
Mertensia virginica (mer-TEN-sia) Virginia Bluebell	15"	Pink-blue flowers for two to three Apr.-May weeks; then plant disappears, native. Light to deep shade; acid soil, self-sows readily. Zones 3-7.	Associates with bleedinghearts, ferns, and early daffodils; among the loveliest; ferns can fill in vacancies after mertensia disappears.
Michaelmas Daisy (see *Aster*) Mistflower (see *Eupatorium*)			

Monarda didyma (mo-NAR-da) (Beebalm, Bergamot)	3'	Native aromatic plant with showy heads of compound irregular flowers, lilac, pink, scarlet. June-Aug. Zones 4-8.	Makes good masses of color. Attracts hummingbirds. Divide every four years.
Myosotis palustris (scorpioides) (my-o-SO-tis) Forget-me-not	1-1½'	Yellow-eyed blue flowers, a few pink, Apr.-Sept.; half shade, self-sows freely. Zones 3-9.	Nice beside brook or pool.
Myrtle (see *Vinca*)			
Nepeta mussini (NEP-et-a) Catnip	1-1½'	Gray-green, silvery, mint-scented foliage. Spikes of lavender flowers, June-July. Faded flowers should be cut off to induce further blooming. For full sun, good drainage, and only medium-good soil. Zones 4-8.	A lovely, billowy, aromatic plant for a wide edge (to 18") of a long border or smaller accents in a strip or island.
Oenothera fruticosa (ee-no-THEE-ra) Sundrops	1½'	Vigorous spreading plant for full sun or light shade; showy yellow cup-shaped flowers throughout the summer. Day-bloomers, not the same as *O. speciosa*, the evening primrose. Zones 4-10.	Nice under a stand of *Lilium tigrinum* or anywhere a sunny patch of garden groundcover is suitable. Absolutely indestructible except in damp clay.

Name	Height	Description, Culture, Zones	Remarks
Paeonia albiflora hybrids (pe-O-nia) Peony (see Chapter 4)	2-3'	Red, pink, white, single, double; late May-June. Sun or light shade. Zones 3-8 (8-9 on West Coast).	Familiar garden peony; single Chinese and double. Needs cold winters.
suffruticosa (Moutan) and *lutea* Tree Peony	3-4'	Same colors, also yellow; mid-May, June. Light shade.	Shrubby tree peony; don't cut back.
Painted Daisy (see *Chrysanthemum*) Pansy (see *Viola*)			
Papaver orientale (pap-AY-ver) Oriental Poppy	2½-4'	Silken red, pink, or white cups or double pompons, brilliant May-June effect, exciting new varieties for sun or light shade; dies down after bloom. Zones 3-8.	Each plant requires about 3' space and a concealer in front, as babys-breath, hardy asters, or phlox to cover six-weeks' summer disappearance. Green winter crown should have mulch under, not over, it where a mulch is required.

Name	Height	Description / Culture	Remarks
Pasque-flower (see *Anemone*)			
Periwinkle (see *Vinca*)			
Phlox (FLOX) (see Chapter 7)		Full sun and an uncrowded planting required by tall types to avoid mildew. Zones 3-9 (best in 4-7) for all species.	Reducing clumps to four or five stems insures big blooms.
carolina (*suffruticosa*) Carolina Phlox	2½-3'	Avoid overhead sprinkling but water deeply in times of drought. June-Aug.	Earlier than *P. paniculata*. White 'Miss Lingard' a favorite.
divaricata (*canadensis*) Blue Phlox	1'	Lavender or white Apr.-May flowering, lovely native. Light shade or sun, border or rock garden.	Exquisite, spreads quickly if in rich soil, watered, fed well. Indispensable groundcover for shade.
paniculata	2-4'	All but yellow; July-Oct.	Hardy summer phlox, no mildew on 'Star Fire'.
subulata Moss-pink	6"	Rose, purple, white; Apr.-May.	Creeping mat growth.
Physostegia virginiana (fy-so-STEE-jia) False Dragonhead	1½-3'	Pink, white, lavender; July-Sept. native. Light, open shade. Zones 3-8.	Coarse, spreading; reliable but best kept out of controlled plantings.
Pinks (see *Dianthus*)			
Plantain-lily (see *Hosta*)			

Name	Height	Description, Culture, Zones	Remarks
Platycodon grandiflora (plat-i-KO-don) Balloon-flower	1-2'	Purple, white; June-Oct. Fairly deep shade here. Zones 3-8.	Fine foliage, appears late, good concealer for bulbs.
Polemonium caeruleum (po-lee-MO-nium) Jacobs-ladder	2'	Upright grower; light to fairly deep shade; rich, moist soil. Zones 2-8.	Fine ferny foliage; dies down then renews, repeats bloom.
reptans	1'	Creeping; blue flowers; May-June.	
Polygonatum biflorum (po-lig-o-NA-tum) Small Solomons-seal	2-3'	Greenish May-June bell flowers strung along arching stems, native. Light to deep shade, rich woods soil. Zones 3-7.	*P. commutatum,* Great Solomons-seal, to 6', too large and coarse for most situations.
Primrose (see *Primula*)			
Primula (PRIM-yew-la)		Leafmold and moisture for all, with deep watering in times of drought. Light, not deep shade; strong hose spray in hot weather to prevent red-spider.	One of the shade gardener's grand opportunities.

auricula Alpine Primrose	6-8"	Hybrids in various colors, yellow or white eye, in umbels; Apr.-May. Top dressing of limestone advised, give winter protection to avoid roots heaving. Zones 3-8.	Strong flower stems rise from ever-green leaf rosette. Handsome strain of giant hybrids. For shaded rock garden or north slope.
denticulata Himalayan Primrose	1'	Lavender, pink, or purple flowers in dense globes on stout stems right after snow melts but before foliage develops. Best where winters are cold. Zones 4-7.	Reliable and enchanting. A white form has slightly larger flowers in looser heads.
japonica Japanese Primrose (Candelabra group)	1-2½'	White, red, pink flowers in whorls spaced out on tall stalks. Brilliant display May-July. Shade and moisture essential. Zones 5-8.	One of the tall Asian primulas; related species, 2 to even 3½', blooms from early summer to Aug. according to species, pastel shades of apricot, clear yellow, magenta-purple, etc.
juliae Julia Primrose	4-6"	Very hardy named hybrids, enduring heat and dryness better than most species. Deep red, lilac, rich purple, white. May. Moderately moist humusy soil in part shade or deeper. Zones 5-7.	Stoloniferous, hence mat-forming. Mixed varieties usually harmonious.

Name	Height	Description, Culture, Zones	Remarks
polyantha Bunch Primrose	1′	Hybrid group in many new and old color combinations, of inch-wide flowers in umbels, and attractive basal leaves. Descended from the English cowslip and oxlip, and long-time favorite and tractable garden plants if in rich, moist soil and part shade. Excellent for edging. May-early June. Zones 3-8.	Divide every second year soon after flowering.
Primula vulgaris English Primrose	9″	Yellow with a darker eye; Apr.-May; lightly fragrant; each on one stem. May work out of soil; divide and replant as needed; water deeply in dry spells.	Nice as an edging plant or in rock garden.
Purple Rockcress (see *Aubrieta*) Red-hot Poker (see *Kniphofia*) Rockcress (see *Arabis*)			

Rudbeckia species and hybrids (rood-BEK-ia) Coneflower	2'	Red, yellow, white; July on, native, part shade. Zones 3-10.	Not the most refined but carefree and showy "daisy" plants for late summer, as 'Gold Drop' and 'White Luster'. 'Goldsturm' blooms Aug.-Oct. in a damp border; all good flowers for drying.
Salvia azurea (SAL-via) Blue Sage	3-4'	Spikes of flowers from sky blue to dull blue-violet; Aug.-Oct. Zones 3-10.	Do not divide or move the roots of this or other species.
pitcheri Pitchers Sage	2-5'	Stems and leaves slightly gray-pubescent. Small bright blue flowers in long spikes, also a white form; Aug.-Sept. Zones 3-10.	Hardiest species in U.S.A. Nice toward back of border.

Sea-lavender (see *Limonium*)

Sea-pink (see *Armeria*)

Name	Height	Description, Culture, Zones	Remarks
Sedum acre (SEE-dum) Goldmoss Stonecrop	2″	Small succulent mat-forming plant with tiny light green leaves and masses of clear yellow 5-petaled flowers in May-June. For dryish soil. Zones 4-7.	Good in paving crevices, or in large rock garden where it can be controlled. Cheerful sight but dangerous spreader.
ewersi Ewer's Stonecrop	9″	Scrambling stems with blue-green leaves ¾″ long, and rounded heads of purple-pink flowers in late summer. Zones 4-6.	Good edging plant and groundcover, neat and controllable. See Chapter 13 for other groundcover sedums.
spectabile Live Forever, Showy Sedum	16″	Vigorous, not invasive, with stalwart stems, gray-green leaves, and large, flattish heads of pink-to-rich-rose flowers in Aug.-Sept. Zones 3-7.	Increase by division. Sun or part shade. Attracts butterflies.
Shasta Daisy (see *Chrysanthemum maximum*)			
Solomons-seal (see *Polygonatum*)			
Speedwell (see *Veronica*)			
Stachys grandiflora (STA-kis) Betony	3′	Whorls of purple two-lipped flowers set in tiers above leafy stems. June-July. Zones 3-9.	
Statice (see *Limonium*)			

Stokesia laevis (sto-KEE-sia) Stokes-aster	1-2'	Lavender, white; July-Aug. Zones 5-10.	Fine in garden, lasting cut flower.
Stonecrop (see *Sedum*) Strawberry (see *Fragaria*) Sunflower (see *Helianthus*) Sweet Rocket (see *Hesperis*) Sweet Woodruff (see *Asperula*)			
Thalictrum aquilegifolium (thal-IK-trum) Meadowrue, Feathered Columbine	3'	Columbinelike foliage, fluffy white or purplish flowers, May-June. Light shade, tolerates full sun with moisture. Rich, humusy soil. Zones 4-8.	All meadowrues are charming open plants for border or woodland; ferny foliage; fine to cut.
polygamum Tall Meadowrue	5-7'	Dainty white flowers in airy panicles, July-Sept. Zones 4-8.	Can appear unexpected anywhere; needs staking, handsome.
rochenbrunianum Lavender Mist Meadowrue	3'	Rosy-lavender flowers with yellow stamens from late spring to Sept. Zones 3-8.	A delicate cloud of color to blend other flowers harmoniously.
speciosum (glaucum) Dusty Meadowrue	3-4'	Fuzzy, yellow, slightly fragrant flowers, blue-gray foliage; lovely in summer bouquets. Zones 5-8.	

Name	Height	Description, Culture, Zones	Remarks
Thermopsis caroliniana (therm-OP-sis) Carolina-lupine	3-4'	Yellow, pealike flowers in spikes, June-July. Full sun, tolerates light shade. Zones 3-8.	Good accent plant, too little grown, charming.
Tiarella cordifolia (ty-a-RELL-a) Foamflower	1'	White flowers, Apr.-July; partial to quite deep shade with moisture and some acidity. Zones 4-7.	Spreads rather slowly; choice plant for border or groundcover.
Tradescantia virginiana (trad-ess-KAN-tia) Virginia Spiderwort	1-2'	Purple, white; June-July; rests after bloom, cut down then, fall crop follows, grasslike leaves, native. Light to quite deep shade with moisture; flowers closed by afternoon, more open next morning. Zones 4-10.	Modern varieties also lovely—white, violet-tinted, pink. Don't miss white 'Iris Pritchard', 'Purple Dome', pink 'Pauline'.
Tritoma (see *Kniphofia*)			
Trollius europaeus (TROL-ius) Globeflower	2'	Rich yellow; May-July. Zones 4-8.	Fine bloom in full sun or light shade with moisture.

Tufted Pansy (see *Viola*)			
Valeriana officinalis (val-ee-ri-AY-na) Garden Heliotrope	4'	Deeply pinnate leaves, blush-white flowers. Zones 3-8.	Strong heliotrope scent. Nice in wild garden and in border.
Veronica incana (ver-ON-ik-a) Woolly Speedwell	1-1½'	Downy gray leaves, long spikes of dark purple, light blue, or pink flowers, June-July. Zones 3-8.	Spreads and flourishes in an open, sandy place.
longifolia subsessilis and hybrids Clump Speedwell	2½'	Wide clumps of rich green foliage and dense compound spikes of lilac blue or pure white flowers; July-Sept. Zones 4-8.	Fine border plant in deep, rich loam.
officinalis Drug Speedwell	1'	Semi-evergreen creeper. Pale blue flowers; May-July, native. Full sun or shade. Zones 3-8.	Low, thick spreader, not a refined grower.
spicata	1½'	Rich blue-violet flowers in branching spikes on stiff stems; July-Sept. Also a dwarf form 6" high, very dense foliage, June-July. Zones 3-8.	Get named varieties, as white 'Icicle', deep pink 'Pavane', or 'Crater Lake Blue'.

Name	Height	Description, Culture, Zones	Remarks
Vinca minor (VIN-ka) Myrtle, Periwinkle		Trailing evergreen; lavender or white Apr.-May flowers. 'Bowles Variety' larger, deeper flowers. Light shade. Zones 4-7.	Colorful and effective, spreads fairly fast if watered well and fed until established.
Viola canadensis (VY-o-la) Canada Violet	1'	Fragrant blue-tinged white flowers, recurrent May-July bloom, sometimes in fall. Deep shade. Zones 3-8.	Good choice for long bloom; blooms earliest for me next to house wall.
cornuta Tufted Pansy	6"	Yellow, white, purple, apricot. Apr.-Oct. Zones 6-9.	Charming small perennial pansy, not always heat-resistant.
cucullata Common Blue Violet	6-10"	Good foliage, deep lavender flowers with darker throat, some bloom all summer. Light shade, longer stems in a moist location. Zones 3-8.	Thrives even in a wet place. Also excellent garden plant.
odorata Sweet Violet	6"	Purple or white flowers, Apr.-May, fall repeat. Zones 3-8.	'Royal Robe' and 'White Czar' fine fragrance.
rotundifolia Roundleaf Violet	4-6"	Fine early yellow purple-striped flowers; nice surprise following the snow. For moist, cool woods, half to deep shade. Zones 3-8.	Thrives under shrubs and evergreens, in rotten wood and leaf-mold; a good groundcover.

tricolor hortensis Pansy	6-8"	In Northern states, if mulched with leaves in late fall, pansies often live over and increase by offsets; light shade better than continuous sun, and in rich soil. A hybrid of three species, perennial but short-lived, often treated as an annual from seed started indoors in late winter. Velvety flowers in many colors. Zones 3-10.
Violet (see *Viola*) Virginia Bluebell (see *Mertensia*) Virginia Spiderwort (see *Tradescantia*) Windflower (see *Anemone*) Yarrow (see *Achillea*)		
Yucca filamentosa Adams Needle	3-5'	Good accent or tub plant; handsome if carefully placed, especially on or near a terrace; sometimes fragrant at night. Tropical-looking clusters of long narrow, evergreen leaves, from which rise sturdy flower-stalks, each bearing in August (earlier in dry summers) large panicles of whitish bells to 2" long. Sandy soil. Zones 4-8.

WHERE TO BUY

Of course there are many other dealers in plants and seeds throughout the nation. Those listed here are ones I can wholeheartedly recommend. Only retail dealers and firms which will accept and ship mail orders are listed, not local nurseries, however excellent, which must be visited for transportation.

* Indicates firms offering hellebores.

Blackthorne Gardens 48 Quincy Street Holbrook, Mass. 02343	**Lilies** (will store bulb orders till spring)
Bluestone Perennials 3500 Jackson Street Mentor, Ohio 44060	**Perennials,** "liners" (smaller plants lower prices), free catalogue
Burnett Brothers, Inc. 92 Chambers Street New York, N.Y. 10007	**Plants and seeds,** color catalogue free
W. Atlee Burpee Co. Hunting Park at Eighteenth Philadelphia, Pa. 19132	**Seeds, chrysanthemum plants, garden aids,** color catalogue free

*Carroll Gardens Westminster, Md. 21157	Perennials, including hellebores, rocks garden plants, free catalogue
Dooley Gardens Rural Route 1 Hutchinson, Minn. 55350	Chrysanthemums, free catalogue
Henry Field Seed & Nursery Co. Shenandoah, Iowa 51601	Perennials, color catalogue free
*Garden Place 6780 Heisley Road Mentor, Ohio 44060	Perennials, including hellebores, free catalogue
Huff's Gardens P. O. Box 267 Burlington, Kans. 66839	Chrysanthemums, free catalogue
*Lamb Nurseries East 101 Sharp Avenue Spokane, Wash. 99202	Perennials, free catalogue
The Lehman Gardens Faribault, Minn. 55021	Chrysanthemums, free catalogue
Lounsberry Gardens P. O. Box 135 Oakford, Ill. 62673	Perennials, ferns, free catalogue
Melrose Gardens 3909 Best Road South Stockton, Calif. 95206	Iris, daylilies, free catalogue
Geo. W. Park Seed Co., Inc. Greenwood, S.C. 29647	Seeds, plants, bulbs, all necessary garden supplies, compost kit, color catalogue free
Putney Nursery, Inc. Putney, Vt. 05346	Ferns, wildflowers, catalogue $.25
Riverdale Iris Gardens 7124 Riverdale Road Minneapolis, Minn. 55430	Iris, free catalogue

Schreiner Gardens, Inc. 3625 Quinaby Road, N.E. Salem, Ore. 97303	**Iris,** catalogue $.50
Louis Smirnow 85 Linden Lane Glen Head P. O. Brookville, N.Y. 11545	**Peonies,** free catalogue
Star Roses & Star Mums The Conard-Pyle Co. West Grove, Pa. 19390	**Chrysanthemums,** free catalogue
Stern Nurseries Geneva, N.Y. 14456	**Perennials,** catalogue $.50
Sunnyslope Gardens 8638 Huntington Drive San Gabriel, Calif. 91775	**Chrysanthemums,** free catalogue
*Thompson & Morgan, Inc. P. O. Box 24 401 Kennedy Boulevard Somerdale, N.J. 08083	**Seeds,** free catalogue
*Wayside Gardens Hodges, S.C. 29695	**Perennials, wide variety of plants,** excellent catalogue in color $1
*White Flower Farm Litchfield, Conn. 06759	**Perennials,** excellent catalogue "The Garden Book" $2.25
Gilbert H. Wild & Son, Inc. Sarcoxie, Mo. 64862	**Peonies, Iris, daylilies,** color catalogue $1.00

INDEX

Name references in italics indicate illustrations.
The illustrations in color are on pages 75–82.